Ecclesial Solidarity in the Pauline Corpus

Ecclesial Solidarity in the Pauline Corpus

Relationships between
Churches in Paul's Letters

James T. Hughes

☙PICKWICK *Publications* · Eugene, Oregon

ECCLESIAL SOLIDARITY IN THE PAULINE CORPUS
Relationships between Churches in Paul's Letters

Copyright © 2019 James T. Hughes. All rights reserved. Except for brief quotations in critical publications or reviews, no part of this book may be reproduced in any manner without prior written permission from the publisher. Write: Permissions, Wipf and Stock Publishers, 199 W. 8th Ave., Suite 3, Eugene, OR 97401.

Pickwick Publications
An Imprint of Wipf and Stock Publishers
199 W. 8th Ave., Suite 3
Eugene, OR 97401

www.wipfandstock.com

PAPERBACK ISBN: 978-1-5326-5874-7
HARDCOVER ISBN: 978-1-5326-5875-4
EBOOK ISBN: 978-1-5326-5876-1

Cataloguing-in-Publication data:

Names: Hughes, James T., author.

Title: Ecclesial solidarity in the Pauline corpus : relationships between churches in Paul's letters / by James T. Hughes.

Description: Eugene, OR: Pickwick Publications, 2019 | Includes bibliographical references.

Identifiers: ISBN 978-1-5326-5874-7 (paperback) | ISBN 978-1-5326-5875-4 (hardcover) | ISBN 978-1-5326-5876-1 (ebook)

Subjects: LCSH: Pauline churches. | Bible. Epistles of Paul—Criticism, interpretation, etc. | Christian communities—Mediterranean Region. | Mediterranean Region—Church history.

Classification: LCC BS2545.P47 H8 2019 (print) | LCC BS2545.P47 (ebook)

Manufactured in the U.S.A.   05/17/19

Contents

Preface | vii

1. Introduction | 1
2. The Meaning of ἐκκλησία | 22
3. Paul's Earliest Letters | 52
4. The Corinthian Correspondence | 93
5. Romans and Philippians | 141
6. Colossians and Ephesians | 164
7. Conclusions | 194

Bibliography | 201

Preface

This book is a revised version of my thesis "Ecclesial Solidarity in the Pauline Corpus: Relationships between Churches in Paul's Letters," completed in 2015 under the skilled and patient supervision of Andrew T. Clarke at Aberdeen University. However, it began life as an MPhil on Ephesians in 2002, working initially with David Peterson at Oak Hill College in London, and I want to express my appreciation to him also for his early encouragement, along with the many other conversation partners who have assisted in the gestation of this project over many years.

I would also like to thank my wife Kirsty and our four children, for their patience and encouragement along the way, and the good folk of Christ Church Greenbank who assisted me in more ways than they knew.

James T. Hughes

Duffield, Autumn 2018

1. Introduction

THIS BOOK IS AN investigation of ecclesial solidarity in the nine letters written to churches within the Pauline corpus, with a focus on interchurch solidarity. In this introduction, I will define ecclesial solidarity and show why interchurch solidarity deserves particular attention (section one), outline my approach to the Pauline corpus (section two), and deal with some additional methodological considerations (section three).

Defining Ecclesial Solidarity

I have chosen to use solidarity here for three reasons. First, solidarity is an essentially non-metaphorical term, referring to the unity of a group. This will be useful when dealing with a number of metaphorical terms and concepts with a sometimes disputed meaning. Second, solidarity is a recognizable term in the discussion of early Christian groups. For example, Ogereau examines the Jerusalem collection, links solidarity with economic equality in the collection, and associates solidarity with sociability, communality, and interdependency,[1] and Horrell links solidarity with difference, fostering group identity and dealing with boundaries.[2]

Third, to choose one of the available biblical terms or metaphors would be to privilege it and to make assertions about the metaphor or the term that are not warranted at this stage, as this dissertation will involve a reexamination of key terminology related to ecclesial solidarity. Here I would argue that the advantages of using a nonbiblical term outweigh the disadvantages.

Ecclesial: Inter- and Intrachurch Relationships

Throughout this study I will use *intrachurch* to refer to relationships within one *local* church, and *interchurch* to refer to relationships between one *local* church and another. I will seek where possible to distinguish between

---

1. Ogereau, "Jerusalem Collection as Κοινωνία," 360–78.
2. Horrell, *Solidarity and Difference*, 2.

the first-century Greek word ἐκκλησία and the subsequent English word "church," which has often come to carry with it wider connotations.

I am defining *local* church as the church that meets within a clearly defined local area. In the Pauline corpus, this local area is a city, as Thessalonica or Corinth, but not a region, such as Galatia or Macedonia. Any given local church may be made up of one or more domestic churches, and this seems to be the case for some of the churches to which Paul writes.[3]

I am defining *domestic* church as that which meets regularly together in a single defined space. I acknowledge that not all these settings are necessary domestic, nor even in a building.[4] However, some form of shorthand definition is helpful, and I have sought to avoid the language of house church, as that has associations with twentieth-century developments.[5]

I will use *universal* and *whole* church interchangeably, but with a preference for *whole* church, given the subsequent theological usage of the "church universal." I will use this term to include every local church extant in the period in which the letters were written. Other descriptions of church, such as *regional* or *provincial* church, will be explained as they occur.

These definitions raise two issues. First, the issue of how the relationship between local and domestic church in any given locality, what Gehring calls "a plurality of house churches within the whole church at one location,"[6] should be defined. Should these be considered intrachurch or interchurch relationships? Whether or not relationships between domestic churches in one local church (or one local area, such as a city) are considered to be intrachurch or interchurch relationships will depend on the context; what may be true of the church in Corinth may or may not be true of the church in Rome, so I will examine these issues as I approach each letter. However, the general principle here would be that relationships between domestic churches are intrachurch when there is a realistic possibility of those churches meeting together.

Second, not all scholars would accept that there is any designation of "church" beyond the local. The use of the word ἐκκλησία noted above for the "whole" church, or for "the totality of Christians"[7] is challenged by some scholars, and this has implications for how ecclesial solidarity is understood.

---

3. See for example Gehring, *House Church*, 130–55; Linton, "House Church Meetings," 233–34. For a somewhat contrary view, see De Vos, *Church and Community Conflicts*, 250–61.

4. See for example Adams, *Earliest Christian Meeting Places*, 201–2.

5. For a discussion of the relationship between house church in the NT and house churches today, see Gehring, *House Church*, 300–11.

6. Gehring, *House Church*, 155.

7. Trebilco, *Self-designations*, 178.

Thus, Knox states "in the New Testament the word 'church' always means 'a gathering' or 'an assembly.'"[8] As for ideas of the universal church, Knox states "It is impossible to discover in the New Testament any other link or relationship of the local churches one with the other than this invisible bond of mutual love of the members one for the other."[9] He argues that using the word church "to describe all our Christian brethren at present living in the world" is a nonbiblical usage.[10] Similarly, Donald Robinson states that "although we often speak of these congregations collectively as the NT church or the early church, no NT writer uses *ekklesia* in this collective way."[11] O'Brien writes: "Although we often speak of a group of congregations collectively as 'the church' (i.e. of a denomination) neither Paul nor the rest of the New Testament uses ekklēsia in this collective way."[12] Finally, after surveying usage in 1 and 2 Thessalonians, Banks concludes: "the idea of a unified provincial or national church is as foreign to Paul's thinking as the notion of a universal church."[13]

The implications of this understanding of ἐκκλησία are significant for this study, in particular for the interchurch dimension of ecclesial solidarity. The argument of Knox and others requires further investigation, which will require engagement with usage in Greek literature and the Septuagint (chapter 2 of this book), before examining the Pauline corpus (chapters 3 to 6).

As can be seen from the foregoing, these definitions are in a sense provisional, and in the conclusion to this study I will comment on their suitability.

Interchurch Relationships: A Neglected Area

This study will highlight interchurch relationships, because they are a neglected area of study for five reasons.

First, interchurch relationships are neglected when the church beyond the local is excluded from the discussion of church. O'Brien asks "What then are the responsibilities which the New Testament sets before the *people of God* who live in the overlap of the ages, between the first and second comings of Christ, and who already partake of the life of heaven while still

---

8. Knox, *Sent By Jesus*, 55.
9. Knox, *Sent By Jesus*, 59–60.
10. Knox, *Sent By Jesus*, 64.
11. Robinson, *Selected Works*, 222.
12. O'Brien, "Church," 92.
13. Banks, *Paul's Idea of Community*, 30.

dwelling on earth?"[14] His answer is to examine Colossians 3:1—4:6, putting his focus squarely on the individual and the local church. Knox states "Interdependence, not independence, is the true Christian relationship. Congregations should be in fellowship with one another."[15] However, the dynamics of that fellowship are not explored. Robinson argues that the New Testament guidance on this is "that there should be *some* point or points at which the members of all churches in the area *sometimes* meet together,"[16] but that what happens when they meet is not stipulated. He is more concerned here to show what is not mandated than what is. The validity of the focus of Knox, Robinson, O'Brien, and others will be examined in chapter 2; here I wish to note this practical outworking of it.

Second, interchurch relationships are neglected by a focus on particular elements of the doctrine of the church. This can be seen in the discussion of the relationship between the "local" church and the "whole" church. Bultmann argues that the "whole" church is the prior idea, because the church as the people of God as a notion came before the local church,[17] and because of the eschatological consciousness of the first church in Jerusalem as the church in the last days.[18] Guthrie is representative of a number of scholars who would disagree with this analysis, arguing from Paul's letters that Paul talks of "the community of believers in a specified locality," and that the universal church only becomes explicit in Ephesians and Colossians.[19] However, in both Guthrie and Bultmann, there is a tendency to view the issue of interchurch solidarity as solved once the universal and local distinction is defined. So Guthrie states: "for any adequate understanding of Paul's view of the nature of the church, both local and universal aspects must be given full weight";[20] however, his conclusion to this section is "that each local group was in its own right a church of God, but none could be isolated from the rest."[21] This conclusion may or may not be valid; it certainly does not offer much in the way of clarifying interchurch solidarity. Similarly, Bultmann's discussion of "church consciousness" is a discussion of life in

---

14. O'Brien, "Church," 116. Emphasis original.
15. Knox, *Sent by Jesus*, 64.
16. Robinson, *Selected Works*, 249.
17. Bultmann, *Theology of the New Testament*, 93.
18. Bultmann, *Theology of the New Testament*, 36–37.
19. Guthrie, *New Testament Theology*, 743. See also Schnelle, *Apostle Paul*, 560–61.
20. Guthrie, *New Testament Theology*, 743.
21. Guthrie, *New Testament Theology*, 744.

the local church, with only a passing reference to the Jerusalem council and the importance of church unity.²²

There is also a related concern with church structures. So Schnelle, having defined the local congregation as representing the whole church in a particular location, states that Paul "knows no hierarchical structure that connects local congregations and the whole church, but each part or manifestation of the church can in turn stand for the whole."²³ While this comment may be a necessary corrective to certain dogmatic positions, it does not answer the question of how one church should relate to another in terms of ecclesial solidarity.

Third, there is a tendency to focus on the local congregation in a way which deliberately or practically excludes discussion of interchurch relationships. Samra focuses exclusively on maturity within the local congregation.²⁴ Hellerman focuses on the church as a family, and his attention is on individual churches. His approach is similar to many, in that once he has defined the community, he then deals with life together, decision-making, and leadership.²⁵ The precise topics may differ in other treatments, but the focus on the internal dynamics of the individual church remains.²⁶ For all the work done on the internal workings of the ἐκκλησία in the first century—for example, how they were led,²⁷ how members related to one another,²⁸ and parallels with other first-century organizations²⁹—there is still need to examine how churches did or should relate to one another.

The focus on the internal dynamics of the community is perhaps most explicit in the work of Banks, who begins his study of the Pauline church by saying "it is the internal dynamics of Paul's communities that we are chiefly concerned to investigate, not the external responsibilities of their members to the world around them."³⁰ In acknowledging only two sets of relation-

---

22. Bultmann, *Theology of the New Testament*, 94–108.

23. Schnelle, *Apostle Paul*, 561.

24. Samra, *Being Conformed*. As an example of this, see 136–52 on 1 Corinthians.

25. Hellerman, *When the Church*, 144–204. See Banks, *Paul's Idea*, 88–117; Guthrie, *New Testament Theology*, 742–78; Schnelle, *Apostle Paul*, 566–73. A discussion of the sacraments is often considered important here: Bultmann, *Theology of the New Testament*, 311–14.

26. See also Roetzel, *Judgement in the Community*, 109–76; Schnackenburg, *Church in the New Testament*, 118–40.

27. See for example Clarke, *Serve the Community*; Clarke, *Secular and Christian*; Clarke, *Pauline Theology*.

28. See for example Chow, *Patronage and Power*.

29. See for example Ascough, *What Are They Saying*.

30. Banks, *Paul's Idea*, 2. See also De Vos, *Church and Community Conflicts*.

ships, those internal to the community and those with the world outside, Banks explicitly (and others implicitly[31]) exclude a third potential set of relationships: those between one ἐκκλησία and another ἐκκλησία: interchurch solidarity.

Fourth, in examining how ἐκκλησία is used in the Pauline corpus, there is a focus on development in Paul's letters. A classic statement of this developmental case in the Pauline corpus can be found in the work of MacDonald. Beginning with the premise that "it is generally held that from the middle of the first century to the middle of the second century the church became more tightly organised,"[32] MacDonald explores various aspects of institutionalization. MacDonald then develops a case for three periods of development in the Pauline corpus, from the community-building institutionalization of Paul's letters, through the community-stabilizing institution of Colossians and Ephesians, to the community-protecting institutionalization of the Pastoral Epistles.[33] In arguing for development, MacDonald argues for changes to attitudes to the world, ministry, ritual, and belief: so, for example, she sees in the Household Codes of Colossians and Ephesians the emergence of stabilization of relationships within and outside the church,[34] with a greater focus on established authority structures,[35] and the cosmological language of Ephesians and Colossians is seen as bolstering the ongoing continuity of the church and of existing relationships, with again a focus on authority.[36]

MacDonald's analysis presents two issues for this study. The first relates to development and authorship: how should the Pauline corpus be approached when looking at interchurch relations? This will be examined below. The second issue is that the arguments about development tend to move the discussion of ἐκκλησία in the Pauline corpus away from interchurch relationships. That can be seen from the topics MacDonald discusses: they are about the internal dynamics of the church, or the relationship between the church and the world. Thus, whilst questions of development present important methodological issues for this study, they have not contributed much to our understanding of the practical realities of interchurch solidarity.

---

31. For example, Bultmann, *Theology of the New Testament*, 308–10.

32. MacDonald, *Pauline Churches*, 2.

33. MacDonald, *Pauline Churches*, 29, and generally. For a similar approach to the Pauline corpus, see Dunn, "Body of Christ," 146–62

34. MacDonald, *Pauline Churches*, 121–22.

35. MacDonald, *Pauline Churches*, 138.

36. MacDonald, *Pauline Churches*, 146, 156.

Fifth, there is a practical neglect of interchurch relationships because of a lack of clarity in determining terminology. The understanding of "church" in the New Testament is not limited to understanding the meaning of ἐκκλησία, and within scholarly literature there is a concern to relate ἐκκλησία to other images of the church, principally the church as a body,[37] as a bride,[38] as a building,[39] and as the people of God.[40] However, there is a lack of agreement over the relationship between the images.

Many view the body of Christ as the principal image.[41] This again promotes a discussion of the priority of the local, the worldwide, or universal,[42] and introduces a host of theological issues and problems relating to origins, anthropology, and imagery.[43] Others begin with the image of the people of God, and here the relationship between the local and the "whole" becomes blurred. So, for example, Brower begins with the global "community of God's holy people,"[44] but focuses on how Paul deals with particular communities. In commenting on 2 Thessalonians 2:13, he identifies Paul's converts as "part of God's elect people, part of God's holy people,"[45] but the application of this is only to holiness within the community.[46] Harrington discusses the people of God, taking Galatians 3:29 as his key Pauline text;[47] and focuses on the development of the people-of-God idea through the Bible, and on the importance of unity as an implication of Galatians 3:29.[48] There is little here on how unity is to be understood or expressed, or on

---

37. Schnelle, *Apostle Paul*, 563–64; Best, *One Body*, 83–159; Schnackenburg, *Church in the New Testament*, 83–85; O'Brien, "Church," 105–14.

38. Best, *One Body*, 169–83; O'Brien, "Church," 114–15.

39. Best, *One Body*, 160–68.

40. Schnelle, *Apostle Paul*, 564–66. Cerfaux, *Church*, 7–8, begins here. See also Schnackenburg, *Church in the New Testament*, 77–81, who focuses on importance of people-of-God imagery.

41. Minear, *Images of the Church*, 173–220. Dunn, *Theology*, 548, states that the body of Christ "is the dominant theological image in Pauline ecclesiology." See also Guthrie, *New Testament Theology*, 744.

42. So Best, *One Body*, 189–92.

43. Dunn, *Theology*, 549–52, provides a helpful summary of issues relating to source. See Dawes, *Body in Question*, 1–78, on issues regarding metaphor in relation to the body of Christ.

44. Brower, *Living as God's Holy People*, 4.

45. Brower, *Living as God's Holy People*, 45.

46. Brower, *Living as God's Holy People*, 45–46.

47. Harrington, *God's People in Christ*, xvii–xviii.

48. Harrington, *God's People in Christ*, 115–16.

the interaction between the local and the "whole."⁴⁹ These studies highlight areas for examination, but also the need for clarity on interchurch solidarity.

Interchurch relationships in the Pauline corpus are then a neglected area of study. In examining ecclesial solidarity, this neglect needs to be addressed. In addition, the foregoing discussion has highlighted a number of points for clarification. I have already highlighted the need for a thorough examination of the meaning of ἐκκλησία, which will begin in chapter 2. In the section below on authorship, I will consider some of the issues raised by the idea of development. Finally, there is a need to establish what will be studied in examining ecclesial solidarity: both in terms of the relationship between ἐκκλησία and other imagery used for the church, but also any other areas that will contribute to our understanding of ecclesial solidarity in the Pauline corpus. It is this issue which I will now address.

Intra- and Interchurch Solidarity

In examining what is meant by solidarity, and how it will be examined, I will first interact with the work of three scholars: Horrell, Trebilco, and Meeks,⁵⁰ who, whilst approaching issues of early Christian⁵¹ identity in slightly different ways, all show the kind of material which might be examined and illuminate the direction I will take in this study.

While Meeks's work on the social world of the apostle Paul is now thirty years old, it remains a foundational text for the study of the social world of Paul. Meeks sets out to ask questions about how the early Christian movement worked, to look at the environment of early Christian groups and "the world as they perceived it and to which they gave form and significance through their special language and other meaningful actions."⁵² Meeks sets Pauline Christianity within its urban, social, and economic context,⁵³ before examining the question of "What makes a group a group?"⁵⁴ Here Meeks

---

49. For a critique of the people-of-God idea see Aletti, "Le Status de l'Église," 153–74.

50. Horrell's work has been chosen because he engages with the issue of solidarity; Trebilco's work provides a close focus on ἐκκλησία amongst other NT self-designations, and Meeks's work remains standard.

51. I acknowledge here that the terminology of "Christian" is anachronistic in discussing the Pauline Church, and therefore I will seek to avoid using it. However, there are occasions when no other term is any better. For a discussion of this see Trebilco, *Self-designations*, 3–4.

52. Meeks, *First Urban Christians*, 8.

53. Meeks, *First Urban Christians*, 9–72.

54. Meeks, *First Urban Christians*, 74.

notes similarities and differences between the ἐκκλησία and other groups,[55] before examining the language of belonging, separation, and boundary,[56] to show how early Christians regarded their own groups. Meeks suggests several useful avenues of inquiry for this investigation. First, some of the material he investigates under the headings of language of belonging and language of separation will be investigated here. Second, Meeks argues that one of the peculiar features of the early Christian groups was "the way in which the intimate, close-knit life of the local groups was seen to be simultaneously part of a much larger, indeed ultimately worldwide, movement or entity."[57] Here Meeks highlights the peculiar way in which the early Christians used ἐκκλησία, the movement of letters, leaders, and messengers between churches, traditions of hospitality, and economic support, particularly the Jerusalem collection.[58]

David Horrell has written extensively on the issue of corporate solidarity. In his 2005 monograph "Solidary and Difference," he examines various ways in which Paul seeks to promote corporate solidarity in Christ. Horrell focuses on reading Paul's ethics, particularly in relation to liberal and communitarian approaches to ethics[59]; nevertheless, his examination of solidarity yields a number of potentially fruitful lines of enquiry. Horrell focuses first on the construction of community, examining baptism and the Lord's Supper, the language of brotherhood, appeals for unity by Paul (particularly in 1 Corinthians 1–4), and the language of the body,[60] to show how "the first and most fundamental moral norm in Pauline ethics is that of corporate solidarity."[61] He then examines holiness language,[62] issues of distinction, diversity, and regard for others in 1 Corinthians 8–10 and Romans 14–15,[63] the use of the example of Christ to promote "other-regard,"[64] and how Christians are to relate to outsiders, with particular reference to Romans

55. Meeks, *First Urban Christians*, 75–84.
56. Meeks, *First Urban Christians*, 85–103.
57. Meeks, *First Urban Christians*, 75. Note that Ascough, "Translocal Relationships," 223–41, argues that the translocal links between associations are more extensive, and the translocal links between Christian groups less extensive than is normally assumed. I will argue in following chapters that translocal links and expectations are both extensive and significant in Paul's letters.
58. Meeks, *First Urban Christians*, 108–10.
59. Horrell, *Solidarity and Difference*, 47–82.
60. Horrell, *Solidarity and Difference*, 101–24.
61. Horrell, *Solidarity and Difference*, 129.
62. Horrell, *Solidarity and Difference*, 133–65.
63. Horrell, *Solidarity and Difference*, 166–203.
64. Horrell, *Solidarity and Difference*, 204–45.

13:1–7.[65] Whilst I will not be examining ecclesial solidarity in order to read Paul's ethics, but rather to understand how Paul fosters solidarity, many of the areas examined by Horrell will feature in this study, in addition to those already covered by Meeks. One noticeable element of Horrell's study is how interchurch solidarity receives only the briefest treatment.[66]

A somewhat different approach to ecclesial solidarity can be seen in the recent work by Paul Trebilco. His stated aim is to examine self-designations, and what they say about "the early 'Christian' movement, its identity, self-understanding, and character."[67] Trebilco highlights four key terms which are relevant for a study of ecclesial solidarity in the Pauline corpus: brothers, believers, saints, and the assembly. In addition, his analysis of "communities of practice," picking up on work in the field of sociolinguistics, highlights self-designations as informing and being informed by group identity.[68] However, Trebilco, like Horrell, does little with the interchurch implications of self-designations other than to describe Christians as part of a large family or worldwide assembly.[69]

There are then several potentially fruitful lines of enquiry for examining ecclesial solidarity in the Pauline corpus in these three works. In addition, there are a small number of other treatments of Pauline ecclesiology which do deal with the issue of interchurch relationships, and here I will summarize the findings of these scholars in order to highlight potential areas for further study.[70] I will do so under three of the headings which have already been mentioned by Meeks: communication, provision (hospitality and support), and belief.

These three areas can be seen in the recent work by Dunn, who argues that Paul's letters suggest that "he inculcated a sense of belonging to and responsibility in relation to a large network of churches, with the Jerusalem congregations as the mother church."[71] In support of this conclusion, he discusses communication: Paul knew lots of people in different churches, traveled extensively (as did other teachers), and hears reports of other churches. He also mentions provision (the collection for Jerusalem) and belief.[72] He

---

65. Horrell, *Solidarity and Difference*, 246–72.
66. Horrell, *Solidarity and Difference*, 115.
67. Trebilco, *Self-designations*, 1.
68. Trebilco, *Self-designations*, 6–9.
69. Trebilco, *Self-designations*, 22–23, 179–80.
70. See also Stenschke, "Significance and Function of References," 185–228.
71. Dunn, *Beginning from Jerusalem*, 655.
72. Dunn, *Beginning from Jerusalem*, 655–56.

concludes that, whilst ἐκκλησία is used for individual churches, Paul did not think of them as "independent and autonomous from each other."[73]

Kloha, Stenschke, and Thompson also argue that interchurch relationships are maintained through communication. Kloha includes Paul's reports on one congregation to another, the exchange of greetings (some from multiple congregations), and the sending of individuals from one church to another here.[74] Stenschke notes the importance of salutations and greetings,[75] and Thompson argues that the survival of the body of Christ was dependent on a network of support, and that a hunger for news, the various early controversies that the letters indicate, and the movement of coworkers all demonstrate this communication happening.[76]

Communication overlaps with the second area, where interchurch solidarity can be observed in shared support and provision. Stenschke notes here the references Paul makes to funding he received,[77] the Jerusalem collection,[78] the provision of hospitality for strangers and visitors,[79] and prayer.[80] Kloha deals with Paul's request for support from the church in Rome, as well as the collection for the church in Jerusalem as evidence of a shared mission.[81]

The third area where interchurch solidarity can be observed is in the area of belief. Kloha argues that the existence of shared beliefs and practices can be seen from the encouragement to read other letters[82] and the appeal to the practice of "the church of God" in 1 Corinthians.[83] Thompson highlights the importance of example and imitation.[84]

This examination of scholarly approaches to solidarity, as well as intrachurch and interchurch relationships, reveals a number of potentially fruitful lines of enquiry. I will examine ecclesial solidarity in the following ways, and for the following reasons.

73. Dunn, *Beginning from Jerusalem*, 657.
74. Kloha, "Trans-Congregational Church," 180–81.
75. Stenschke, "Significance and Function of References," 217–21.
76. Thompson, "Holy Internet," 56–60.
77. Stenschke, "Significance and Function of References," 195–96.
78. Stenschke, "Significance and Function of References," 204–5.
79. Stenschke, "Significance and Function of References," 208–17.
80. Stenschke, "Significance and Function of References," 200–201.
81. Kloha, "Trans-Congregational," 183.
82. Col 4:16; Kloha, "Trans-Congregational," 181.
83. Kloha, "Trans-Congregational," 181–82; see also Stenschke, "Significance and Function of References," 206–7.
84. Thompson, "Holy Internet," 56–60.

First, foundational to an understanding of ecclesial solidarity is an understanding of the range of meaning of ἐκκλησία. This is the word that Paul uses from his earliest letters for the "church," and therefore needs to be examined. This examination will begin in chapter 2, and then continue through the following chapters looking at the Pauline corpus.

Second, there are also a potentially large number of images used for the church, such as temple, body, bride, or building, and descriptions of the church, such as brothers, people of God, and holy people, which also need to be examined. Here, my focus in chapter 3 and following will be on those images and descriptions which are prominent in the letters, and which might contribute to a deeper understanding of ecclesial solidarity between churches.

Third, there are several different activities done by and between churches which foster group solidarity, such as the appeal to the word or Christian tradition, communication between churches, hospitality, and mutual support. At the same time, in the Pauline letters, Paul as apostle and as one to be imitated looms large. In examining these areas in chapter 3 and following, I will focus on the role of Paul, looking at all these areas, again with a particular focus on interchurch relationships. Two areas will not be explored in this book, due to limitations of space: the ecclesial implications of baptism and the Lord's Supper, and of various designations for "church leaders" in the Pauline corpus.

This approach to ecclesial solidarity should allow access to the neglected question of how interchurch relationships in the Pauline corpus are intended to function, examining what the implications of interchurch solidarity are.

Approaching the Pauline Corpus

In the section entitled "Interchurch Relationships: A Neglected Area," I highlighted one of the questions raised by MacDonald's analysis of development in the Pauline corpus: how should the Pauline corpus be approached when looking at ecclesial solidarity? The fact that not all of the thirteen letters that bear Paul's name as author and/or cosender[85] are universally considered to have been written by him cannot be ignored in an analysis of the Pauline corpus; however, it is not my intention in this thesis to offer any significant contribution to debates on authorship. Nor is this a study of

---

85. On the role of these coauthors (or cosenders), see Fulton, "Phenomenon," 230–34.

development in the Pauline corpus. The challenge is to find a methodology which takes account of these issues.

First, one of the reasons for treating some letters as post-Pauline is because their content is considered to have developed beyond, or in some cases against, Paul's ideas as expressed in the letters with undisputed authorship. For example, one of the reasons Lincoln argues that Ephesians is pseudonymous is because of the development in content in relation to Colossians, particularly ecclesiological developments,[86] and a number of authors see the development from church as "assembly or gathering" to universal church as indication of a later setting, moving towards "early catholicism."[87] I am seeking to avoid a methodology which establishes "Paul's" view before looking at the "later" letters. As I noted, some of the development cruxes in relation to ecclesiology are the areas which I am planning to investigate. So, the question of whether ἐκκλησία is used universally in the Pauline corpus,[88] or how body imagery is used by Paul, are often resolved in terms of authorship and development. This tends to prevent engagement with the issue of how the whole and local ἐκκλησία might relate to one another. If authorship questions can be left to one side, then there is the possibility of a more fruitful engagement with the Pauline corpus.

Therefore, this is a study of the nine Pauline letters written to churches,[89] which seeks to identify similarities, differences, and developments without seeking to establish whether they are down to authorship or cosenders. Rather, this study presupposes that issues of authorship may be informed by the findings of this study, rather than needing to be presupposed.

Second, there is disagreement about the amount of development, and how much development can be anticipated from a single author. So, for example, when discussing titles of church leaders, Clarke argues for "a pattern of notable consistency" across Pauline communities, with no significant difference in institutionalization between the earlier and the later letters.[90] Best argues that even across five letters (1 Thessalonians, Galatians, 1 and 2 Corinthians, Philippians), we should not expect "surface consistency" from Paul, but neither would we expect "great variations" from him.[91] Certainly, development should not be assumed, and development should not be as-

---

86. Lincoln, *Ephesians*, li–liv.
87. So Käsemann, "Ephesians and Acts," 288.
88. Dunn, *Theology*, 541.
89. This is not to deny that Philemon and the Pastoral letters apply to local churches, but to set some necessary limits to the study due to space.
90. Clarke, *Pauline Theology*, 77.
91. Best, *Paul and His Converts*, 25–26.

sumed to indicate a different author, and this might argue against using a three-part scheme like MacDonald's, particularly one which divides along lines of assumed authorship.[92]

Third, I wish to avoid a scheme which prioritizes certain letters for determining Pauline ecclesiology. Yet any scheme must begin somewhere. My proposal is to look at these letters in *approximate and relative chronological order*. I propose to look at the Pauline corpus in a number of chapters, approaching them diachronically rather than synchronically. These letters are ordered as they would have been written by Paul, but the order also follows that of MacDonald and others who would view a number of these letters as Post-Pauline. The scheme I am proposing is as follows:

I will look first (in chapter 3) at Paul's earliest letters: Galatians, 1 and 2 Thessalonians. I am dating Galatians to around AD 49–50, based on a south Galatian destination, agreeing with those who argue that Paul uses the term provincially rather than ethnically,[93] and that the narrative of Galatians fits best with Acts 11:30/12:25 or Acts 15.[94] Paul's authorship of 2 Thessalonians has been challenged on theological, historical, and literary grounds.[95] However, a plausible account can be given for all three of these areas that enables 2 Thessalonians to be grouped with 1 Thessalonians by noting how the rest of the NT treats eschatology,[96] the importance of the signature in 2

---

92. MacDonald, *Pauline Churches*, 3–4.

93. Burton, *Galatians*, xxvii. See also Magda, *Paul's Territoriality*, 82–102, who argues that Paul's toponymy is consistently Roman, and that this is consistent with Paul using Galatia as a designation for the Roman province. See also Longenecker, *Galatians*, lxx who notes Ramsay's research showing that provincial Galatia included these cities during the time in which Paul was writing.

94. Both Longenecker, *Galatians*, lxxiv–lxxxiii, and Morgado, "Paul in Jerusalem," 60–67, argue for an identification of Galatians 2:1–10 with Acts 11:30/12:25, and therefore date these events, and Galatians, before the Jerusalem council, to AD 49. However, Silva, *Interpreting Galatians*, 132–39, and Phillips, *Paul, His Letters and Acts*, 80–81, both argue for a later date based on the identification of Galatians 2:1–10 with the Jerusalem council. Given the polemical nature of Galatians, it seems unlikely that Paul in writing a historical narrative would risk missing out a visit to Jerusalem which might undermine his claim to independence, whilst at the same time, it is hard to account for why he would avoid the rhetorical and polemical opportunity presented by the decree of the Jerusalem council to demonstrate to his readers that his position was the correct one. However, even if Galatians 2:1–10 and Acts 15 describe the same event, Galatians still belongs to the earlier part of the 50s and can still be considered one of Paul's earliest letters.

95. Hughes, *Early Christian Rhetoric*, 82–83. See also Malherbe, *Letters to the Thessalonians*, 365; Nicholl, *From Hope to Despair*, 4–8; Green, *Thessalonians*, 60–61.

96. Green, *Thessalonians*, 63; Witherington, *1 and 2 Thessalonians*, 10–11; Malherbe, *Letters to the Thessalonians*, 365–66.

Thessalonians 3:17,[97] and the different rhetorical purposes of the letters.[98] This offers sufficient basis to examine the ecclesiological content of the letter by placing it amongst Paul's earliest letters. 1 Thessalonians is generally dated to approximately AD 50. For the present, I will adopt the working assumption that 2 Thessalonians was written soon after, with both letters probably originating from Corinth.[99]

In chapter 4, I will cover the Corinthian correspondence. 2 Corinthians has been subject to a number of partition theories, which have impacted upon how this letter (or letters) is seen to relate to the concerns and problems described in 1 Corinthians.[100] Whilst recognizing that it is not possible to prove the literary integrity of 2 Corinthians, there are two reasons why I will treat 2 Corinthians as a unity in this study.[101] First, there is no textual evidence for the separate existence of parts of 2 Corinthians, or for the editorial composition of one letter from a number.[102] Second, I would argue that the integrity hypothesis is a plausible hypothesis because the assumptions it makes are reasonable; for example, finding a digression rather than a split at 2:14 and 7:5,[103] and noting overlap in terminology between 2 Corinthians 1–7 and 8–9.[104] If necessary, the issue of the relationship between the letters will be revisited in the conclusion. 2 Corinthians was probably written quite soon after 1 Corinthians,[105] around AD 55.[106]

97. Nicholl, *From Hope to Despair*, 9–11; Jewett, *Thessalonian Correspondence*, 181–86.

98. Witherington, *1 and 2 Thessalonians*, 29–36; Jewett, *Thessalonian Correspondence*, 68–87; Debanné, *Enthymemes*, 54–55. Note here Nicholl, *From Hope to Despair*, 187–98, who develops an extensive argument for a setting of 2 Thessalonians within Paul's ministry.

99. Bruce, *1 & 2 Thessalonians*, xxi; Malherbe, *Letters to the Thessalonians*, 73.

100. For example, Mitchell, *Paul, the Corinthians*, 6–8, who argues for five different letters.

101. Harris, *Second Epistle*, 42–43, notes the large number of twentieth-century commentators and writers who have held to the hypothesis that chapters 1–13 constitute a single document, despite the arguments to the contrary of those who propose partition as the "scholarly consensus."

102. Barnett, *Corinthian Question*, 232, raises the problem of beginnings and endings of letters being removed to form one letter, and the difficulty of understanding why that would have happened.

103. Harris, *Second Epistle*, 14.

104. Harris, *Second Epistle*, 27–29; see also Hall, *Unity*, 100–102.

105. So, Harris, *Second Epistle*, 64–67, dates 1 Corinthians to AD 55 and 2 Corinthians to AD 56. Witherington, *Conflict & Community*, 352, dates 1 Corinthians to 53 or 54, 2 Corinthians not before late 55, and probably in AD 56.

106. The following commentators all adopt dates for 1 Corinthians between AD 53 and 57: Fitzmyer, *First Corinthians*, 43; Thiselton, *First Epistle*, 29–32; Garland, *1*

Chapter 5 will cover Romans and Philippians, as belonging to the next period of Paul's ministry. I am assuming Romans to have been written from Corinth.[107] I will treat the letter as a unity, as the arguments for Romans 16 being an integral part of the letter are sufficient from a textual, rhetorical, and theological point of view, and more persuasive than any of the alternatives,[108] although the unitary nature of the letter is not essential to this study. I am also treating Philippians as a single letter,[109] written by Paul, from prison or house arrest in Rome,[110] to the church in Philippi which he founded.

Chapter 6 will examine Colossians and Ephesians. Here a pragmatic decision to treat Colossians and Ephesians separately from Philippians, which belongs to the same time period if all three letters were written by Paul, has been made to avoid assuming common authorship.

This scheme is not an attempt to find five periods of development within Pauline understanding of interchurch relations. Rather, it is an attempt to look at things in an approximate and relative order; but I will note similarities and dissimilarities throughout the thesis.

In general terms, I would defend this scheme because it gives the scope to look at ecclesial solidarity in the Pauline corpus, whilst remaining open, as far as possible, on authorship. It will also allow sufficient attention to be given to some aspects of the setting of each letter.

Methodology

In this chapter, I have sought to define ecclesial solidarity, particularly identifying interchurch solidarity as a neglected area. I have also outlined my approach to the Pauline corpus. However, two methodological questions remain unresolved, which I will address here: first, my approach to the study of the meaning of words, and second, my general approach to exegesis.

Corinthians, 20.

107. The letter is generally dated to AD 56 to 58, although the precise dates are not critical to this study. So, Moo, *Romans*, 3; Kruse, *Romans*, 2; Jewett, *Romans*, 19–20.

108. Lampe, "Roman Christians," 216–30.

109. Witherington, *Philippians*, 15–17; Fee, *Philippians*, 21–23; Alexander, "Hellenistic Letter-Forms," 242–46.

110. Witherington, *Philippians*, 9–11; Fee, *Philippians*, 34–37; O'Brien, *Philippians*, 19–26.

Approaching Word and Language Study

Chapter 2 of this study will examine the meaning of the word ἐκκλησία in Greek literature prior to the first century, and throughout this study I will be concerned with the meaning of words. However, ever since Barr's critique of "certain methods . . . of using linguistic evidence from the Bible,"[111] word study has been a precarious enterprise that needs to be undertaken cognizant of recent developments in linguistics and lexical studies.[112] In this section, I will briefly outline these developments before outlining my own approach.

I will begin here with the work of Thiselton, as he outlines the concerns of Saussure and Barr and provides a summary of semantics in biblical studies into the 1970s, including the work of Nida on transformations and kernel sentences.[113] He summarizes the problems of traditional assumptions about language,[114] highlighting the importance of context,[115] and the arbitrary nature of grammatical constructions.[116] He argues that, whilst context is critical, words do have meaning, and therefore word studies are not without value.[117] He also distinguishes between synchronic and diachronic approaches to language study.[118]

Thiselton's general approach is similar to that of Cotterell and Turner, whose position can be summarized as follows: "the significance of the words cannot arbitrarily be changed by the individual if his signals are to be correctly perceived by others. On the other hand it is not possible arbitrarily to insist that the significance of the signs shall not change."[119]

Cotterell and Turner then make several arguments which are relevant to this study. First, they note the respective places of diachronic and synchronic study of language, and the limits of both.[120] Second, in their

---

111. Barr, *Semantics of Biblical Language*, 1.

112. On Barr's critique, see also Cotterell and Turner, *Linguistics*, 106–28; Thiselton, "Semantics," 80–85; Piñero and Peláez, *Study of the New Testament*, 457–63; Du Toit, "Contributions," 295–303.

113. Thiselton, "Semantics," 95–98.

114. Thiselton, "Semantics," 76–78.

115. Thiselton, "Semantics," 78–79.

116. Thiselton, "Semantics," 85–88.

117. Thiselton, "Semantics," 83–84. He notes here that Barr's critique of the *Theological Dictionary of the New Testament* relates not to word study per se, but "illegitimate totality transfer."

118. Thiselton, "Semantics," 80–82.

119. Cotterell and Turner, *Linguistics*, 18.

120. Cotterell and Turner, *Linguistics*, 25–26.

discussion of the nature of meaning,[121] they define *discourse meaning* (in relation to 1 Corinthians) as "searching for the meaning of what Paul expressed when it is understood as the record of an (admittedly lengthy) contextualized utterance."[122] Using this sense of discourse meaning, this study seeks to examine the discourse meaning of Paul's letter to churches, in relation to ecclesial solidarity. Third, Cotterell and Turner note the importance of defining relevant "presupposition pools," to understand the referent of an expression, and therefore its significance;[123] in chapter 2, I will be diachronically studying the potential presupposition pool of ἐκκλησία. Fourth, they provide a model for analyzing different senses of a word, emphasizing the importance of synchronic analysis;[124] synchronic analysis of the meaning of ἐκκλησία and other key terms is a key component of chapters 3 and following of this study.

More recently, Gene Green has advocated relevance theory as "a framework within which we may understand the way words mean in context."[125] Relevance theory emphasizes the importance of context, and the need for gaps between the meaning of a sentence and an utterance to be filled by the hearer; hearers (or readers) must interpret to understand.[126] Furthermore, all concepts are ad hoc, arising for specific purposes at particular times.[127] This may appear to lead to linguistic indeterminacy, and the arbitrary change which Cotterell and Turner argue against. However, relevance theory argues that communication is constrained by the principle of relevance: that the communication received is worth processing, and that the addressee will decode the utterance following the path of least effort.[128] Green concludes that traditional approaches to word study based on semantic range are inadequate given the ad hoc nature of concepts, and therefore the focus must be on understanding the shared knowledge of writer and first readers, the context.[129]

121. Cotterell and Turner, *Linguistics*, 53–71.
122. Cotterell and Turner, *Linguistics*, 64.
123. Cotterell and Turner, *Linguistics*, 100–101.
124. Cotterell and Turner, *Linguistics*, 178.
125. Green, "Lexical Pragmatics," 800.
126. Green, "Lexical Pragmatics," 803–4. For further examples of this in practice, see Wilson, "Relevance Theory," 136–39.
127. Green, "Lexical Pragmatics," 806–7. For discussion of the relationship between metaphor, narrowing and relevance theory, see Wilson, "Relevance Theory," 139–42; Wilson, "Relevance and Lexical Pragmatics," 343–60. For an analysis of ad hoc meaning see Hanks, "Word Meanings Exist," 125–34.
128. Green, "Lexical Pragmatics," 807–8.
129. Green, "Lexical Pragmatics," 808–12. See also Hanks, "Word Meanings," 133.

Finally, I want to note the insight of sociolinguistics, recognizing that language is used for group definition; shared language can be used to reinforce identity.[130] For example, Trebilco argues that early Christ-followers used designation for the other creatively, to define and redefine outsiders and insiders;[131] language needs to be understood in its social context.

In the light of these developments in linguistic and lexical theory, my own approach is as follows. First, studying the use of words remains a worthwhile endeavor. Whilst the meaning of words is not fixed, nor is it entirely arbitrary. Meaning is constrained; therefore, it is reasonable to assume that when Paul communicates, he is using words to be understood. Therefore, the referents are understandable, and there is some relationship between meaning in a specific context and meaning elsewhere.

Second, diachronic and synchronic approaches are complementary if carefully handled. This is particularly the case in approaching the meaning of ἐκκλησία because, as has already been noted, the semantic range of this term has been disputed. In seeking to understand Paul's use of the term, one of the useful lines of investigation is diachronic, recognizing that this provides a context, not a prescriptive semantic range, for understanding Pauline usage.

Third, and most importantly, words must be understood in context. Therefore, this study will focus on contextual interpretation. My purpose is to seek to discover Paul's intentions from a close examination of the text in context.

Careful word study remains a legitimate endeavor. I will now examine the second methodological consideration here, my general approach to exegesis.

Approach to Exegesis

There is an obvious overlap here between this section and the previous one, as exegesis involves the meaning of words and sentences. However, here I will comment briefly on three other considerations when approaching the Pauline corpus.

First, this study is rhetorical, in that it is concerned with how Paul seeks to persuade his audience. It is a synchronic analysis, concerned with the text itself.[132] I am seeking to understand, not critique, Paul's construction

---

130. Trebilco, *Self-designations*, 11–13; Adams, *Constructing the World*, 25–28.
131. Trebilco, "Creativity at the Boundary," 201.
132. Piñero and Peláez, *Study of the New Testament*, 500.

of reality.¹³³ My focus is then on the intentions of the author, insofar as those intentions are revealed by the text, and with sensitivity to how the text would have been understood by its first hearers or readers.¹³⁴ However, this study is not tied to any particular approach to the rhetoric of the letters,¹³⁵ but recognizes the letters as letters and speeches.¹³⁶

Second, in this study I will be examining a number of Pauline metaphors, and therefore it is appropriate to briefly outline my approach to metaphor, an area of significant scholarly interest in recent years, where various approaches have been proposed.¹³⁷ A recent example is the work of Gupta, who argues for a series of interpretative principles to allow for richer interaction with metaphorical language. These principles involve identifying metaphors, then interpreting them according to five principles: exposure (whether author and reader share a common field of knowledge), analogy (is similar usage found elsewhere, in the same general historical context?), contextual coherence (establishing the metaphor within its literary context), history of interpretation, and intertextual influence.¹³⁸ In dealing with metaphors in this study, I will be concerned with the issues Gupta summarizes, although I will not be formally adopting any particular methodology. Rather, I will be seeking to recognize that which is common to all approaches: attention to what is being done in metaphorical language, and attention to how that operates in context.¹³⁹

---

133. In that sense, this is a study of the rhetoric *in*, not *of*, the bible. For this distinction see Amador, "Word Made Flesh," 53–55.

134. I acknowledge that this is disputed territory. Lategan, "New Testament Hermeneutics," 65–105, summarizes the hermeneutical issues relating to a historical, structural, or reader-response approach. See also Lampe, "Rhetorical Analysis," 21, who argues that whether Paul used rhetorical elements deliberately is irrelevant, if the focus is on what the ancient recipients could detect.

135. For critiques of this approach see, for example, Weima, "What Does Aristotle," 458–68; Porter and Dyer, "Oral Texts," 323–41.

136. For a reconstruction of how this may have worked, see Richards, *Paul and First-century*, 201–9.

137. See, for example, Gupta, "Towards a Set of Principles," 169–71; Aasgaard, *Brothers and Sisters*, 23–31. See also Dawes, *Body in Question*, 25–78, for a fuller interaction with various authors, again highlighting the importance of interpretation in context.

138. Gupta, "Towards a Set of Principles," 171–75.

139. For a similar approach to metaphor that does not work within an explicit methodological framework, see Longenecker, "Metaphor of Adoption," 71–78.

Conclusion

The purpose of this introductory chapter has been to define ecclesial solidarity, to show why interchurch solidarity is worthy of particular attention, to outline my approach to the Pauline corpus, and to deal with a number of methodological issues. In doing this, I have also highlighted the need to examine more fully how ἐκκλησία should be understood, and therefore chapter 2 will be devoted to this. In chapters 3 to 6, I will examine Paul's letters in five roughly chronological sections, as explained and justified above. In chapter 7, I will return to some of the issues raised in this chapter regarding authorship, as well as indicating what can be said from the Pauline corpus about ecclesial solidarity.

2. The Meaning of ἐκκλησία

IN CHAPTER 1, I noted that the range of meaning of ἐκκλησία in the Pauline corpus was contested, and that this challenge focuses on the preservation of the root meaning of ἐκκλησία as assembly, and therefore argues against the traditional conception of the church as "local" and "universal,"[1] replacing it with the idea of the church as "local" and "heavenly." Therefore, in this chapter I will reexamine some of the evidence for the usage of the term, looking at Greek literature, and then the Septuagint and related literature. I will then summarize these findings, before Paul's use of ἐκκλησία is examined in chapters 3 to 6. In addition, in the last section of this chapter, I will review some of the work done in recent years on the size and location of first-century churches, so that ecclesial solidarity in Paul can be examined in historical context.

Greek Literature

Argument from Greek Usage for a Local-only Usage of ἐκκλησία

A key element of the argument for a restricted range for the word ἐκκλησία in the Pauline corpus (and in the NT more widely) is that in Greek literature outside the NT, the word means an assembly, actually assembled. The almost exclusive use of the term for an assembly of citizens is noted,[2] and some argue that this indicates that the assembly only existed when assembled.[3] For O'Brien this is significant, as it shows that ἐκκλησία means an assembly,

---

1. That the universal church exists is a theological commonplace. See for example Calvin, *Institutes of the Christian*, 1012–13.

2. See also here Hoehner, *Ephesians*, 287, who states that the word is always used for an assembly in secular Greek, citing Aristotle, Thucydides, Herodotus, and Polybius. Winter, "The Problem," 205–7, argues that the word is transliterated into Latin and used in the semantic field of *politeia*.

3. O'Brien, "The Church," 89. See also Knox, *Selected Works Volume II*, 19; Campbell, "The Origin and Meaning," 132; Ward, "Ekklesia," 165.

not an "organization" or "society."[4] Perhaps the clearest statement of this position comes from O'Brien: "Attested from the fifth century BC onwards, *ekklēsia* denoted the popular assembly of the full citizens of the Greek city-state. This assembly, in which fundamentally political and judicial decisions were taken (cf. Acts 19:39; at vv. 32 and 41 an unconstitutional assembly is also called an *ekklēsia*), was regarded as existing only when it actually assembled."[5]

This understanding of Greek usage is not unique to these authors,[6] but can be traced back to the influential article by Schmidt in *TDNT*. Schmidt states that in secular Greek, ἐκκλησία denotes a popular assembly and relates it to the Greek polis.[7] Schmidt's stance is largely followed in other dictionary articles. For example, Roloff concludes: "in classical Greek as well as in Hellenistic literature, it became a technical expression for the assembly of the people, consisting of the free men entitled to vote."[8] Roloff does note wider applications for any public assembly.[9] Trebilco draws the distinction between the ἐκκλησία and the βουλή; the ἐκκλησία only existed when assembled, the βουλή continued in existence.[10]

A second element of Greek usage is also noted: the derivation of the word from εκ-καλεω, being called out. So, Schmidt states that ἐκκλησία means the called-out ones, and sees this as significant for Christian usage: those called out of the world.[11] Coenen also notes the etymology, the idea of calling out, and the use of the term originally as the summons of an army.[12] However, as Roloff points out,[13] the etymological origins of the term are lost in the shift in terminology to a technical expression for assembly. Campbell argues that ἐκκλησία is more often any assembly, rather than an assembly

---

4. O'Brien, "The Church," 89; Knox, *Selected Works Volume II*, 20–1; Robinson, *Selected Works Volume 1*, 231.

5. O'Brien, "Church," 90. See also Robinson, *Selected Works*, 222, 231; Banks, *Paul's Idea*, 27–28, (supported by four references to Thucydides and two to Philo).

6. See for example Schnelle, *Apostle Paul*, 560; Becker, *Paul, Apostle to the Gentiles*, 427.

7. Schmidt, "ἐκκλησία," 513, citing Acts 19:32 and 19:39f.

8. Roloff, "ἐκκλησία," 411. See also Coenen, "Church," 291

9. Roloff, "ἐκκλησία," 411.

10. Trebilco, *Self-designations*, 165–66; also Ward, "Ekklesia," 165; Campbell, "Origin and Meaning," 132. See also Clarke, *Serve the Community*, 15–16 for general distinctions between ἐκκλησία and βουλή.

11. Schmidt, "ἐκκλησία," 513. See also Knox, *Selected Works*, 10, who makes the calling of God a link between the church in the New and Old Testaments.

12. Coenen, "Church," 291.

13. Roloff, "ἐκκλησία," 411.

duly summoned, and that ἐκκαλεῖν is not used of convening an ἐκκλησία.[14] Further, as Johnston notes, Schmidt's point about the importance of the idea of being called out in the New Testament can be maintained, but it is not a part of the word ἐκκλησία.[15] I do not therefore think that the etymology of the word is of any great significance for understanding Paul's use of the term, and will focus my attention exclusively on Greek usage.

Ἐκκλησία in Greek Literature

Here I will provide a survey of the use of ἐκκλησία in Greek literature from the fifth-century BC to the first century BC. This survey seeks to be comprehensive enough in scope to challenge or confirm previous conclusions on the use of the term; however, it is not a complete survey of all usage: I am not looking at inscriptional or similar evidence, and this survey will focus on authors who use the term a significant amount. Here I will examine a sufficiently representative sample of Greek literature before the first century AD, from a variety of genres,[16] beginning in the fifth century BC and working through to the first century BC.

Thucydides's *History of the Peloponnesian War*, still largely accepted as generally accurate if incomplete,[17] was written from c. 431–c. 400 BC.[18] As such, it is one of the first texts to extensively use ἐκκλησία, and therefore a good place to begin this study. In terms of genre, Thucydides writes history, although with literary skill.[19] Three features of his use of ἐκκλησία emerge from a survey of his work.

First, ἐκκλησία is a political assembly, called together to make decisions.[20] This may involve hearing the arguments of ambassadors from other

---

14. Campbell, "Origin and Meaning," 131. See also Ward, "Ekklesia," 165.

15. Johnston, *Doctrine*, 35–36.

16. I have used *Thesaurus Linguae Graecae* (*TLG*) as the basis for this survey. *TLG* lists 1,074 occurrences of ἐκκλησία before the first century AD. By excluding spurious and fragmentary works, and treating the Septuagint and Philo separately in this discussion, I am left with a sample of approximately eight hundred occurrences in Greek literature across more than a dozen authors ranging from the fifth to the first century BC. I take this to be a sufficient sample for this investigation.

17. For a recent brief discussion of this, see Rusten, "Thucydides and His Readers," 3–4.

18. See Denniston, "Thucydides," 1516–17 for likely dating.

19. See for example Dover, "Thucydides," 44–59, for recognition of the literary character of the work, and Dihle, *History of Greek Literature*, 164–69, for Thucydides as historian.

20. See Thucydides, *History* 2.13; 3.41; 4.29; 4.118; 5.46; 5.77; 6.72; 8.69; for

places, such as *History* 1.31, where an assembly of the Athenians is called to hear the arguments of the Corcyraeans and Corinthians,[21] deciding that a treaty has been broken,[22] responding to popular unease,[23] responding to attacks or threats,[24] meeting in times of revolution,[25] a leader defending his conduct,[26] and getting ready for war.[27] The overwhelming sense here is of the assembly as a place of persuasion and decision in time of war or conflict. The assembly mentioned by Thucydides in 3.36, and again in 3.41, is worthy of particular note, as it is often referred to as an example of the continuous existence of the βουλή, whilst the ἐκκλησία is temporary.[28] Certainly 3.36 and 3.41 refer to an assembly which meets and refers back to the decrees of a former assembly, although in 3.36 the former assembly has to be inferred from the context, and the βουλή is not mentioned here. The distinction between βουλή and ἐκκλησία may be maintained, but not from these two references.

Second, the assembly is normally that of a Greek city-state, although there are occasions when an assembly of soldiers is in view.[29] When the plural is used, it is used for a series of assemblies meeting consecutively.[30]

Third, there are some indications of the way in which the assembly operates. There are some observable distinctions between the role of the

---

examples of assemblies being called and passing resolutions. "Political" here is taken to be that which concerns the city, the *polis*, or wider political entity.

21. See also Thucydides, *History* 1.44 where a second assembly is called to decide on what they had heard at assembly of 1.31, or 6.88 where the assembly is a place of appeal for envoys from other places, similarly 6.8.2.

22. Thucydides, *History* 1.87, where an assembly of the Lacedaemonians decides that a treaty had been broken.

23. Thucydides, *History* 3.36, where an assembly of the Athenians is convened because of popular unease about actions against the Mytilenaeans.

24. Thucydides, *History* 6.36, an assembly at which Hermocrates speaks about attacks from Athens. See also 6.51, an assembly of the Catanaens votes to side with Athens (with an army at the gates).

25. Thucydides, *History* 8.86, an assembly where envoys of the four hundred spoke on purpose of the revolution.

26. Thucydides, *History* 2.60.

27. Thucydides, *History* 6.8–9.

28. See Campbell, "Origin and Meaning," 132n3; Ward, "Ekklesia," 135n7; Trebilco, *Self-designations*, 166n11. Both Campbell and Ward refer to 3.46 here, but the reference they cite is found in 3.41.

29. Thucydides, *History*, 8.81 (three times), an assembly where the majority of soldiers are won to a certain course of action, and where Alcibiades spoke. See also 8.67, 76.

30. Thucydides, *History* 6.6.

assembly and the council,[31] and comments about the time for the assembly to meet,[32] about reinstating the assembly,[33] about voting methods,[34] about why an assembly was not called,[35] and about how the assembly was distracted.[36] It is not my concern here to establish the mechanics of Greek city-state politics in the fifth century BC. However, these indications show the concern with the right ordering of and the role of the popular assembly.

Aristophanes also writes about the Athenian assembly, although with the satirical and critical edge of "Old Comedy."[37] In his earlier plays, the assembly gathers, or fails to gather,[38] can be wronged or polluted,[39] makes decisions,[40] should be properly constituted,[41] and is dissolved.[42] Later plays show a more satirical view of the assembly,[43] which perhaps climaxes with *Thesmophorizusae* and *Ecclesiazusae*, both of which feature women in assembly.[44] This suggests a shared understanding of the assembly by Aristophanes' audience, as certainly not a place for women, which could then be satirized. One final reference in Aristophanes is worthy of note, as

31. It is here in 5.45 and 46 that the distinction between the βουλή and ἐκκλησία can be clearly seen, as the βουλή in 5.45 call the δῆμος into assembly. Thucydides writes that, due to the machinations of Alcibiades, the Lacedaemonians expressed different views in council and in assembly.

32. Thucydides, *History* 8.94.

33. Thucydides, *History* 8.97.

34. Thucydides, *History* 1.87.

35. Thucydides, *History* 2.22, because of Pericles's fear of the decision that the assembly would make.

36. Thucydides, *History* 6.51.

37. See Harsh, *Handbook of Classical Drama*, 264–66, for brief comments on Aristophanes's style. Harsh dates his productive period between 427 and 388 BC.

38. Aristophanes, *Ach.* 19, where it is the day of assembly, but the Pnyx is deserted; *Ach.* 28, where the protagonist is first into the assembly whilst other lag; *Eq.*, 936, where the assembly waits.

39. Aristophanes, *Ach.* 56; *Eq.*, 305, where the chorus sings of the pollution of the assembly.

40. Aristophanes, *Ach.* 169, where the assembly about the Thracians pay; see also *Plut.* 725, where the assembly as place of Athenian business, and *Plut.* 950, where the assembly contrasted with council.

41. Aristophanes, *Eq.* 746, where Demos is exhorted to convene an assembly.

42. Aristophanes, *Ach.* 173.

43. See for example Aristophanes, *Vesp.* 32, where the verb is used of assembling of sheep, in the Pnyx, to be addressed by a pig.

44. See Aristophanes, *Thesm.* 277, an assembly of women at the festival (to try Euripides); also 301–4, 376. In *Eccl.*, the women are planning to sneak into the assembly to ensure proper decisions are made; see, for example, 89. The same assembly is in view in 20, 270, 289, 352, 376, 490, 501, 548 (with comments about payment), and 740.

it implies the possibility of personification of the assembly: in *Ecclesiazusae*, Blepyrus misunderstands Praxagora as implying that the assembly has had a child.[45] Too much should not be made of this individual reference, but it does suggest, along with Aristophanes's general satirical tone, that there was flexibility in how ἐκκλησία might be used.

Xenophon, writing in the early years of the fourth century BC, uses ἐκκλησία in a similar way to Thucydides.[46] The ἐκκλησία is a political assembly called to make decisions.[47] Second, the assembly is that of the Greek city-state,[48] although on a number of occasions an assembly of soldiers is in view.[49] The plural is used for a series of assemblies.[50] Third, there are indications about how the assembly operated,[51] including offices, and relationships between ἐκκλησία and βουλή.[52]

There are comparatively few references to ἐκκλησία in Plato,[53] and a similar pattern emerges from them.[54] Two points of interests emerge. First, the use of ἐκκλησιασταί for assembly-men, which remains a very rare

---

45. Aristophanes, *Eccl.* 549–50.

46. See Tuplin, "Xenophon," 1628–29, for Xenophon's life between c. 430 and c. 362 BC.

47. Xenophon, *Hell.* 1.7 the assembly is the place for deciding disputes; in 1.4 and 6.5, it is the place for decision making; 1.7, assembly called (also 2.2 and 6.5); 1.7 and 5.2, testimony before assembly; 1.7, assembly being persuaded; 2.4, assembly dismissed.

48. Xenophon, *Hell.* 6.4, Lacedaemonian assembly; 1.6 Milesian assembly.

49. Xenophon, *Hell.* 1.1 (twice), assembly of troops. Xenophon, *Anab.* 1.3, 4; 5.6.

50. Xenophon, *Mem.* 4.4; *Apol.* 20.6.

51. In Xenophon, *Hell.* 1.7, the assembly is the place for sorting disputes, but decision-making is delayed because of the lateness of hour, and a new proposal from the Senate is considered for the following day. Also, in 1.7, decisions of a former assembly are referenced (similarly in 2.1 and 2.2), and supporters are being sneaked into the assembly. 2.2 also sees the assembly in action, and in 3.2, Xenophon describes the assembly as angry; in 6.5.36.6, there is uproar in the assembly. In 3.3, Xenophon notes when the "little assembly" was not called. See also Xenophon, *Mem.* 3.7, where the assembly is made up of tradesmen.

52. Xenophon, *Hell.* 1.4, βουλή, and ἐκκλησία

53. Annas, "Plato," 1190–91, notes that the precise order and dating of Plato's writings is difficult; however, they can be dated to the first half of the fourth century BC, as Plato lived c. 429–347 BC.

54. *TLG* lists seventeen, of which at least three are probably spurious, for which see also Annas, "Plato," 1190. In addition to those mentioned here, see Plato, *Gorg.* 456b, 481e; Plato, *Prot.* 319b; Plato, *Leg.* 764a, 850b; Plato, *Apol.* 25a.

occurrence in the literature,⁵⁵ and second, the plural used for assemblies conceived of in general.⁵⁶

I will consider the ten Attic Orators together for convenience.⁵⁷ Unsurprisingly, they have a particular focus on the Athenian assembly.⁵⁸ As in Thucydides, the assembly is a place of decision-making and dispute,⁵⁹ the place where laws are made,⁶⁰ taxes raised,⁶¹ and where people come or are brought to explain their actions.⁶² They are concerned with the right operation of the assembly, and distinguish between the role of the ἐκκλησία and the βουλή. Arguably, Demosthenes provides one of the clearest distinctions between the two when he quotes the decree of Callisthenes: "In the archonship of Mnesiphilus, at an extraordinary *assembly* convened by the Generals and the Presidents, with the approval of the *Council*."⁶³ Demosthenes also appears at times to use ἐκκλησία and δῆμος interchangeably: the δῆμος has given authority to the βουλή, in the ἐκκλησία.⁶⁴

The ten Attic Orators are also concerned with the following of due process and right conduct, particularly the failure of opponents to observe

---

55. So Plato, *Apol.* 25a; Plato, *Gorg.* 452e. See Liddell et al., *Greek-English Lexicon*, 509, for two occurrences in Aristotle: *Pol.* 1275a and *Rhet.* 1354b.

56. Plato, *Euthyd.* 290a; Plato, *Resp.* 492b.

57. The ten Attic Orators are Aeschines, Andocides, Antiphon, Demosthenes, Dinarchus, Hypereides, Isaeus, Isocrates, Lycurgus, and Lysias, and cover a period of approximately 120 years, the "Golden Age" of Greek rhetoric. See Carey, "Attic Orators," 212.

58. Although note Demosthenes, *Cor.* 213, assembly of Thebans; Aeschines, *Tim.* 180, assembly of Lacedaemonians.

59. See, for example, Demosthenes, *Cor.* 143; Demosthenes, *Fals leg.* 53; Demosthenes, *Mid.* 13, 197; Demosthenes, *Timocr.* 11; Demosthenes, *Exord.* 6.1; 14.1; 34.1, 2; 47.3. See also Isocrates, *De pace* 25, 66, 68; and Isocrates, *Big.* 7; Andocides, *On the Mysteries*, 11, 82; Aeschines, *Tim.* 81, 180; Aeschines, *Fals. leg.*, 82–83, 85; Dinarchus, *Demosth.* 95.

60. Demosthenes, *Timocr.* 23; *1 Aristog.* 50.4.

61. Demosthenes, *Timocr.* 97 records the need for tax for the expenses of assembly, of religious services, and of the βουλή.

62. In Demosthenes, *Aristocr.* 31, the assembly is the place of arrest, whilst in Demosthenes, *3 Philip.* 1, the assembly is the place for denouncing wrongs of Philip. See also Demosthenes, *Cor.* 132; Demosthenes, *Mid.* 163, 193–94, 197. Finally, see Aeschines, *Tim.* 60, where deeds are exposed before the whole town in the assembly.

63. Demosthenes, *Cor.* 37 (see Demosthenes, *Demosthenes*). Emphasis added. The same distinction can be seen in Demosthenes, *Cor.* 73, 169 (where the council goes to the council houses, and the assembly to the place of assembly). See also Demosthenes, *Timocr.* 11; Aeschines, *Ctes.* 125.

64. Demosthenes, *Fals. leg.* 154.

due process,[65] such as when Aeschines accuses Ctesiphon of passing legislation when the assembly was on the point of adjourning, most people having left,[66] or of calling the assembly on the day of the sacrifice to Asclepius, against previous custom.[67]

There are times when decrees and proceedings of previous assemblies are quoted,[68] a notable example of this being the discussion of the role of the assembly in the crowning of Ctesiphon.[69] They note how the assembly can become bored,[70] corrupted by wicked orators,[71] and otherwise wrongly influenced.[72] It is a place of decision, but also of indecision and inconsistent decision, as Isocrates writes: "we are behaving so illogically that we do not have the same opinion about the same situation even on the same day. Rather, we condemn something before we get to the Assembly, and then once we get there, we vote for it; then a little later, after we leave the Assembly, we complain about the decisions we made there."[73] It is a political body, but nevertheless has "religious" content.[74] The plural is used for consecutive assemblies.[75]

Aristotle[76] shows some similarities with the Attic Orators. In *Athenian Constitution*, he is concerned with attendance, offices, location, payments,

---

65. See for example Demosthenes, *Fals. leg.* 19, 34–35, 58, 185; Demosthenes, *Mid.* 8–9; Demosthenes, *Cor.* 122–23; Demosthenes, *Aristocr.* 97; Demosthenes, *Timocr.* 21–22, 25–26, 80; Demosthenes, *Chers.* 32–34; Demosthenes, *3 Philip.* 4, 6; Aeschines, *Tim.* 22, 26, 33, 35; Aeschines, *Fals. leg.* 60, 68; Aeschines, *Ctes.* 149; Dinarchus, *Aristog.* 16.

66. Aeschines, *Ctes.* 126.

67. Aeschines, *Ctes.* 67.

68. Demosthenes, *Cor.* 7, 29, 55, 73, 75; Demosthenes, *Halon.* 19; Demosthenes, *Mid.* 10; Demosthenes, *1 Aristog.* 20; Aeschines, *Ctes.* 24, 27.

69. Aeschines, *Ctes.* 32, 34–36, 43–44, 47–48, 204.

70. Demosthenes, *Mid.* 154.

71. Demosthenes, *1 Aristoge.* 9.

72. Demosthenes, *Mid.* 162.5. Lysias, *Against Erarosthenes* 71, 73, 75, 77; Lysias, *Against Agoratus* 17; Aeschines, *Tim.* 86.

73. Isocrates, *De pace* 52, see also 59. Quoted from Isocrates, *Isocrates II*, 147.

74. "Political" should not be read as "secular" and therefore taken to exclude religious in the ancient world. See for example Aeschines, *Fals. leg.* 158, where the assembly needs to be purified; Dinarchus, *Demosth.* 47, where Demosthenes is cursed at the assembly; Demosthenes, *Fals. leg.* 70, for an imprecation read at the assembly. See also Schmidt, "ἐκκλησία," 514n28 for other references.

75. Sometimes this is translated distributively, as in "every assembly," or with the singular. See Demosthenes, *Cor.* 191, 207, 234, 273; Demosthenes, *Mid.* 153; Demosthenes, *Lept.* 94; Demosthenes, *Andr.* 68; Demosthenes, *1 Aristog.* 13, 41–42, 47, 64; Isocrates, *Panath.* 13; Aeschines, *Tim.* 121, 178, 180; Aeschines, *Fals. leg.* 145; Aeschines, *Ctes.* 69, 146, 175; Dinarchus, *Demosth.* 99.

76. Nussbaum, "Aristotle," 165, dates him to 384–322 BC, with his writing period

and other rules for the assembly,[77] as well as deception in the assembly.[78] *Politics* gives further insights into the potential workings of the assembly: the responsibility of the richer citizens to attend,[79] the designation of assembly members as officials,[80] how the assembly works differently in oligarchy and democracy,[81] how the assembly should be sovereign in democracy,[82] as well as more examples of various practices in various places.[83] Perhaps most interesting here is Aristotle's discussion of the relationship between the individual "base" members of the assembly and collective sovereignty. In discussing the right of the assembly, despite being made up of common people, to judge, he argues that "although each individual separately will be a worse judge than the experts, the whole of them assembled together will be better or at least as good judges,"[84] and "it is not the individual juryman or councilor or member of the assembly in whom authority rests, but the court, the council and the people,"[85] indicating that the assembly has a corporate existence, and that the whole is greater than the individual parts. Theophrastus[86] deals with behavior in the assembly.[87]

Polybius[88] uses ἐκκλησία in similar ways to those noted here; however, some differences of emphasis emerge: ἐκκλησία is used for an assembly

---

beginning after 367 BC.

77. Aristotle, *Ath. pol.* 4.3; 7.3; 41.3 (twice); 42.4; 43.4; 44.4; 62.2.

78. Aristotle, *Ath. pol.* 15.4; 34.1.

79. Aristotle, *Pol.* 1266a.

80. Aristotle, *Pol.* 1275a (twice), 1275b.

81. Aristotle, *Pol.* 1292b (twice), 1293a, 1294b, 1297a (eight times), 1298b, 1300a, 1318b, 1319a, 1320a.

82. Aristotle, *Pol.* 1317b (three times).

83. For places, see Aristotle, *Pol.* 1272a, Crete; 1275b, 1285a, Sparta. For practices see Aristotle, *Rhet.* 1354b and 1358b for the role of the assembly in judging cases, and 1418b for the Messinian assembly as a place of rhetoric.

84. Aristotle, *Pol.* 1282a (in Aristotle, *Aristotle*).

85. Aristotle, *Pol.* 1282a (in Aristotle, *Aristotle*).

86. Theophrastus (c. 371–c. 287 BC) is included as a successor of Aristotle. See Sharples, "Theophrastus," 1504–5.

87. Theophrastus, *Char.* 4.2; 26.5; 29.4a.

88. Derow, "Polybius," 1209–11, dates him between c. 200 and c. 118 BC. The move from Theophrastus to Polybius here is significant, representing the move from classical to Hellenistic Literature and the increasing significance of Rome as subject matter for Greek authors. See Dihle, *History of Greek Literature*, 290–92.

of soldiers,[89] and it is used for assemblies in various places.[90] Notably, it is used for the Achaean or Aetolian general assembly or congress suggesting a representative function.[91] In discussing the Roman state, ἐκκλησία is used for the popular assembly, as distinct from the Senate, a similar distinction to the ἐκκλησία and the βουλή distinction noted before.[92]

Diodorus of Sicily, probably writing between 56 and 30 BC,[93] writes of assemblies in various places, and the number of times that assembly is used here (and the wide variety of places where assemblies are noted, well beyond the traditional Athenian orbit) should be noted.[94] He also refers to assemblies of soldiers,[95] and to the Second Panhellenic congress of 194 BC as an assembly.[96] Still, the assembly does what it has always done: being summoned,[97] listening to speeches and making decisions,[98] responding

---

89. Polybius, *Histories* 1.45.2; 1.69.9; 3.34.9; 3.45.1, 5; 4.72.7; 6.39.2; 11.31.1; 11.32.1. See also 11.27.6 and 11.27.7 for an assembly of mutineers summoned and surrounded.

90. Polybius, *Histories* 2.4.1, Medionians; 16.31.1, 4, Abydus; 22.5.10; 29.11.2, 4, Rhodes; 5.74.4; 5.75.10; 5.76.3, Selge; 16.26.1, Athens; 27.1.12, Thebes; 28.5.1.2, Arcania.

91. Polybius, *Histories* 4.15.8; 4.7.2; 5.1.7, 9; 21.3b.2; 22.12.5, 7; 22.10.10, 12; 23.5.17; 28.3.7; 28.4.1, 2; 38.11.7.

92. Polybius, *Histories* 3.85.8; 4.34.7; 6.12.4; 23.14.4.

93. Sacks, "Diodorus Siculus," 472–73. For brief remarks on purpose and style, see Rebenich, "Historical Prose," 291–92.

94. Diodorus of Sicily, *History* 9.20.1; 11.42.1, 6; 12.33.2; 12.39.2, 5; 13.5.1; 13.69.1; 13.73.6; 13.101.6; 14.3.5; 17.15.1, 2; 18.64.3; 18.65.6, Athens; 11.72.2; 11.92.2; 13.19.4; 13.28.3; 13.87.4, 5; 13.88.1; 13.91.3, 4; 13.92.4; 13.94.4, 5; 13.95.2, 6; 13.96.3; 14.45.2; 14.46.1; 14.64.5; 14.70.3; 15.74.5; 16.10.3, 4; 16.20.6; 19.9.1, 5; 20.4.6; 20.7.2; 26.15.2, Syracuse; 12.9.4, Croton; 12.17.2, 5; 12.19.1; 13.4.4, Catania; 12.55.10, Mytilenaeans; 13.83.4, Centoripa; 14.38.4, Heracleia; 15.75.1, Scotussa; 15.7.9; 15.78.4, Thebes; 16.27.2, Delphi; 16.25.1, Boetians; 13.94.5, Geloan; 26.10.1, Capua; 31.5.3, Rome; 31.42.1, Arevaci; 33.5.4, Aradus. This expansion is in keeping with his desire to look at world history from a Roman perspective.

95. Diodorus of Sicily, *History* 11.26.5 (twice); 11.35.2; 14.21.6; 15.54.1, 4; 16.4.3; 16.18.2, 3; 16.79.2; 17.94.5; 18.30.2; 18.39.2.6; 19.25.7.4; 20.42.3; 30.20.1. See also 17.74.3; 17.109.2 for the Macedonians on campaign with Alexander; 19.61.1.4; 19.81.2.2, assembly under arms.

96. Diodorus of Sicily, *History* 28.13.1; this assembly is of the leading men of all Greece. As such, it is of a different nature than the normal Greek pattern, as those present represent others, rather than all eligible men being present.

97. Diodorus of Sicily, *History* 4.53.1 by Jason; 30.16.1 by Ptolemy; 31.11.1 by Aemilius.

98. Diodorus of Sicily, *History* 18.74.1.

to kings and rulers,[99] and occasionally being rebellious,[100] even when the historical context is not that of the Classical period.

Diodorus also refers to an assembly of priests in Egypt.[101] The plural is used for a series of assemblies as elsewhere,[102] although there is one example of the plural potentially being used for assemblies meeting concurrently.[103] Diodorus also refers to a general or common assembly, a κοινῇ ἐκκλησία.[104]

The widening of the scope of assembly in Diodorus is noteworthy, and can also be seen in Dionysius of Halicarnassus, whose major work *Roman Antiquities* was published in 7 BC.[105] He uses assembly in many of the ways noted previously.[106] So assemblies are called and dispersed,[107] they listen to speeches, envoys and defenses,[108] they declare war,[109] there is a concern with due process,[110] and assemblies can be unruly and ill-advised.[111] At particular moments of Roman history, Dionysius presents the assembly as

---

99. Diodorus of Sicily, *History* 20.24.4; here the king is Eumelus.

100. Diodorus of Sicily, *History* 34/35.2.15, a rebellious assembly where the citizens of Enna are put to death; 36.4.4, slaves and rebels hold and assembly.

101. Diodorus of Sicily, *History* 1.58.4.

102. Diodorus of Sicily, *History* 13.63.6; 16.3.1; 17.108.3; 20.63.2; 21.9.1. Perhaps clearest here is 36.16.1, which records a series of assemblies over two years.

103. Diodorus of Sicily, *History* 30.1.1.

104. Diodorus of Sicily, *History* 11.50.3.1, Sparta (a general assembly distinct from the council of 11.50.2); 16.32.2, 16.68.5, Delphi; 16.78.2.3, Rhegium; 19.5.1, Susiane; 19.51.1, Macedonian; 19.67.4, Acarnaians.

105. Dionysius of Halicarnassus, *Ant. rom.* 1.3.4. For a brief survey of Dionysius's Atticism and Greek presentation of Roman history, see Rebenich, "Historical Prose," 292–94.

106. Note that at over two hundred occurrences, his *Roman Antiquities* contains the greatest number of uses of ἐκκλησία of the literature cited.

107. Dionysius, *Ant. rom.* 2.6.1, called by Romulus; 2.56.5, dispersed by Romulus; 10.3.3, 6, called and dismissed by Tribunes; 10.13.7; 10.15.3; 10.16.1, called by Verginius against the Senate and consuls. See also 6.43.2; 7.7.5; 7.38.1; 7.57.4; 8.72.4; 10.18.2; 10.19.4; 10.25.3; 10.40.3; 11.61.1.

108. Dionysius, *Ant. rom.* 10.48.2, where the assembly is the place to call for trial; 4.17.3; 4.48.3, assembly against Tarquinas; 7.26.1, place for Marcius's defence; 7.36.4, place that will decide punishment of Marcius Coriolanus. See also 5.11.2; 6.82.3; 6.88.1; 7.14.2; 8.75.1; 9.37.2; 9.54.5, 6; 10.5.2; 10.15.7; 10.47.3; 10.55.1; 10.56.1, 11.5.4; 11.46.3; 11.53.3; 11.54.5.

109. Dionysius, *Ant. rom.* 8.11.1, 2.

110. Dionysius, *Ant. rom.* 8.77.1, 2, the quaestor has the right to assemble the people; 6.67.2; 7.17.2, the sanctuary of Vulcan as place where assembly met; 8.6.2, Marcius complains over the failure of due process in the summoning of the tribal rather than the centuriate assembly; 11.10.4, poorest not summoned to assemblies under Decemvirate.

111. Dionysius, *Ant. rom.* 7.23.3, unruly assembly; 9.25.3, tribunes incite people against Patricians; 9.48.1, fight breaks out in the assembly after Appuis refuses to leave.

THE MEANING OF ἐκκλησία 33

having a crucial role in decision-making,[112] and ἐκκλησία is used of meetings of various peoples in various places.[113] There is a distinction between the assembly and a council, generally here the Senate.[114] The assembly can be of soldiers.[115] The plural is used for a series of assemblies, or assemblies in general.[116]

However, there are also particular features of Dionysius's usage. First, he distinguishes between the centuriate assembly[117] and the tribal assembly.[118] The assembly is also described as being divided by curiae.[119] He talks of the assembly of the people,[120] of a general or common assembly,[121] and often specifically states that the assembly is of the army/soldiers, rather than it being inferred from the context.[122]

There is also an occasion where he records rival assemblies being called, by Appius at the sanctuary of the Vulcan, and by Valerius at the

---

112. Dionysius, *Ant. rom.* 4.71.5; 4.76.4; 7.14.5, in relation to Brutus and Valerius; 4.71.2, 6; 4.75.1–2, 4; 4.78.1; 4.84.5; 4.85.1, assembly in Rome summoned against the power of Tarquin. See also 4.8.3; 4.9.6; 4.10.1–2, 6; 4.20.3; 4.23.1; 4.34.1; 4.35.3; 4.37.2; 5.1.2; 5.4.1; 5.10.1; 5.17.2.

113. Dionysius, *Ant. rom.* 1.47.4, Achaeans; 3.2.4; 3.22.2; 3.30.2, 5; 3.31.1, Albans; 4.56.4; 4.57.2; 4.58.3, Gabini; 5.3.2, Tarquinii; 3.36.2; 4.57.1; 5.57.2–4; 4.58.4, Romans; 8.4.2, 3, Volscians; 5.52.5, Latins; 5.60.1.2, Fidenae; 5.34.2.2; 5.34.4.2 Tyrrhenians.

114. Dionysius, *Ant. rom.* 6.87.1; 10.43.3, where a decree of the Senate is read in assembly; 7.15.4; 7.16.1, 4; 7.7.1; 7.17.2, 6; 7.27.1; 7.27.3; 10.31.1, where the role of the Senate, assembly, consuls and tribunes is discussed; 8.43.7; 9.48.3, decree to Senate first and then to assembly; 10.33.4, 6; 10.34.2; 10.35.4, the role of the assembly in power struggles between consuls and tribunes. See 6.16.1; 6.30.2; 6.40.1; 6.43.3; 6.69.4; 6.70.2; 6.81.2; 6.83.2; 6.89.2; 6.96.2, for times when the Roman assembly of people (not the Senate) make decisions.

115. Dionysius, *Ant. rom.* 3.13.1; 3.27.3; 4.85.3; 6.6.1; 6.94.1; 7.6.4, 5; 8.54.5; 9.8.4; 9.10.5; 9.13.3; 9.50.6.

116. Dionysius, *Ant. rom.* 2.8.4.6, calling of the Plebians in Rome with the horn to assemblies in general.

117. Dionysius, *Ant. rom.* 8.82.6; 8.90.5; 10.32.4; 10.50.1; 10.56.2; 10.57.6; 11.45.1.

118. Dionysius, *Ant. rom.* 7.59.1; 7.59.2.1; 11.45.2.7. Section 7.59 contains a discussion of the workings of the centuriate and tribal assemblies and notes the novelty of what happens in the trial of Marcius Coriolanus. Similar discussions of the relationship can be found in 9.41.2, 4; 9.46.4; 9.49.3 highlights tribal assemblies as the place where tribunes and aediles chosen. See 2.7 for an explanation of the relationship between tribes and curiae as instituted by Romulus.

119. See for example Dionysius, *Ant. rom.* 2.57.3; 2.58.3; 2.60.3.1.

120. Dionysius, *Ant. rom.* 7.11.4; 7.15.4; 7.58.4; 8.70.1; 9.1.3; 9.54.1; 10.28.1; 11.50.1.

121. Dionysius, *Ant. rom.* 9.1.2, here of the Tyrrhenians.

122. Dionysius, *Ant. rom.* 7.6.4; 9.13.3.

Forum.¹²³ This is the only example of concurrent assemblies in the same city recorded in the literature I have surveyed.

The plural is used a number of times.¹²⁴ Often there are comments on the makeup of these assemblies: the inclusion of the baser elements, or their fractious nature.¹²⁵ Assemblies are involved in the overthrow of the Senate,¹²⁶ and the distinction between centuriate and tribal assemblies also applies here.¹²⁷ The plural can also be used for assemblies in general.¹²⁸

Dionysius's extensive and varied use of ἐκκλησία follows the general pattern and contours established here, from Thucydides onwards. However, the widening of the scope of assembly to include the history of the Roman Republic, and the tendency to be more explicit on what kind of assembly is meeting, show how usage in the first century BC was in some ways different from that in the fifth and fourth century BC. If Dionysius and Diodorus are included in the literature survey, it is no longer the Greek city-state that is primarily in view, and ἐκκλησία can be used for bodies which would not have been recognizable as assemblies by the Athenians and others.

Implications of Greek Literary Usage

In looking back over all the authors sampled here, several things can be noted. First, the broad contours of the standard definition of ἐκκλησία still stand: it is a temporary gathering of appropriate men called to decide on a variety of topics pertaining to the wellbeing of the city-state or area. It is a local body, although there are a few occasions noted above where a more representative body is in view.

Second, it is a political body.¹²⁹ That is, the ἐκκλησία is concerned with decisions about war, taxes, and making decisions. It can be influenced, corrupted, misused, and manipulated. Even when it is the army that assembles, the decisions remain political: whether and when to attack or withdraw. This is a common thread throughout the literature and is significant for

---

123. Dionysius, *Ant. rom.* 11.39.1–3.

124. Dionysius, *Ant. rom.* 11.39.1–3; 10.26.5; 10.54.6; 12.1.11.

125. Dionysius, *Ant. rom.* 4.23.6; 8.14.4; 8.58.3; 8.71.4, 5; 8.72.1; 8.73.1; 9.17.5.8.

126. Dionysius, *Ant. rom.* 9.43.4.

127. Dionysius, *Ant. rom.* 11.45.1, 3; 11.53.1 for centuriate assemblies; 11.45.1–3 for tribal assemblies.

128. Dionysius, *Ant. rom.* 40.20.1, the rights granted to the rich in the assembly. See also Dionysius, *Isocr.* 2; Dionysius, *1 Amm.* 11; Dionysius, *Thuc.* 48–49.

129. I will designate this usage a "*polis* assembly" or "*polis*" to distinguish from other uses.

this investigation because it raises the question of how Paul can use such a clearly political word and apply it to a group which does not represent all, in fact which normally represents very few, of the eligible voters in any city, and which includes women.

Third, as the review above has shown, different authors have different emphases. These emphases can be related to genre; compare the austere decision-making of Thucydides's assembly with the frivolous mockery of Aristophanes. However, the variety also lies in subject matter, so Dionysius and Diodorus's inclusion of Roman history changes how they discuss ἐκκλησία and what can be included in the term. Similarly, Plato's more philosophical discussion of the nature of the assembly introduces the term assemblymen, and Aristotle hints at the conception of the ἐκκλησία as a corporate body; the same may be true in Aristophanes's idea of the assembly having a child. When considering Paul's usage, it must be recognized that both the genre and subject matter of his writing are different. The literature I have surveyed does not include many epistles, tends to be for general consumption by an elite audience rather than to a particular community or communities, and has a high-political bias, the doings of great men.

Fourth, and critically for this study, it is legitimate to ask what role the use of the term ἐκκλησία between the fifth and first centuries BC has had in determining how Paul can use the term. Whilst the general contours are clear, there is enough variety here to suggest that the term can have a wider application, such as to a gathering of soldiers, and that the term can be applied in new ways, as noted above in the usage of Dionysius and Diodorus. The general contours of the term are as frequently described in the scholarly literature; however, there is significant flexibility in how ἐκκλησία is used. I would argue that this leaves scope for Paul, not writing about city politics, and writing in a different genre and with a different subject matter, to use the word differently. It is true that ἐκκλησία is generally used for an assembly in a city, but arguably the Greek background provides one semantic range for understanding ἐκκλησία which may or may not be followed and expanded by Paul.[130]

Ἐκκλησία in the Septuagint and Philo

In this section, I will examine the occurrences of ἐκκλησία in the Septuagint and Philo.[131] In doing so, I will examine three issues. The first arises from the

130. For a similar position, see Giles, *What on Earth*, 230.

131. I have chosen not to examine Josephus, as his writings do not predate the Pauline corpus. For a comment on his use of ἐκκλησία, see Du Toit, "*Paulus Oecumenicus*,"

foregoing discussion of Greek literature, and from the discussion of whether Septuagint or Greek literary usage was most influential on NT authors: how the Septuagint related to Greek usage elsewhere. For example, Schmidt argues strongly that, whilst there is an analogy between NT and Greek usage of ἐκκλησία, the significance of the term comes from the Septuagint;[132] in reexamining Septuagint usage, I will examine the relationship to the wider Greek literary tradition.

Second, there is a need to consider the arguments made about Septuagint usage by O'Brien, Robinson and others. There is the contention that the assembly is always assembled. So, Robinson states that ἐκκλησία was used "for the congregation of Israel. It did not apply to the members of the society of Israel whether assembled or not assembled, but to their actual meeting together."[133] There is the argument that certain assemblies have special significance for understanding the NT usage of ἐκκλησία; O'Brien states, "Of particular significance, however, are those instances of *ekklēsia* (rendering *qāhāl*) which denote the congregation of Israel when it assembled to hear the work of God on Mt. Sinai, or later on Mt. Zion where all Israel was required to assemble three times a year."[134] There is also the question of who is involved in the assembly; whether it is an assembly of the whole nation, or a representative assembly.[135]

Third some comments will be made on ἐκκλησία as a translation of the Hebrew word קָהָל, and the relationship between עֵדָה and קָהָל' in seeking to determine the range of meaning for ἐκκλησία in the Septuagint.

Ἐκκλησία in the Septuagint and Greek Literature

Ἐκκλησία is used to describe groups gathered together for various purposes, in a way which largely parallels Greek literary usage elsewhere, but

---

134n68.

132. Schmidt, "ἐκκλησία," 514. He notes how ἐκκλησία became a technical term transliterated into Latin, and how the church avoided describing itself as a cultic society, despite the popularity of the term. See also Trebilco, *Self-designations*, 166–67. See also Du Toit, "Paulus Oecumenicus."

133. Robinson, *Selected Works*, 231. See also Knox, *Sent by Jesus*, 55.

134. O'Brien, "Church," 90. For the same argument, see O'Brien, *Colossians*, 57–58. So also, Knox, *Selected Works*, 24, who argues that the key text is Deuteronomy 4:10. He also links the rock in Matthew 16:18 to Deuteronomy and Numbers 20:10.

135. O'Brien, "Church," 90, argues that the whole nation is involved in Deuteronomy 4:10; 9:10; 18:16; 31:30; Judges 20:2, but that chief representatives are present in 1 Kings 8:14, 22, 55.

with some differences of nuance related to the genre of the works being discussed. In all these occurrences, an actual assembly assembled is in view.

The cognate verb is used for the act of gathering, for a gathering of the assembly,[136] of the people more generally,[137] of elders and officials,[138] a mustering for war,[139] and a gathering of the Jews of Susa.[140] This usage is similar to the general contours previously noted.

The noun ἐκκλησία is used to describe a gathering of prophets,[141] a gathering of armies,[142] an army confronted by a prophet and some leaders,[143] and a gathering for a judicial function, such as in Nehemiah 5:7 and 5:13, where Nehemiah gathers an assembly to deal with the nobles.[144] The reference in Nehemiah 5 may well be the closest of anything in the Hebrew Bible to the working of a Greek assembly, with the emphasis on holding the nobles to account, and a decision agreed upon by the whole assembly,[145] although the covenant renewal element of this assembly and therefore its links with assemblies such as those in Deuteronomy should not be underplayed.[146]

In keeping with the different genre of writings here, ἐκκλησία is used where the setting of worship is more explicit than in Greek usage. For example, in Psalm 25,[147] the assembly of the wicked in v. 5[148] is contrasted with

---

136. Lev 8:3, 4; Num 20:8, 10; Josh 18:1; Judg 20:1. Note that in all these cases it is a gathering of the συναγωγή. See also Jeremiah 33:9; 43:9; 1 Maccabees 6:19 (assembling the people) and 1 Maccabees 12:35 (assembling the elders).

137. Deut 31:12; 1 Chr 13:5; 15:3; 2 Chr 15:9; 24:6.

138. Deut 31:28; 1 Kgs 8:1; 1 Chr 28:1; 2 Chr 5:2, 3.

139. 2 Sam 20:14, 1 Kgs 12:21, 2 Chr 11:1.

140. Esth 4:16. See Schmidt, "ἐκκλησία," 527–28.

141. 1 Sam 19:20.

142. 1 Sam 17:47. See O'Brien, "Church," 89, the gathering of an army in preparation for war.

143. 2 Chr 28:14. See O'Brien, "Church," 89, who includes this reference with 1 Samuel 17:47, although the assembly here happens after returning from battle.

144. Neh 5:7, 13; see also Mic 2:5. Giles sees Nehemiah 5:13 as a reference to Israel as "a religio-political entity" (Giles, *What on Earth*, 234). However, an actual assembly is summoned in 5:12. It may then be a representative assembly.

145. Summers, "Nehemiah 5:1–13," 184–85, notes the town-meeting elements of the passage, and how this is a political gathering because it is concerned with the affairs of the *polis*, the city or community.

146. On covenant renewal see, for example, Levering, *Ezra and Nehemiah*, 158.

147. Eng: 26.

148. Ps 25:5 (Eng: 26:5). "The 'coming together' of an unruly and potentially dangerous crowd" (O'Brien, "Church," 89–90). As Gray, *I & II Kings*, 206–7 notes, also citing Qumran, the use of ἐκκλησία in this way shows that the word does not have specifically religious connotations.

the regular assemblies in v. 12,[149] whilst in Psalm 88:6, God is praised in an assembly of the holy ones in heaven,[150] and the Holy Ones in view are most likely heavenly begins, not human.[151] This is not a usage noted elsewhere in the Greek literature, however in all these instances, there is still an actual assembly in view.

In those works in the Septuagint which are not part of the Hebrew Bible, the relationship with the use of ἐκκλησία in wider Greek literature, and yet the distinctive character of these assemblies can be seen. Perhaps clearest is Judith,[152] where four times the assembly of the people of Bethulia is mentioned.[153] Here we have a local assembly after the Greek pattern, and the assembly here questions, laments, and summons.[154] However, in two of the four occurrences in Judith, there are explicit requests to God for help, from or associated with the assembly.[155] So here we have a Greek assembly of the *polis*, but one with a particular character because the population are Israelites.

In 1 Maccabees, assembly is used in a number of ways. In 1 Maccabees 2:56, assembly refers to the testimony of Caleb in the assembly of Numbers 13:26, and thus the whole assembly of Israel in the wilderness is in view.[156] It is also used for a body of faithful soldiers,[157] for a theoretically comprehensive gathering after the restoration of the altar in the temple,[158] for a great assembly, whose precise composition is unclear, but which looks in its behavior to follow the general pattern of a Greek polis assembly,[159] and for diplomacy at the assembly in Jerusalem.[160] With the exception of 1

---

149. Craigie, *Psalms 1–50*, 226, notes the implicit contrast with wicked assembly in v. 5.

150. Ps 88:6 (Eng: 89:7).

151. Tate, *Psalms 51–100*, 409, 420.

152. Wills, "Book of Judith," 1075, dates Judith to around 100 BC, which would fit with a widespread understanding of the Greek *polis*, and its extensive application outside Greece, for which see Diodorus and Dionysius.

153. Jdt 6:16, 21; 7:29; 14:6.

154. Jdt 6:16; 7:29; and 14:6 respectively.

155. Jdt 7:29; 6:21.

156. Note here use of ἐκκλησία for the assembly, and συναγωγή, in Numbers 13:26, further indication of overlap of terminology.

157. 1 Macc 3:13.

158. 1 Macc 4:59. See Doran, "First Book of Maccabees," 72, noting a number of links between this passage and earlier sacred assemblies. For later associations of the festival here, see Bartlett, *1 Maccabees*, 74.

159. 1 Macc 5:16. Doran, "First Book of Maccabees," 77, notes how the Maccabees are constantly portrayed as consulting the people.

160. 1 Macc 14:19.

THE MEANING OF ἐκκλησία   39

Maccabees 2:56, these occurrences follow the pattern observed here: local assemblies with particular Jewish characteristics.

The book of Sirach contains several references to the assembly. In many of them, a specific assembly is not in view, but the assembly in general, where wisdom exalts,[161] where the acts of the righteous will be recognized,[162] or where the adulteress will be punished.[163] One use relates closely to the Greek assembly, where Sirach discusses how craftsmen are not sought for the βουλή or the ἐκκλησία[164] and Sirach calls upon the people and the leaders of the ἐκκλησία to listen.[165] ἐκκλησία is also used for a gathering of a mob.[166] Du Toit argues that Ben Sira is important given the marks of interculturality in the document, that Sirach has "the meeting of a Greek δῆμος in mind," and that a local assembly is in view here.[167] However for a number of reasons, I don't think Du Toit's conclusion can be established with such certainty. First, in Sirach 50:13 and 20, the assembly in view is the assembly of all Israel at Sinai,[168] and in Sirach 46:7, the assembly in the wilderness.[169] Although these are past occurrences, at 39:10, Sirach parallels the praise of the scribe by the assembly and by nations, suggesting that an assembly of all Israel may be in view here too. Second, most of the references in Sirach are general in nature, which, allied with the poetic genre of the work, makes it impossible to be certain that Sirach generally has a local assembly in view. He certainly sometimes has an assembly of all Israel in view and may have that assembly in view on other occasions, however theoretical it might be in Sirach's historical setting.

Looking at the references from Judith, 1 Maccabees, and Sirach as a whole, the influence of the Greek *polis* is discernible. However, I do not detect a straightforward line of development towards a local assembly.

161. Sir 15:5.

162. Sir 31:11. For similar uses of the assembly in general, see Sir 21:17; 39:10; 44:15. A similar generalized reference can be found in Psalms of Solomon 10:6.

163. Sir 23:34.

164. Sir 38:33, and see the passage in general, Sir 38:24–34. See also Skehan and Di Lella, *Wisdom of Ben Sira*, 451, who underline this by noting that the craftsmen lack qualifications for the assembly.

165. Sir 33:19.

166. Sir 26:5.

167. Du Toit, "*Paulus Oecumenicus*," 135–36

168. Du Toit, "*Paulus Oecumenicus*," 136, does recognize this cultic occasion. Marcos, *Septuagint in Context*, 316, notes the Greek panegyric tradition here, but how this is still an assembly of all Israel. This underlines the mixed nature of Sirach, and the need to avoid sharp division between Septuagint and Greek literary usage.

169. The same assembly to which 1 Maccabees 2:56 referred, Numbers 13:26.

Instead, in all the occurrences mentioned here, we have an actual assembly assembled, which shares many characteristics with the assembly of the *polis*, but which also has a particular Jewish character.

Turning to Philo, a similar pattern can be observed. There are times when Philo has in mind the Greek *polis* assembly,[170] other occasions when the assembly in view is more general but owes more to Moses and Sinai,[171] and one occasion when Philo refers to a divine assembly of the gods, referring back to Plato in the Timaeus.[172] Here we see Greek usage with a particular Jewish character, and in the final example, a particular usage driven by the context.

There are then marked similarities between Greek literary usage of ἐκκλησία and the Septuagint, although those similarities vary depending on the genre of the literature and its historical origins. Certainly, the idea of an assembly actually assembled remains prominent. At the same time, usage in the Septuagint and Philo has distinctive characteristics, as outlined previously.

The ἐκκλησία of all Israel

We now turn to examining those occurrences of ἐκκλησία, which are said to have particular significance, the gathering of the whole congregation of Israel, a comprehensive assembly. There are several occasions when a comprehensive assembly gathers. The first such assembly is at Horeb and is discussed in Deuteronomy.[173] Knox highlights Deuteronomy 4:10 as a key text in identifying this assembly,[174] and here Moses refers back to Horeb, speaking to a people who did not stand there as if they did,[175] and calls them to remember what they saw and heard. This highlights both the foundational nature of the assembly at Horeb, but also its inclusiveness, which seems to extend beyond those who were there. Deuteronomy 5:22 is similar, and further establishes the essential characteristic of this assembly: the

---

170. Philo, *Abr.* 20; Philo, *Ios.* 73; Philo, *Decal.* 39; Philo, *Spec.* 1.55; 2.44; Philo, *Prob.* 6, 138.

171. Philo, *Deus* 111; *Somn.* 2.187.

172. Philo, *Aet.* 13.

173. Deut 4:10; 9:10; 18:16. This assembly, of course, features in Exodus, although it is not translated with ἐκκλησία.

174. Knox, *Selected Works*, 24.

175. McConville, *Deuteronomy*, 105–6, notes that only Moses stood before the Lord at Horeb.

people are (vicariously) addressed by God.[176] Also in Deuteronomy, there are a number of occasions when those who are excluded from the assembly are noted.[177] As Du Toit notes, the existence of entry conditions suggests a closed group, and therefore an ongoing entity, not restricted to the time of meeting, an idea which is seen more clearly still in Nehemiah 13:1–3, where those of foreign descent are not just excluded from assembling, but are excommunicated from the people.[178] Finally, Deuteronomy 31:30 recognizes that there is an assembly on the edge of the promised land who hear about Horeb, and who are to put the commands from Horeb into practice.

Deuteronomy then establishes a pattern for the assembly of all Israel as the place where God's word is heard, and as a gathering. However, the crossgenerational nature of the assembly in Deuteronomy 4, and the exclusions in Deuteronomy 23, suggest that, whilst Deuteronomy deals with an actual assembly, that assembly represents an ongoing reality. The assembly has some kind of existence when not assembled.

Later assemblies follow a similar pattern to those in Deuteronomy.[179] The comprehensiveness of the assembly at Mizpah is emphasized by the penalties enacted on those who fail to turn up.[180] In Ezra 10,[181] the call to the assembly includes the explicit injunction that those who fail to attend will be expelled. This injunction only makes sense if those involved are considered to be part of the assembly even in their absence, suggesting a persistent reality. Nehemiah 8 emphasizes that all the exiles have assembled,[182] and how this assembly includes women and children.[183]

The Psalms present a challenge for interpretation here, as the generalized nature of many of the references to ἐκκλησία make precise identification of the assembly in view difficult, but it is possible that some of the

---

176. See McConville, *Deuteronomy*, 131–32, for the foundational nature of this assembly.

177. Deut 23:2–4, 9.

178. Du Toit, "*Paulus Oecumenicus*," 135. See also McConville, *Deuteronomy*, 131.

179. Josh 9:2 (Eng: 8:35).

180. Judg 20:2; 21:5, 8.

181. Ezra 10:1, 8, 12, 14.

182. Neh 8:2, 17. Duggan, *Covenant Renewal*, 85, notes the emphasis on community here, emphasized seven times in these verses with five different expressions.

183. Duggan, *Covenant Renewal*, 104–5.

references in the Psalms to the great assembly,[184] or blessed assembly,[185] or to an assembly of the people,[186] are comprehensive, [187] as also in Joel's call for all to come to a sacred assembly at Zion.[188]

The comprehensive assembly, patterned after the example of Sinai, is a recurring theme in the usage of ἐκκλησία in the OT. However, some of these references are not wholly comprehensive, for ἐκκλησία is also used for a representative assembly. Significant here are the references to the assembly that gathers for the dedication of the temple in 1 Kings 8. In 1 Kings 8:1–2, the composition of the assembly is described: it is made up of the elders, heads, and chiefs (v. 1), and all the men of Israel (v. 2).[189] However, this group is then referred to as the whole assembly of Israel in 1 Kings 8:14, 22, and 55, and the size of this assembly of all Israel is emphasized in 1 Kings 8:65.[190] Other examples of this usage are the assembly David calls to establish Solomon's succession,[191] the assembly at Gibeon,[192] and the assembly described in 1 Chronicles 13:2 and 4, where an assembly which does not include all Israel is described as the whole assembly of Israel,[193] suggesting that here again there is a representative role: some can be considered in lieu of the whole.[194]

---

184. Ps 21:26 (Eng: 22:25); 39:10 (Eng: 40:10). In context, perhaps also Psalm 21:23 (Eng: 22:22) can be included here, as well as the assembly of the many of Psalm 34:18 (Eng: 35:18). A similar usage can be detected in some of the Sirach references noted earlier.

185. Ps 25:12 (Eng: 26:12); Ps 67:27 (Eng: 68:28). See also Psalm 149:1, the assembly of the saints. Hossfeld and Zenger, *Psalms 3*, 648, talk of a cultic community here.

186. Ps 106:32 (Eng: 107:32). Note the parallel here with the elders. Hossfeld and Zenger, *Psalms 3*, 108, argue that the elders here are not an official body.

187. The same can be said of Proverbs 5:14 and Job 30:28, which may have a more localized assembly in view.

188. Joel 2:16.

189. Whether or not all the men of Israel is to be taken as an expansion of v. 1, or whether those listed in v. 1 are counted as all the men of Israel is not essential here, as either way this is not an actual assembly of all Israel. O'Brien notes this representative use, of a "congregation of tribal leaders, or patriarchal chiefs" in 1 Kings 8 ("Church," 90). See also Gray, *I & II Kings*, 207 who regards the presence of tribal representatives at the ceremony as possible.

190. See also 2 Chr 6:3, 12, 13; 7:8.

191. 1 Chr 28:2, 8; 29:1, 10, 20. This assembly is not comprehensive (28:1), yet functions in 20:8 as all Israel, the assembly of the Lord.

192. 2 Chr 1:3, 5.

193. This assembly is clearly not comprehensive, as it sends out for the "rest of our brothers."

194. 2 Chr 10:3 may be an exception to the general pattern of representative assemblies, as there are no indications that the assembly is representative. However, the

A similar pattern can be seen in other assemblies in 2 Chronicles. Their comprehensive nature is emphasized, but that comprehensive nature does not mean all Israel was present. So, in 2 Chronicles 20:5,[195] Jehoshaphat's assembly is of Judah and Jerusalem, although the chronicler notes that people came from every town of Judah,[196] suggesting that not everybody came. A similar dynamic is at work in 2 Chronicles 23:3, where the whole assembly makes a covenant, but it is clear that those present are representatives of the people.[197] Even the assembly which Hezekiah calls in 2 Chronicles 30[198] is not completely comprehensive, because some refuse to come.[199] These are comprehensive assemblies in that they represent the will of the people, even when not everybody is present. They are assembled, but they also represent people who are not there.

One feature of a number of these assemblies is a reference back to the gathering at Horeb.[200] This is explicit in 1 Kings 8, where the temple as the successor to the tabernacle and new home for the ark of the covenant is noted. It is also a feature of 2 Chronicles 29–30, where the invitation to the whole of Israel is noted,[201] as is the fact that nothing like this had happened since the days of Solomon,[202] and what is being celebrated is the Passover.[203] The assemblies in later Israelite history may have become representative, as the tribes no longer traveled together; however, the aspiration remained for a united people gathered together. This desire can perhaps also be seen in the use of ἐκκλησία to describe the traveling company of returning exiles—one of the things being celebrated here is the exiles returning together as a company.[204]

---

logistics of gathering all Israel, and the way in which they can be sent away and reconvened in three days (10:5), may indicate that it was functionally representative.

195. See also 2 Chr 20:14.

196. 2 Chr 20:4.

197. 2 Chr 23:2. A similar dynamic is at work in 2 Chr 29:23, 28, 31, 32; 30:2, 4, where a more limited assembly is in view.

198. 2 Chr 30:2, 4, 13, 17, 23–25.

199. 2 Chr 30:10–11.

200. Examples of a tendency to refer back to the wilderness wanderings in general can be seen in 1 Maccabees 2:56 and Sirach 46:7, which both refer back to Numbers 13:26.

201. 2 Chr 30:6.

202. 2 Chr 30:26.

203. See also Japhet, *1 and 2 Chronicles*, 913–15, who notes that these chapters contain material not in the 2 Kings account, and highlights the frequency of קָהָל in the Hezekiah periscope (928). Both these observations indicate the importance of Horeb, as Hezekiah's idealized kingship climaxes in a restoration of the assembly.

204. Ezra 2:64; Neh 7:66. Giles, *What on Earth*, 234, sees here references to Israel as

Philo quotes the exclusion from the assembly of Deuteronomy 23 regularly,[205] underlining the foundational character of this assembly for Jewish self-identity, even after the return from exile.

I agree with O'Brien and others that the Sinai assembly is significant for understanding ἐκκλησία in the Septuagint. However, part of that significance lies in two features of the comprehensive assembly which need to be noted. First, the assembly has some form of existence, even when it is not assembled. Second, people can be considered part of the assembly, even when they are not there, whether that is because they should have been there, or because others are representing them.

Other Terminology for the Assembly

Turning now to examine the relationship between עֵדָה and קָהָל' and ἐκκλησία and συναγωγή, two issues are relevant to this study.

The first is the relationship between ἐκκλησία and συναγωγή. ἐκκλησία is used to translate קָהָל, which is generally translated "convocation" or "assembly."[206] However, קָהָל is not only translated ἐκκλησία, but also συναγωγή.[207] In particular in Genesis, Leviticus, and Numbers, קָהָל is translated by συναγωγή twenty-one times, and in Ezekiel and Jeremiah nineteen out of twenty times.[208] This suggests a terminological overlap between ἐκκλησία and συναγωγή, and this has raised the question as to why Paul and other New Testament authors chose to use ἐκκλησία, when other terms, such as συναγωγή, were available. Schmidt[209] argues that ἐκκλησία was a wider and more significant term than συναγωγή, while Giles[210] argues that there is significant overlap between the two terms. It could also be argued that ἐκκλησία helps to draw a distinction between Jewish and

---

"a religio-political entity," arguing that the note of assembly is absent. I think it is better to see these two references as a record of the company of the traveling exiles as they returned, a company that was assembled as it traveled.

205. Philo, *Leg.* 3.8, 81; Philo, *Post.* 177; Philo, *Ebr.* 213; Philo, *Conf.* 144; Philo, *Migr.* 69; Philo, *Somn.* 2.184. Implicit references: Philo, *Mut.* 205; Philo, *Virt.* 108. *Spec.* 1.325 builds more general applications to assemblies from Deuteronomy 23.

206. See Schmidt, "ἐκκλησία," 527 for the four occasions when the translation is from the stem קהל. See Johnston, *Doctrine*, 36 for a sample summary of usage.

207. According to Giles, *What on Earth*, 233, קָהָל appears 123 times in the Old Testament; seventy-three times it is translated by ἐκκλησία, and thirty-five by συναγωγή.

208. Coenen, "Church," 292.

209. Schmidt, "ἐκκλησία," 517, although he also notes on 518 that συναγωγή can be used of the Christian community.

210. Giles, *What on Earth*, 237–38.

Christian gatherings,[211] or that the comparative neutrality of the term allowed the early Christians considerable scope to define what it meant for them. At this remove and without any explicit New Testament guidance, it is difficult if not impossible to answer this question with any certainty, and certainly any necessarily tentative conclusions regarding why ἐκκλησία was chosen should not direct how the term should be understood in its New Testament and, specifically here, Pauline context. It may well be as simple as the fact that συναγωγή was a word already in use by others.

Second, עֵדָה is also used to refer to the assembly or congregation, and is usually translated in the LXX συναγωγή, and never ἐκκλησία.[212] A distinction in meaning is sometimes made between עֵדָה and קָהָל. So Ward argues that עֵדָה is used of the society itself, the people of God, whereas עֵדָה denotes the actual assembly,[213] and Campbell argues that this can be seen in how five-sixths of the occurrences of עֵדָה are found in the books concerned with the journeying of Israel to the promised land: Exodus, Leviticus, Numbers, and Joshua.[214] Coenen draws a distinction between עֵדָה as the summons to assembly, of the people or the עֵדָה,[215] and עֵדָה as the community assembled, and the community as a people.[216] He argues that עֵדָה is the word for "community," and קָהָל the word for the ceremonial expression that results from the covenant.[217] Giles argues for the assimilation of the עֵדָה idea of community to the קָהָל idea of assembly. Giles argues that there are places where קָהָל is used instead of עֵדָה such as in Deuteronomy,[218] or where קָהָל replaces עֵדָה, such as in 2 Chronicles 23:1-3.[219] Therefore, קָהָל can be used in much the same way as עֵדָה, for the community, whether gathered or not.[220] Giles argues that the best translation for ἐκκλησία as it is used in the New Testament is "community," noting the "pedigree" of this translation stretching back to Luther and Tyndale.[221]

---

211. Best, *Ephesians*, 623; Schnelle, *Apostle Paul*, 560.
212. Coenen, "Church," 292.
213. Ward, "Ekklesia," 166.
214. Campbell, "Origin and Meaning," 133.
215. Coenen, "Church," 292
216. Coenen, "Church," 294.
217. Coenen, "Church," 295. He finds similar usage in the Qumran on 296. For a similar distinction see Johnston, *Doctrine*, 36-37.
218. Giles, *What on Earth*, 233.
219. Giles, *What on Earth*, 234.
220. Giles, *What on Earth*, 235.
221. Giles, *What on Earth*, 241-43. For a more general critique of this view, see Peterson, "Locus," 212-13.

However, I would argue that trying to find a clear distinction between the terms עֵדָה and קָהָל which can then inform the discussion of ἐκκλησία and συναγωγή, seeks to read too much into the evidence for two related reasons.

First, קָהָל can be translated by both ἐκκλησία and συναγωγή, and therefore there is an interchangeability of terms here, as the translation choice seems to depend on which biblical book is being considered.[222] Similarly, עֵדָה and קָהָל overlap in meaning, for the assembly described as עֵדָה in Exodus is rendered by קָהָל in Deuteronomy. The interchangeability of terms is confirmed by the references to Numbers 13:26 in 1 Maccabees 2:56 and Sirach 46:7, which both use ἐκκλησία to describe an assembly originally rendered συναγωγή, as a translation of עֵדָה, and Philo refers to the Sinai gathering as ἐκκλησία, in passages where the Septuagint does not use ἐκκλησία.[223]

Second, the meaning of ἐκκλησία is not inherent to the word, but is determined by the context. My analysis of occurrences from both the Septuagint and Greek literature has shown that ἐκκλησία is an assembly, but what kind of assembly, or whether the assembly is representative, or whether it overlaps in meaning with other terms depends on the context of the usage. This is a similar observation to that made about the afore-mentioned *ekkaleo* idea; the significance of being called out in the NT is determined contextually, not etymologically; the precise nuance of ἐκκλησία in any given author should also be determined from their contextual usage, where usage elsewhere is a guide but not determinative.

Conclusion

Three things should to be noted here from the use of ἐκκλησία in the Septuagint and Philo. First, I have argued above that there is considerable overlap between usage in the Septuagint and wider Greek literature, and that in both cases the meaning of the term is driven by the context. Therefore, the distinctions that are drawn between 'Greek' and 'Jewish' usage should not be drawn too sharply.[224] The Septuagint represents a contextual nuancing of a term capable of a range of meanings in Greek literature.[225]

---

222. See Schmidt, "ἐκκλησία," 529.

223. Philo, *Post.* 144; Philo, *Her.* 251; Philo, *Decal.* 32, 45.

224. Compare Du Toit, "*Paulus Oecumenicus*," 132–43.

225. Compare Schmidt, who describes ἐκκλησία as "a wholly secular term," given meaning by the context, by who constitutes the assembly ("ἐκκλησία," 527).

Second, several interesting contextual interpretations emerge from the Septuagint. There is the generalized idea of the assembly found in the Psalms and Sirach, where the precise composition is elusive. There is the representative assembly idea, which emerges particularly in the later historical books. Finally, the exclusions of Deuteronomy 23 and other strictures on attendance suggest that people are members of the assembly even when the assembly is not assembled. There are also some unique uses, such as for an assembly of heavenly beings or an assembly of gods, which indicate the flexibility in the possible application of ἐκκλησία.

Third, in my discussion of עֵדָה and קָהָל' and ἐκκλησία and συναγωγή, I have emphasized the importance of the context, not a set of ideas considered inherent to the term, in determining meaning.

Ἐκκλησία in Greek Literature and the Septuagint

From this study on Greek literature, I noted the overwhelmingly political dimension of ἐκκλησία, and the primary usage as a local body which assembles to make decisions. I also noted some flexibility of usage depending on author, and some unusual uses. I concluded that Paul, writing in a different genre and with different concerns, could make use of the flexibility of the term in an analogous way to Polybius, Diodorus, and especially Dionysius, as they extend the Greek polis to include Roman assemblies of various kinds.

From my examination of the Septuagint, I noted the significant commonality between Septuagint and Greek literary usage, genre-related differences, and the importance of the assembly of all Israel. I further noted the idea of a representative assembly, and some indications that the assembly existed even when not assembled. I have emphasized the importance of context in determining meaning.

There are three implications for understanding ecclesial solidarity in Paul from my examination of Greek literature and the Septuagint, about what might be expected from the Pauline corpus.

First, it is to be expected that ἐκκλησία will be used for a local church in a given city or other similar geographical area. If Greek usage is followed, then the plural might be used to refer to a series of consecutive assemblies or churches; it would be unusual for it to be used for different assemblies in the same location. Septuagint usage might suggest that sometimes representative assemblies are in view, and that there would be an ongoing concern for the comprehensive assembly.

Second, a certain level of flexibility might be expected from the Pauline corpus, as a political term is applied to a group which functions in a different way. Whilst the Septuagint usage might be instructive here, the comprehensive assembly seen above was an assembly of Israel, and when other assemblies are in view, such as at Bethulia, they are often political in nature and owe much to Greek literature. There needs to be a recognition that the context into which Paul writes, to groups in various geographical locations around the Mediterranean which nevertheless have some form of commonality, would impact his use of ἐκκλησία in ways similar to, but not necessarily restricted to, Septuagint usage, or that of Dionysius and Diodorus, as compared to Thucydides.

Third, these two observations underline the importance of context in understanding Pauline usage. Therefore, in examining occurrences of ἐκκλησία in the Pauline corpus, I will seek meaning first from the context of the letter and Paul's use elsewhere, neither ignoring nor prioritizing usage in Greek literature and the Septuagint.

In coming to Paul, we come with a term used for an assembly assembled, but which is also capable of related but different usage.

Contextualizing ἐκκλησία in the First-century World

In the final section of this chapter, I will seek to summarize some of the findings of recent studies of the first-century world as they relate to how ἐκκλησία should be understood, to ensure that the exegetical examination of the Pauline context takes account of relevant historical and social information.

For the purposes of this study, there are two key questions to be answered. First a question of location: where did early Christians meet? Second, the question of size: how large were these gatherings?

It is generally assumed that ἐκκλησίαι in the mid-first century met in houses, or domestic spaces. Edward Adams has challenged this consensus, arguing that early Christian meetings were not almost exclusively in houses[226] by casting doubt on the certainty with which the NT evidence is normally approached,[227] before providing evidence for the possible usage of other places such as shops, workshops, warehouse cells, barns,[228] hotels and inns, rented dining rooms and bathhouses,[229] and gardens, watersides,

---

226. Adams, *Earliest Christian Meeting Places*, 9–15
227. Adams, *Earliest Christian Meeting Places*, 18–44.
228. Adams, *Earliest Christian Meeting Places*, 156.
229. Adams, *Earliest Christian Meeting Places*, 179–80.

urban open space, and tomb sides.[230] He wants a wider perspective "which acknowledges the importance of houses as Christian meeting places during this period, but insists that Christian groups could plausibly have met in a variety of other available places too."[231] As I noted in chapter 1, this is a necessary observation and corrective. However, most of the settings outlined by Adams would still present the same challenges of size and possible patronage; the church would be meeting in a shop or a warehouse with an owner, and someone would need to be responsible for renting the dining room or bathhouse. Even in the Mediterranean climate, none of the outdoor settings suggested by Adams would be suitable as a permanent meeting place. Granted that the meeting places for the early church were not almost exclusively houses, the fact remains that a room where size restrictions and ownership were potentially relevant remain the overwhelmingly picture.

Gehring has traced the importance of houses for Christians from the ministry of Jesus based in Peter's house in Capernaum,[232] through the "upper room church" of early Christianity in Acts 1–5,[233] to the extensive evidence for ἐκκλησίαι meeting in houses in the Pauline mission,[234] noting the likely size and shape of a number of the houses that may have been used by early Christians for gathering and worship.[235] Other studies show that to talk of a "house" as the location for the ἐκκλησία means recognizing the variety of houses in the first-century world. Jewett argues that the appropriate setting for at least some of the ἐκκλησίαι that met in houses in Rome is the blocks of *insulae*: small rented apartments where the poor lived a precarious existence.[236] In his study of houses in Pompeii, Oakes demonstrates a variety of different housing types within one block,[237] and then indicates how a "craftworker" house in Pompeii may indicate the kind of houses that people would have met in in Rome.[238] Horrell examines some buildings east of the theatre in Roman Corinth, suggesting that they might, with the judicious use of a "disciplined imagination" provide a context for understanding the kind of dwellings that Christians could have met in in first-century

230. Adams, *Earliest Christian Meeting Places*, 196–97.
231. Adams, *Earliest Christian Meeting Places*, 200.
232. Gehring, *House Church*, 35–42.
233. Gehring, *House Church*, 63–69.
234. Gehring, *House Church*, 131–54.
235. Gehring, *House Church*, 31–35, 65–69.
236. Jewett, *Romans*, 53–55.
237. Oakes, *Reading Romans*, 1–45.
238. Oakes, *Reading Romans*, 69–97. Note that Oakes argues against Jewett's tenement churches, as does Balch, "Paul, Families, and Households," 259.

Corinth.²³⁹ As noted, Adams adds further spaces. The precise location of the ἐκκλησίαι to which Paul wrote is almost certainly beyond us; however, these studies indicate both that Christians generally met in *domestic* spaces in the Greco-Roman world, defining *domestic* as a privately-owned space which was not just used for church meetings.²⁴⁰

The variety of domestic spaces leads naturally into the second question: that of size. How big were Christian ἐκκλησίαι in the first century? A variety of answers have been given to this question, but the element they share is that the size of the ἐκκλησία was sometimes limited by the size of the space in which it met. Oakes estimates that his "craftworker church" from Pompeii could accommodate around forty individuals,²⁴¹ and that the same ἐκκλησία in Romans, where property was generally smaller, would have accommodated around thirty.²⁴² It is likely that in many situations, this size of meeting space may well have accommodated everybody, and was not therefore a limitation. De Vos estimates the Christian community in Thessalonica at around twenty-five members, who would have met in an *insula*,²⁴³ and thirty members in Philippi who met in an *insula*.²⁴⁴ However, it appears that in some situations, the size of meeting space limited or adversely affected the ἐκκλησία. Thus, Murphy-O'Connor argues, based on his analysis of the space in a villa at Anaploga that some of the problems in the ἐκκλησία in Corinth stemmed from the fact that there was not a building available that could hold the forty to fifty (or more) people that made up the ἐκκλησία there.²⁴⁵ Other authors have noted that there appear to have been a variety of "house churches" in Rome, and that this appears to have contributed to some of the issues Paul addresses in his letter.²⁴⁶ On the other hand, Gehring argues that there would have been wealthy Christians able to rent an upper room in Jerusalem able to contain the whole ἐκκλησία,

---

239. Horrell, "Domestic Space," 367–68.

240. See the survey of various views on size and location in Adams, "First-century Models," 63–68. See also Linton, "House Church Meetings," 234–38.

241. Oakes, *Reading Romans*, 80–84.

242. Oakes, *Reading Romans*, 89–97.

243. De Vos, *Church and Community Conflicts*, 154.

244. De Vos, *Church and Community Conflicts*, 250–61.

245. Murphy-O'Connor, "House-Churches," 129–34. See also Banks, *Paul's Idea*, 35–36, who argues for a church size of around thirty to forty-five people, and Richards, *Paul and First-century*, 41, who estimates church size at forty to fifty based on "the house of the tragic poet" in Pompeii.

246. Watson, "Two Roman Congregations," 203–15, argues for separate Jewish and gentile congregations, whilst Lampe, "Roman Christians," 216–30, identifies seven or eight congregations and divisions. See also Jewett, *Romans*, 61–62.

around 120 individuals,[247] whilst De Vos argues that the whole ἐκκλησία of around one hundred met in Corinth perhaps once per month in a "club room" provided by Gaius.[248]

For the purposes of this study, it is not necessary to decide between these alternatives; rather, to recognize the issue that this discussion of size raises, the distribution of the early ἐκκλησίαι within particular geographical locations. We also see here a clarification as to what is meant by a domestic church: a domestic church is likely to be a gathering where size is ultimately restricted by space, and where a size of forty to fifty was probably much more common than spaces that could accommodate a hundred or more.

Although provisional and somewhat speculative, this understanding of local and/or domestic ἐκκλησία will help inform the investigation of ἐκκλησία in later chapters.

---

247. Gehring, *House Church*, 66, 68.
248. De Vos, *Church and Community Conflicts*, 195–205.

3. Paul's Earliest Letters

IN THIS CHAPTER I will examine ecclesial solidarity in Paul's earliest letters, 1 and 2 Thessalonians and Galatians, in relation to the three areas outlined in chapter 1, taking account of the exploration of the meaning of ἐκκλησία undertaken in chapter 2.

Ecclesial Solidarity and ἐκκλησία

In chapter 2, I noted three things of relevance for the examination of the use of ἐκκλησία in Paul's earliest letters: first, that usage for a local church is to be expected, but also that a representative use might be anticipated; second, flexibility linked to genre and purpose; and third, the importance of context. Here I will examine the seven occurrences of ἐκκλησία in Paul's earliest letters—seeking to understand them in context—and examine how they contribute to our understanding of ecclesial solidarity, looking first at any similarities and differences from Greek literary usage, before examining any implications these occurrences have for intra- and interchurch solidarity.

Paul's Early Use of ἐκκλησία

In each of the three letters examined here, Paul writes to a group or groups of believers addressing them either as a church: τῇ ἐκκλησίᾳ Θεσσαλονικέων (1 Thess 1:1; 2 Thess 1:1); or as a number of churches: ταῖς ἐκκλησίαις τῆς Γαλατίας (Gal 1:2). The similarities here with Greek usage have been frequently noted:[1] Paul refers to an ἐκκλησία meeting in a particular geographical location, recognizing the existence of assemblies in various places.[2] The ἐκκλησία in each place is an identifiable group, which gathers

---

1. See for example Banks, *Paul's Idea*, 29.

2. While there are some indications that there may have been multiple congregations in Thessalonica, due to the size of the city, the fame of the church, and the reference to "leaders" in 1 Thessalonians 5:12 (see Witherington, *1 and 2 Thessalonians*, 4; Malherbe, *Letters to the Thessalonians*, 14; Green, *Thessalonians*, 7–8; Gehring, *House Church*, 133), there is no direct evidence of multiple meeting places for the church

together. It is noticeable that, as Paul's earliest extant uses of ἐκκλησία they come without explanation. Paul presumes that his readers will understand what an ἐκκλησία is,[3] and it is often argued that the secular understanding of an assembly lies behind this term. In part, this is no doubt true, for common usage would provide a baseline understanding of what Paul understands an ἐκκλησία should be, and one which he could reasonably expect all his readers to understand.

However, the similarities with Greek usage should not be overstated, because the ἐκκλησίαι to which Paul writes are very different than the *polis* ἐκκλησίαι his readers would have been familiar with. They are not a *polis*, nor a group of soldiers, nor—to follow Septuagint usage—are they self-evidently a part of Israel assembled at Sinai or Zion. Nor is it likely that a link between ἐκκλησία and voluntary association would be obvious here, given the small number of times that ἐκκλησία is used for voluntary associations. It is possible that ἐκκλησία had already developed a particular meaning for the early Christians by the time Paul wrote his letters.[4] However, this common understanding of ἐκκλησία would have been shared with the Thessalonians and Galatians by Paul, and is only now accessible through close examination of these letters.

One of the ways Paul addresses his understanding of ἐκκλησία is found in 1 Thessalonians 5:12–22, where he addresses the conduct of the ἐκκλησία,[5] a topic frequently noted as being of concern in the Greek *polis* assembly.[6] In 1 Thessalonians 5:12–22, Paul exhorts members of the ἐκκλησία to behave in a certain way,[7] and these exhortations clarify Paul's understanding of ἐκκλησία in three ways.

---

in Thessalonica. This would suggest that no firm conclusions about the existence or otherwise of multiple house churches in Thessalonica at the time Paul wrote should be drawn, and therefore I will treat the Thessalonian correspondence as having been written to one local and domestic church.

3. The assumption that the term already meant something when Paul used it can be traced through a number of commentators. For example, Chrysostom, *Galatians*, 4; Luther, *Galatians*, 38–39; Calvin, *Galatians, Ephesians, Philippians and Colossians*, 10–11.

4. Various authors offer suggestions as to how the term was used by the early church before Paul wrote his letters, and where the term originated. See, for example, Trebilco, *Self-designations*, 183–98; Du Toit, "*Paulus Oecumenicus*," 138–40; and Van Kooten, "Ἐκκλησία τοῦ θεοῦ," 522–48.

5. See for example Malherbe, *Letters to the Thessalonians*, 308–9, who entitles 5:12–22 "On Intracommunal Relations."

6. See for example Thucydides, *History*, 1.87; 2.22; 6.51; 8.94, and chapter 2 of this book.

7. Green, *Thessalonians*, 246–47, argues that 1 Thessalonians 5:12–22 forms a set outline of teaching, noting similarities with Romans 12:3–17.

First, a number of these exhortations can be seen to reflect behavior that would be expected in the assembly. The Thessalonians are to recognize (εἰδέναι)[8] and esteem their leaders[9] who "labor in the Lord" (1 Thess 5:12–13), they are to behave in a way which is peaceable (1 Thess 5:13), and they are called on to admonish, encourage, help, and be patient with various groups (1 Thess 5:14), doing good rather than evil (1 Thess 5:15). There are similarities here with Greek literary usage, where the procedural concerns noted by the ten Attic Orators indicate a concern with right behavior in the assembly,[10] but there is nevertheless a shift from concern for procedural irregularity and oratory deception to a concern for "pastoral care."[11] Paul's understanding of what should take place in the believers' ἐκκλησία is very different from what was expected of a *polis* assembly.

Second, there are a number of exhortations within this section that go beyond behavior in the assembly. At least three deal with behavior at all times, which must include when the ἐκκλησία is not assembled (1 Thess 5:16–18). This suggests that the ἐκκλησία encompasses an ongoing set of relationships even when not physically assembled, much as was implied by the exclusions from the assembly in Deuteronomy 23, as Paul feels able to encourage collective behavior that is expressed in actions which take place both within and beyond the confines of the assembly.[12]

Third, there is no indication at the end of 1 Thessalonians 5 (or in Galatians and 2 Thessalonians) that the ἐκκλησία is dissolved, which was a frequent occurrence in Greek literature,[13] and can also be seen in Solomon's

---

8. For understanding the word in this way, indicating that the Thessalonians were to recognize legitimate leadership, see Clarke, *Pauline Theology*, 84; and Green, *Thessalonians*, 248.

9. For a discussion of leadership titles in 1 Thessalonians 5:12 and elsewhere, see Clarke, *Pauline Theology*, 71–74.

10. See, for example, Demosthenes, *Fals. leg.* 19, 34–35, 58, 185; Demosthenes, *Mid.* 8–9; Demosthenes, *Cor.*122–23; Demosthenes, *Aristocr.* 97; Demosthenes, *Timocr.* 21–22, 25–26, 80; Demosthenes, *Chers.* 32–34; Demosthenes, *3 Philip.* 4, 6; Aeschines, *Tim.* 22, 26, 33, 35; Aeschines, *Fals. leg.* 60, 68; Aeschines, *Ctes.* 67, 126, 149; Dinarchus, *Aristog.* 16.

11. The phrase is Malherbe's. See Malherbe, *Letters to the Thessalonians*, 323–27, for comments on "psychagogy" here.

12. A contrast can be drawn here with Aristophanes, for whom the assembly is often a place removed from the realities of life. For example, in Aristophanes, *Vespae* 32, where the verb is used of assembling of sheep, in the Pnyx, to be addressed by a pig, or in *Ecclesiazusae*, where the women are planning to sneak into the assembly to ensure that proper decisions are made. Also compare Sirach 38:33, where craftsmen are not the right kind of people for the assembly, to Paul's emphasis on the need for hard work here from all members of the ἐκκλησία.

13. For example, Xenophon, *Hell.* 2.4; Dionysius, *Ant. rom.* 2.56.5; 10.3.6.

dismissal of the people in 1 Kings 8:66, or the sending away of the assembly for three days in 1 Kings 12:5.

Paul's early use of ἐκκλησία indicates similarities with the usage noted in chapter 2, as Paul first uses ἐκκλησία for an assembly of people gathering in a particular location. However, these similarities should not mask the differences that I have noted above.

Intrachurch Solidarity

The three uses of ἐκκλησία at the start of these letters indicate little directly about ecclesial solidarity. Intrachurch solidarity in these letters will be explored through the imagery used and the language of imitation. However, one common feature of these uses is how they indicate that the core identity for the ἐκκλησία is in another. In 1 Thessalonians 1:1 and 2 Thessalonians 1:1, the ἐκκλησία is in God the Father and the Lord Jesus Christ.[14] Whether the preposition here is taken instrumentally or with an incorporative sense,[15] it expresses identity and belonging, and reminds Paul's readers that their ecclesial solidarity is founded in God and Jesus. This picture is reinforced by the instructions in 1 Thessalonians 5:12-24, which begin and end with reference to the Lord Jesus Christ, who legitimates those who labor (v. 12), who will return and who has called the Thessalonians into existence as a group (v. 23-24). The same can be said of Galatians 1:2, for the Galatians are reminded of the formation of their identity in 1:3-4, receiving grace and peace from the Father and Jesus, having been rescued by Jesus according to the Father's will. Ecclesial solidarity for these local congregations in Thessalonica and Galatians is founded on the work of the Lord Jesus Christ, and this reality is fundamental to their identity.

Interchurch Solidarity

The focus of this study is on the neglected area of interchurch solidarity, and so here I will look at four references to ἐκκλησία which may have a

---

14. 1 Thessalonians 1:1 and 2 Thessalonians 1:1 are very similar. The only difference is that 1 Thessalonians 1:1 reads "to the church . . . in God the Father," whereas 2 Thessalonians 1:1 reads "to the Church . . . in God our Father." Malherbe, *Paul and the Thessalonians*, 79 notes that this qualification is unusual, and argues that the "in" should be understood instrumentally, the assembly being called into existence by God. He takes this to be evidence of the eschatological dimension of the letter.

15. Malherbe, *Letters to the Thessalonians*, 99, takes it instrumentally. Bruce, *1 & 2 Thessalonians*, 7 argues for an incorporative force; Green, *Thessalonians*, 85, is similar.

translocal reference, and indicate the potential for solidarity between local ἐκκλησίαι.

First, in 1 Thessalonians 2:14 and Galatians 1:22, Paul refers to churches in or of Judea. When compared to the plural in Galatians 1:2, a pattern can be seen: the plural is used to designate multiple congregations in a region.[16] A number of commentators have suggested that Paul uses ἐκκλησίαι to refer to churches in a province,[17] and Bruce argues that this is distinguished from ἐκκλησία used to refer to the church in a city.[18] Certainly, it does seem to be Paul's early practice to use the plural to refer to a group of ἐκκλησίαι in one province or area. This is not a usage noted either from Greek literature or the Septuagint, for this is not a representative usage, but rather a grouping of ἐκκλησίαι. Whether or not the usage should be described as provincial, if it implies some kind of relationship between ἐκκλησίαι in a region, then it would have implications for interchurch solidarity, and there are indications that this is the case in each of the occurrences. In Galatians 1:2 the churches in Galatia are addressed together, and are addressed with the same designators, most notably brothers. In Galatians 1:22, the churches of Judea are described as having a common identity in Christ. In 1 Thessalonians 2:14 the churches of Judea are considered to be an imitable group, who have suffered together, who are again described as in Christ Jesus.

Four of the seven earliest references to ἐκκλησίαι are in the plural. Paul's frequent and early use of the plural for multiple churches suggests it is natural for him to talk of "local churches," and a group of associated churches in more than one locality. Already in the earliest letters, Paul is adopting a usage of ἐκκλησία which is not shared with either the Septuagint or Greek literature,[19] in using the plural to suggest some kind of common identity and bond in Christ Jesus. As presented in Greek literature, *polis* assemblies in different cities are likely to be competing rather than cooperating. The

---

16. Malherbe, *Letters to the Thessalonians*, 386, notes that five out of the seven occurrences of ἐκκλησίαι in Paul follow this pattern.

17. So, for example, in 1 Thessalonians 2:14, Judea is taken to cover the whole area of Palestine, so Green, *Thessalonians*, 141; Malherbe, *Letters to the Thessalonians*, 168; or at least a wider geographical area involving Galilee and Samaria, so Bruce, *1 & 2 Thessalonians*, 45. Significant for the idea that Paul thought in terms of Roman provinces is Magda, *Paul's Territoriality*, 82–102, who argues that Paul's toponymy is Roman, particularly in Romans 15:19 and Colossians 3:11, but also in 1 Thessalonians 2:14; 1 Corinthians 16:1, 5, 19; 2 Corinthians 1:1, 8; Galatians 3:1.

18. Bruce, *Galatians*, 103, argues that the plural in Galatians 1:2 is an indication that this letter is sent to a province rather than to a city.

19. The one exception here may be the PanHellenic league, although this was a representative assembly.

precise nature of this interchurch solidarity will be explored here and in the following chapters.

Second, in 2 Thessalonians 1:4, Paul refers to the churches of God in general; Paul writes about how he boasts in the Thessalonians among ταῖς ἐκκλησίαις τοῦ θεοῦ. This can be taken as a reference to the churches where Paul is,[20] or a more general reference.[21] In context, these churches are ones in which Paul is able to boast about the Thessalonians. This would certainly include Corinth, and likely extends to Achaia and Macedonia, and, if communication between churches in the first century was as widespread as some suggest,[22] then it could be a wider group. However, we have already seen that Paul has some kind of regional usage for ἐκκλησία, and therefore the question this occurrence raises is why Paul did not take advantage of that usage here, to refer to the churches in Achaia, or Achaia and Macedonia? I would argue here that, in the context of persecution, suffering, and the day of the Lord, which dominates this letter, Paul is deliberately widening the perspective of the Thessalonians. They are not to think provincially here, but more widely, of all the churches of God. In addition, all these churches share with the Thessalonians in being churches of God, a reminder that the core identity for the ἐκκλησία is in another.

Third, there is one singular reference to the church in Galatians 1:13 which may refer to churches in more than one locality, when Paul writes of his persecution of τὴν ἐκκλησίαν τοῦ θεοῦ. Bruce argues that this should be taken as a reference to one church, the church in Jerusalem.[23] It is argued that the doctrine of the church in Galatians is primitive, as befits its early date,[24] in contrast to the more universal usage in the prison epistles,[25] and therefore Paul would not use ἐκκλησία in a universal sense.[26] Others take τὴν ἐκκλησίαν τοῦ θεοῦ in a more general or universal sense, to refer to all

---

20. Ellicott, *Thessalonians*, 95, takes this as a reference to the churches in Corinth and its neighborhood. So also Bruce, *1 & 2 Thessalonians*, 145. Green, *Thessalonians*, 281–82, suggests the same reference as in 1 Thessalonians 1:6–7, the churches in Macedonia and Achaia.

21. Calvin, *To the Romans*, 388. Witherington, *1 and 2 Thessalonians*, 191, sees a reference to multiple local assemblies that Paul has founded or is founding. Malherbe, *Letters to the Thessalonians*, 386–87 sees a reference to all the churches, but primarily those in Achaia.

22. See for example Thompson, "Holy Internet."

23. Bruce, *Galatians*, 90.

24. So Longenecker, *Galatians*, lxxxiii–lxxxviii; also Lightfoot, *Galatians*, 73.

25. Longenecker, *Galatians*, 6.

26. Banks, *Paul's Idea*, 30.

those Christians that Paul sought to persecute in his former way of life.[27] Burton argues that, whilst Paul uses the term the church of God sparingly, he uses it for the church in general, particularly in reference to persecution.[28]

Is then Galatians 1:13 a reference to a single church, the church in Jerusalem, or to the church in general, because it includes within it churches beyond Jerusalem? In the narrative of Acts, Saul's persecuting zeal extended beyond Jerusalem to Damascus,[29] and this would indicate that τὴν ἐκκλησίαν τοῦ θεοῦ here extends beyond one local church. This would be a change from what might be expected from Greek literature. However, we have already seen that ἐκκλησία is used distinctively and flexibly and by Paul. Furthermore, the fact that at the same time as referring to the *church* of God in Galatians in a letter in which Paul writes to multiple *churches*, or that in 2 Thessalonians 1:4 Paul refers to the *churches* of God as a general term for a group of churches, or perhaps all churches, does not stop Paul from employing a different but complementary usage here. I would argue that the most natural reading of this verse is that Paul has a conception of "the church of God" as an entity; that he sometimes used ἐκκλησία as a collective term for Christians considered as a whole, rather than only for the church in one locality. This usage for the "whole" church needs to be further explored in the chapters that follow.

What then is the significance of the term τὴν ἐκκλησίαν τοῦ θεοῦ? Elsewhere in these three letters, ἐκκλησία is used both with and without further specification. In 1 Thessalonians 1:1 and 2 Thessalonians 1:1, the church is described as being *in* God and Christ; in 1 Thessalonians 2:14, we read of τὴν ἐκκλησιῶν τοῦ θεοῦ *in* Judea, and in Galatians 1:22 the churches of Judea are *in* Christ. However, in Galatians 1:2, the churches are simply *in* Galatia. Given that, in Galatians 1:2, ἐκκλησία could be used without further specification for Christian churches, it seems unlikely that the distinction here is between a Christian and a civic or *polis* assembly. However, neither is this necessarily a technical term for "the church universal," given the way in which Paul is also happy to talk about the churches of God, and described the church, even in just these three letters, with a variety of modifiers. Here

27. Longenecker, *Galatians*, 28; Burton, *Galatians*, 45–46. Lightfoot, *Galatians*, 81 notes the similarity of this more universal usage to Acts 8:3. Martyn, *Galatians*, 154 takes Paul to be referring to a "fundamentally political entity, God's expanding beachhead in the world." See also Giles, *What on Earth*, 114, and Meeks, *First Urban Christians*, 229n163, 229n164.

28. Burton, *Galatians*, 419–20.

29. Assuming that Acts can be used at least as a rough chronological outline of the spread of the early church. On the general agreement between Acts and Paul's letters on the early geographical spread of Christianity, see Phillips, *Paul, His Letters, and Acts*, 72–73.

in Galatians 1:13, in the midst of Paul's argument about his former behavior, in the midst of a discussion of Judaism, τὴν ἐκκλησίαν τοῦ θεοῦ is most likely a reference to the fact that, in being a zealous Jew, Paul was actually opposing God, in Jerusalem and beyond, and is therefore a polemical point against his opponents in Galatia—who, he would argue, are doing the same. In addition, it is a reminder that the core identity of the ἐκκλησία is found in relation to God. Galatians 1:13 then indicates a wider reference than the local church, a reference to the "whole church," and is also a reference to a church which finds its core identity in God.

Paul's earliest letters, particularly 1 and 2 Thessalonians, have been seen as the place where Paul's primary understanding of the ἐκκλησία as a local church is established. However, not only is Paul concerned with the local ἐκκλησία, but he also operates with a conception of ἐκκλησίαι operating regionally and more widely, and can also use ἐκκλησία for the whole church. I will now explore how Paul's use of ἐκκλησία relates to the other imagery he uses for the church.

Ecclesial Solidarity in Imagery Used for the Church

In chapter 1, I outlined a number of areas which I will consider under this heading, including images such as body or temple, but also other descriptors such as the language of family. I will include only those relevant to these three letters here: the language of ἐν Χριστῷ in Galatians, the language of brotherhood, and the language of holiness in the Thessalonian correspondence.

Σῶμα and the Language of Incorporation

There is one reference to σῶμα in Galatians (6:17) where Paul refers to bearing the marks of Jesus on his body. However, this is not a reference to the body as a corporate entity, but to the physical sufferings of Paul as an apostle of Jesus Christ. Similarly, 1 Thessalonians 5:23 is a reference to "the whole of you, spirit and soul and body." This is most naturally taken as a reference to each individual being ready for the return of Christ. In the sense of a corporate entity, σῶμα is not used in Galatians or 1 and 2 Thessalonians.

However, in Galatians, there are two passages where the language of incorporation may be present. First, in Galatians 1:22, the churches of Judea are ἐν Χριστῷ. Bruce argues here for the term as incorporative, denoting

Christ's people as members of his body.³⁰ Given the absence of body terminology in Galatians, this is potentially quite significant, if it were to indicate that, from Paul's earliest letters, his idea of the ἐκκλησία could be linked to his understanding of incorporation. At this stage, however, it remains just a possibility.³¹

The main group of references to incorporation in Galatians is found in 3:26–28.³² Here, in the space of three verses, the Galatians are described as ἐν Χριστῷ Ἰησοῦ twice (v. 26 and v. 28) and having been baptized εἰς Χριστόν (Galatians 3:27). The first reference, in v. 26, could be a reference to incorporation, or to faith in Christ as the means whereby the Galatians have become sons of God, or to both.³³ Then, Galatians 3:27 refers to being baptized into Christ, and in v. 28 Paul talks about all being one in Jesus Christ. How is εἰς used in v. 27? It could be taken to mean "with reference to" Christ, so that just as faith is in Christ, so also baptism is into Christ, or it could be given an incorporative force.³⁴ I would argue for the incorporative force here on the basis of v. 28, where ἐν Χριστῷ is seen as the unifying factor, bringing together Jew, Greek, slave and free, male and female, and making them all one. It is possible to detect the beginnings of ἐν Χριστῷ having a corporate dimension. This has two implications for ecclesial solidarity. First, the emphasis in this section falls on the unity of the Galatians—they are one in Christ Jesus, and since they span multiple ἐκκλησίαι, this emphasizes intrachurch solidarity. Second, people are either one of the conditions listed in v. 28, or the other. Given what has already been observed concerning the

---

30. Bruce, *Galatians*, 104. Burton, *Galatians*, 63, talks of the intimacy of fellowship between these communities and the risen Jesus. Martyn, *Galatians*, 176, takes this as a reference to being in the new realm God is now establishing in Christ. In Best, *One Body*, 6–7, Christians form a community in Christ.

31. 1 Thessalonians 1:1 and 2 Thessalonians 1:1, with their references to the church in God, in Christ, may also tend in this direction.

32. There are a number of other references to being *in Christ* in the epistle. Some relate to individuals: Galatians 2:4, 2:17; 5:6. In 3:14, Christ is the agent whereby the gentiles receive the blessing given to Abraham. It is the grouping of references in 3:26–28 which are the most significant for this study. See also Longenecker, *Galatians*, 153.

33. Longenecker sees Christ as the distinctive object of faith, and describes the verse as having a "local sense" (*Galatians*, 152–53). Burton sees Christ as the one in whom believers live, taking Christ as the basis of sonship as a "secondary and suggested thought" (*Galatians*, 202–3). Lightfoot has both senses here: "You are sons by your union with, your existence in Christ" (*Galatians*, 149). Bruce, *Galatians*, 184, sees an incorporative sense here.

34. With reference to Christ: Longenecker, *Galatians*, 155; Burton *Galatians*, 203. Incorporation: Bruce, *Galatians*, 185. Calvin, *Galatians, Ephesians, Philippians and Colossians*, 68 argues for a strong unity so that God sees Christ and not the believer. Best, *One Body*, 66–68, argues for the same meaning as ἐν Χριστῷ in vv. 26 and 28.

interchurch dimensions of ἐκκλησία in this letter, the interchurch dimension of the oneness in Christ Jesus must not be ruled out here, and therefore, whilst Paul's primary concern here seems to be to remind the Galatians of their position in Jesus Christ, nevertheless, in doing so he suggests a picture of corporate identity across and beyond Galatia.

Family Language: Brotherhood

In this section, I will examine how Paul uses the language of brotherhood in his earliest letters.[35] Brotherhood is an important term for this study, because of the frequency with which Paul uses the term,[36] and because family imagery, including brotherhood, is imagery which entails solidarity. In particular, 1 Thessalonians has the highest frequency of occurrences of ἀδελφοί per chapter in any of Paul's letters.[37] I will consider first how the term would have been understood by Paul and his readers before examining how Paul uses the term in his earliest letters.

Brotherhood in Classical Antiquity

The language of brotherhood needs to be understood in the context of the ancient family, and of ancient Mediterranean understandings of brotherly love. There are three features of ancient Mediterranean family and kinship relationships which are relevant to my examination of brotherhood in the

---

35. Although I use the word "brothers" throughout this section, Paul's use of ἀδελφοί in his earliest letters and elsewhere can often legitimately be translated brothers and sisters, and therefore my choice to use "brothers" here should not be taken to exclude the translation "brothers and sisters." See Trebilco, *Self-designations*, 24–25. Aasgaard, *Brothers and Sisters*, 7–8, chooses "sibling," but notes the problems with that choice.

36. Aasgaard, "'Role Ethics' in Paul," 516. Aasgaard notes that the ἀδελφ root is used metaphorically 120 times in seven of Paul's letters. See also Horrell, "From ἀδελφοί to οἶκος θεοῦ," 311, for a table showing the use of "ἀδελφοί/ἀδελφοή as "Fictive Kinship Terms Referring to Fellow Christians." For the three letters under consideration here, he notes nineteen uses for 1 Thessalonians, eight for 2 Thessalonians, and ten for Galatians. See also Burke, *Family Matters*, 165; Banks, *Paul's Idea*, 54–55; Horrell, *Solidarity and Difference*, 111.

37. See Burke, *Family Matters*, 165n3 for a table showing that the term occurs nineteen times in 1 Thessalonians, nine times in 2 Thessalonians, and with much more frequency than in Romans, 1 and 2 Corinthians, Galatians, and Philippians. Trebilco, *Self-Designations*, 28–30, has a table which summarizes this information, and also notes how frequency depends on Paul's relationships with the recipients and the content of the letter.

Pauline corpus. First, family in the ancient Mediterranean world did not necessarily mean the nuclear family, but could include a wider group of individuals, either those who lived in the same household,[38] or those connected to a household through patronage structures.[39] Second, kinship relationships in the ancient Mediterranean world implied responsibility, particularly a responsibility to protect the group or certain members of it. Osiek and Balch note the importance of honor and shame and how that related to protection of the family, and particularly of women as the "weaker" sex.[40] Third, kinship responsibilities emphasize group identity,[41] and a concern about group goals, and the position of the group.[42] This group identity tends to demarcate the group from other groups;[43] Best argues that "brothers" serves to distinguish the community from those outside "by creating a bond between those within."[44] Kinship language was used in the ancient Mediterranean world to denote boundaries and responsibilities.

Ancient understandings of brotherly love can be gleaned from a number of sources. The most complete work on this subject is Plutarch's *On Brotherly Love*,[45] where he writes to Nigrinus and Quietus, who practice brotherly love,[46] lamenting its rarity.[47] Plutarch then extols the virtues of φιλαδελφία, how it brings unity to brothers and joy to parents,[48]

---

38. Osiek and Balch, *Families*, 5–35, note the way in which living space influenced family structures; a large dwelling meant a large household, a small dwelling a small household. For a discussion of whether more emphasis should be given to the nuclear family, see Clarke, *Serve the Community*, 82–86. For an example of varied living spaces in one block and how families might have lived there, see Oakes, *Reading Romans*, 1–45.

39. Osiek and Balch, *Families*, 54, highlight the importance of patronage in ancient society.

40. Osiek and Balch, *Families*, 38–41.

41. See also Hellerman, *When the Church*, 31–33; Meeks, *First Urban Christians*, 74–84.

42. See for example Malina, "Collectivism," 22.

43. Thompson, "Paul, Plutarch," 223–24, notes Plutarch's demarcation between the family and outsiders.

44. Best, *Paul and His Converts*, 132. See also, for example, Horrell, "From ἀδελφοί to οἶκος θεοῦ," 296–97.

45. Although a contemporary of Paul, Plutarch is taken to be representative of general understandings of brotherly love in the first century. See Aasgaard, *Brothers and Sisters*, 93–106.

46. Plutarch, *Frat. amor.* 478b.

47. Plutarch, *Frat. amor.* 478c.

48. Plutarch, *Frat. amor.* 480c.

demonstrates love for parents,[49] and is a good example for children.[50] The familial solidarity expressed by brotherly love can perhaps be most clearly seen in Plutarch when he emphasizes the need for brotherly love in situations where it might be threatened and lead to familial disharmony, such as when a father dies,[51] or when a friend fails to be, in Plutarch's terms, a good friend.[52] A similar understanding can be seen in Jewish sources:[53] in 4 Maccabees, the brotherly love between the seven brothers tortured by the tyrant is praised,[54] as the brothers encourage one another to withstand torture, and Philo's *Embassy to Gaius* criticizes Gaius for failing to show brotherly love.[55] Josephus provides three examples of commendable brotherly love.[56] Perhaps the most interesting of these is the final one, between Joseph and Solymius, where Solymius's brotherly love entails giving his own daughter to Joseph to save him from a beautiful actress. In these examples drawn from Jewish sources, brotherly love involves standing together, and the willingness to make sacrifices for a brother.[57] It is also worth noting that the sibling relationship was often long-lasting; Hellerman gives various examples[58] to illustrate his argument that "the closest family bond in ancient Mediterranean society was not the bond of marriage. It was the bond between siblings."[59]

49. Plutarch, *Frat. amor.* 480f.
50. Plutarch, *Frat. amor.* 480f.
51. Plutarch, *Frat. amor.* 483c.
52. Plutarch, *Frat. amor.* 491b: good friends should help brothers to be bound together.
53. See Aasgaard, *Brothers and Sisters*, 71–74, for other examples of the spread of the concept of φιλαδελφία.
54. 4 Macc 13:16, 23; 14:1.
55. Philo, *Legat.* 87.
56. Josephus, *A J.* 2.161, Joseph and his brothers; 4.26, Moses and Aaron; 12.189, between Joseph and Solymius in Alexandria.
57. See also Aasgaard, "Role Ethics," 519; Burke, *Family Matters*, 97–127; Thompson, "Paul, Plutarch," 223–24.
58. Hellerman, *When the Church*, 40–50.
59. Hellerman, *When the Church*, 40. Note also the discussion of what kind of relationships are implied by brotherhood. Horrell, "From ἀδελφοί to οἶκος θεοῦ," 296–97, states that the term "conveys no sense of hierarchy or superiority," but the context might imply it. Clarke, "Equality or Mutuality," 160–63, disputes the idea that brotherhood language is egalitarian, arguing rather that it is inherently hierarchical; there is mutuality, solidarity, mutual dependence, and a commitment to overcoming differences in brotherly language in the ancient world, but not equality. Burke, *Family Matters*, 97–127, also argues against the idea that reciprocity means equality, arguing that there is evidence of hierarchy in brotherly relations, whilst Trebilco, *Self-designations*, 35–37 notes that in 1 Thessalonians 5.12, the leaders are also brothers.

In the first-century world, then, family could encompass more than just blood relations. It was a key group that needed to be protected and defended. Sibling relationships were often strong.[60] Paul's choice to use brotherhood and fictive kinship extensively in his earliest letters will be examined against this background.

Brotherhood and Intrachurch Solidarity

The use of kinship and sibling language to encourage and promote intrachurch solidarity is frequently noted.[61] A brief survey of these three letters demonstrates two ways in which sibling language contributes to intrachurch solidarity.

First, "brothers" is used to encourage a shared identity. Paul outlines what is true of the brothers to whom he writes. In 1 Thessalonians 1:4,[62] they are loved by God, and in 1 Thessalonians 5:4, the brothers are of the light, not the darkness, an identity that is in God (5:4), and that is further reinforced in 5:5 by more family language: they are "sons of light." In 2 Thessalonians 1:3, Paul gives thanks for the brothers because of their growth in faith and love, and in 2:13 because they were chosen as the "firstfruits" to be saved. Finally, in Galatians 4:28 and 4:31, the Galatian brothers are described as children of the free woman, not the slave, and in Galatians 6:18, all the brothers are to receive the grace of Christ in their Spirit. Paul is also concerned with their knowledge: in 1 Thessalonians 4:13, Paul wants them to know as brothers about those who have "fallen asleep," and in 1 Thessalonians 5:1, the emphasis falls on what they already know as brothers. In Galatians 1:11, Paul addresses brothers to highlight that his gospel is not a human gospel, and in Galatians 3:15, Paul shares a human example with brothers. Here, the language of brotherhood fosters intrachurch ecclesial solidarity, by emphasizing a shared identity in God and Christ, and membership of a new family.

Second, there are several exhortations about behavior within the community which indicate a concern that shared identity should result in shared

---

60. For a similar summary, see Horrell, *Solidarity and Difference*, 112.

61. Thompson, "Paul, Plutarch," 226; Horrell, "From ἀδελφοί to οἶκος θεοῦ," 302.

62. 1 Thessalonians 1:4 appears without explanation, suggesting that it was natural for the Thessalonians to be addressed as brothers, presumably because that was Paul's usage in Thessalonica. Malherbe, *Letters to the Thessalonians*, 110, suggests that Paul is drawing here on the experience of the proselyte to Judaism. See for example, Philo, *Virt.* 179, who does encourage proselytes to be viewed as kinsmen. However, whether or not this is the origin of the language for Paul, the origin of the language for the Thessalonians would have been Paul.

behavior. In 1 Thessalonians 4:1, the brothers are exhorted in the Lord Jesus to continue to live as instructed by Paul and to please God. Paul's use of the vocative indicates that they are being exhorted here because they are brothers and have a shared identity in Jesus Christ. In 2 Thessalonians 2:15, the brothers are exhorted to stand firm and hold to the traditions[63] taught by Paul; in 2 Thessalonians 3:6, they are commanded to keep away from the idle brother; and in 2 Thessalonians 3:13, they are to continue to do good. Finally, in Galatians 5:13, the brothers called to freedom are exhorted not to use freedom to serve the flesh, but to serve one another.

In the context of exhortation, the discussion of idleness[64] in 2 Thessalonians 3:6–15 shows how Paul uses brotherhood language, when he talks about how to deal with a brother. The Thessalonians are dealing with a brother (3:6) even when they are to avoid close association with the brother (3:15). This suggests that the bonds of fictive kinship within the Thessalonian Church are to be maintained, despite behavior which might ultimately lead to some kind of exclusion from communal activity such as fellowship meals.[65]

One of the purposes Paul has in encouraging shared behavior and shared identity is to resocialize the Thessalonians, who would have experienced a dislocation from previous identity groups by becoming Christians. Burke argues that the language of brotherhood is used to resocialize those who have left existing social practices behind as a result of turning from idols.[66] Similarly, Furnish[67] argues that, in a context where the Thessalonians are facing opposition from friends and family, Paul calls for the Thessalonians to expand the love they have within the community to outsiders; the community is resocialized and then enabled to interact with others, and Malherbe relates kinship language to the feelings of abandonment and inward distress felt by the Thessalonian Christians as a result of their conversion.[68]

---

63. Malherbe, *Letters to the Thessalonians*, 440, notes the positive connotation of traditions here as Paul's ethical teaching.

64. Malherbe, *Letters to the Thessalonians*, 317, prefers the translation "disorderly" here and elsewhere in these two letters. The precise translation of ἀτάκτως is not critical here.

65. Malherbe, *Letters to the Thessalonians*, 460.

66. Burke, *Family Matters*, 170. See also Barclay, "Conflict in Thessalonica," 514. The language of brotherhood may not be the only way Paul seeks to strengthen the community; see for example, de Silva, "Worthy of His Kingdom," 50, on the use of the language of honour and shame in this regard.

67. Furnish, "Inside Looking Out," 108–13.

68. Malherbe, *Paul and the Thessalonians*, 46–52. See also Trebilco, *Self-designations*, 31.

The language of brotherhood is then a potent way of helping new, suffering Christians to be and behave as members of a new community, and of encouraging intrachurch solidarity.

Brotherhood and Interchurch solidarity

The implications Paul's language has for interchurch solidarity are frequently neglected in discussions of brotherhood, and it is these implications that I will now explore.

First there are a number of references which emphasize the relationship between Paul and the church or churches to which he writes. This is clearest in 1 Thessalonians. In 1 Thessalonians 2:1, Paul talks about the knowledge the brothers have about his ministry in Thessalonica, which he again recalls in 2:9. In 2:17, he expresses his fervent desire to see them again. In 3:7, he affirms that he is reassured about the brothers because of Timothy's favorable report. Finally, in 1 Thessalonians 5:25–26, he asks for their prayers and offers greetings with a holy kiss. The Thessalonians are his brothers, and he emphasizes how he has behaved and is behaving as a brother towards them. They know of Paul's conduct among them, and he wants them to know of his continued care and concern for them, and particularly his heartfelt anguish for them, which demonstrates his brotherly affection. Although he can't be present, he wants to offer them a visible sign of affection, a holy kiss,[69] and he wants to receive their affection, expressed through prayer.[70] Paul is not just a brother to the Thessalonians—he also uses parental language, and the solidarity expressed here is not between churches, but between Paul and the Thessalonians. However, this usage does highlight the possible applicability of brotherhood language beyond the local congregation.

Second, there are several occasions in Galatians where there appears to be a wider sense of brotherhood than that which pertains solely to the local congregation, and this wider sense tends towards interchurch solidarity. In Galatians 1:2, Paul writes with all the brothers to the churches of Galatia. The precise identification of these brothers is not the issue here.[71] What is significant is that they are considered brothers, not just of Paul, but also (I would argue), by implication, brothers of the Galatians, because, as we have already seen, Paul considers himself to be a brother to the Galatians. Whilst Paul is clearly the author of the letter, there is a sense in which brothers are

---

69. Malherbe, *Paul and the Thessalonians*, 341.

70. For similar examples, see 2 Thessalonians 3:1; Galatians 4:12; 5:11.

71. For an identification of who the brothers are, see, for example, Longenecker, *Galatians*, 5–6.

communicating to a family which transcends the local church. In addition to brotherly relations between Paul's brothers and the Galatian churches, there should also be brotherly relations between the Galatian churches, as can be seen from Galatians 4:28 and 4:31. In the allegory of Hagar and Sarah in 4:21-31, Paul describes two sets of people: those under law and those who are free in Christ.[72] The brothers in all the Galatian churches belong to those who are free in Christ, for they are identified collectively in Galatians 4:28 and 4:31 as children of the promise, children of the free woman, and therefore, by implication, brothers,[73] whether they are Jews or gentiles.[74]

Third, there is one place in 1 Thessalonians where brotherhood is explicitly applied beyond the local congregation: in 1 Thessalonians 4:9-12, where the language of brotherhood and brotherly love is also used in relation to other churches, all the brothers throughout Macedonia.[75] The Thessalonian believers are to love each other, and they are to continue to love all the brothers in Macedonia.[76] This brotherly love is taught by God, indicating its foundational nature for the community.[77] In addition, 1 Thessalonians 3:12 calls for love to increase for each other and everyone else, indicating that love is to extend beyond the immediate community.[78] Taken with the references already noted in Galatians and the relationship between Paul and the churches to which he wrote, we can see that from his earliest letters, Paul was conscious of a brotherhood which, although primarily expressed in the local church, nevertheless transcended the local congregation, and that, by implication, brothers in different congregations have a relationship with and responsibilities to each other that can be described as brotherly

---

72. Bruce, *Galatians*, 226.

73. It is also possible that there is an implicit brotherly relation in 1 Thessalonians 2:14, where the Thessalonians are imitators of the churches of Judea, as fellow sufferers of persecution, perhaps implying brotherly imitation of brothers.

74. Trebilco, *Self-designations*, 30-31.

75. Whilst this reference is generally neglected, Horrell, *Solidarity and Difference*, 115, does briefly explore the implications of 1 Thessalonians 4:9. See also Stenschke, "Significance and Function of References," 204.

76. See Aasgaard, *Brothers and Sisters*, 154-57 on the structure of this section of 1 Thessalonians.

77. See Aasgaard, *Brothers and Sisters*, 157-58 on whether love in general is God-taught, or brotherly love in particular. Aasgaard opts for love in general. Either way, emphasis here is on foundational importance of brotherly love.

78. Furnish, "Inside Looking Out," 109-10. Malherbe, *Letters to the Thessalonians*, 213 takes the reference to "all" in 1 Thessalonians 3:12 as love for pagans within the assembly; Green, *Thessalonians*, 178; Witherington, *1 and 2 Thessalonians*, 103; Bruce, *1 & 2 Thessalonians*, 72; Ellicott, *Thessalonians*, 47, take this as a reference to people in general who were not members of the church. Either way, love was to extend beyond the local community.

love.[79] Therefore, the language of brotherhood is not just the language of intrachurch solidarity; it is also used for interchurch solidarity.

However, having said that brotherhood carries implications for interchurch solidarity, it is then necessary to establish what those implications are, to determine what responsibilities between brothers apply between local churches. Green argues that financial support for Christians in general is most likely in view here.[80] Horrell focuses on hospitality, material goods, and "mutualism," seen most clearly in the collection project.[81] However, given the level of responsibilities that brotherly language implied in the ancient world,[82] I would argue that the expression of brotherly love between congregations is to go beyond finance and hospitality. The Thessalonians are not described as friends with believers in other places;[83] they are brothers,[84] and therefore have responsibilities. By extension, just as the Thessalonians must not wrong their brothers in Thessalonica,[85] so they must not wrong their brothers in Macedonia, and beyond.[86]

For two reasons, more is at stake here than just hospitality, mutual mission, and financial support, important as they are.[87] First, because in 1 Thessalonians 4:11–12, Paul moves from love for the brothers in Macedonia to living a life that will win respect from the surrounding community.[88] This could be considered a return to concerns which only impact upon

---

79. Meeks, *First Urban Christians*, 109, talks of a universal brotherhood of believers which Paul and the other leaders of the gentile mission sought to foster. Given Paul's concern to reinforce community identity, it would seem strange for him not to take advantage of the idea of there being a community which transcended the local.

80. Green, *Thessalonians*, 206. Malherbe, *Letters to the Thessalonians*, 245, talks of preaching the gospel and hospitality. Burke, *Family Matters*, 210–13, also opts for hospitality.

81. Horrell, *Solidarity and Difference*, 115. See also Stenschke, *References*, 204.

82. E.g., Burke, *Family Matters*, 126–27.

83. Malherbe, "Exhortation," 252–53.

84. On the choice of the language of brotherhood over the language of friendship, see Malherbe, *Paul and the Thessalonians*, 104.

85. E.g., 1 Thessalonians 4:6.

86. Although only the Macedonians are mentioned in 4:10, the churches of Judea are mentioned in 2:14 as a model for imitation. It seems reasonable, then, to include them within the group who the Thessalonians were to treat as brothers.

87. Aasgaard, *Brothers and Sisters*, 160, presents a different suggestion: that their brotherly love is shown by being a model missionary centre in Macedonia, as in 1 Thessalonians 1:7. However, I would argue that the context of 4:9–12 indicates that it is behavior within the community and before outsiders that is in view here.

88. Note the link that Dodd, *Paul's Paradigmatic 'I'*, 218, makes between the Thessalonians' behavior in 4:10b–12 and the example of Paul in 2:9.

the Thessalonian community, and the issues there with work.[89] However, given the fact that the reputation of the Thessalonians for faith reverberated through Macedonia and Achaia,[90] so too would any reputation they might have or gain for being unwilling to work. Brotherly love then implies an on-going responsibility at the level of how a church behaves, not just how a church treats other believers when they meet; how the Thessalonian Christians conducted themselves would have an impact on their brothers in Macedonia, Achaia, and beyond.[91] Second, given the strong emphasis on brotherly responsibilities, and given the collective nature of ancient family structures, to use the word "brother" is to evoke a pattern of strong relationships. This would be an encouragement to the Thessalonians to recognize their solidarity with and mutual responsibility for their brothers, whether near or far.[92] Two implications follow from this.

First, the language of brotherhood in Paul's earliest letters implies a strong interchurch solidarity, going beyond the realm of hospitality and financial support to the realm of collective identity and behavior. Given that these are the primary realms in which Paul's language of brotherhood operates in intrachurch solidarity, we can see an overlap which begins to suggest that intrachurch solidarity as expressed through brotherhood is also at the same time interchurch solidarity, for all that the Thessalonians do in the local church has the potential to impact upon their brothers elsewhere.

Second, I have noted uses of ἐκκλησία which imply interchurch relationships. Here we see the language of brotherhood applied to interchurch relationships, suggesting that interchurch solidarity could be expressed through a shared brotherly identity and shared brotherly behavior.

---

89. See Burke, *Family Matters*, 223–24. Aasgaard, *Brothers and Sisters*, 161–65, argues in a similar way, that Paul makes use of the "family ethos" here. He notes the need for the group to be united, as well as for worthy representatives of the message, but does not acknowledge that this has, in the context of 4:9–12, implications beyond Thessalonica.

90. 1 Thess 1:7–10.

91. Malherbe argues that these references to other Christian groups indicate that the Thessalonians "are not alone in the world but are members of a worldwide fellowship in which they enjoy exemplary standing" (*Paul and the Thessalonians*, 75–76). Here we might observe a pattern developing, whereby the positive actions of the Thessalonians have a positive impact on other Christian groups, but are also beneficial to the Thessalonians in their precarious situation.

92. On this see, for example, Aasgaard, *Brothers and Sisters*, 160–61.

Holiness Language and Holy People

The language of holiness appears in a number of places in 1 Thessalonians, and twice in 2 Thessalonians,[93] although it is absent from Galatians.[94] Holiness in seen in the context of the return of Christ: Paul twice prays that the Thessalonians will be holy at the coming of Jesus;[95] the Thessalonians are to greet one another with a holy kiss;[96] and holiness is the key emphasis of the exhortatory section in 4:1–12, where living a life worthy of the Lord is described in terms of becoming holy (4:3), acting in holiness (4:4), and a call to holiness (4:7) explicitly linked to possession of the Holy Spirit (4:8). A number of scholars have highlighted the importance of holiness in 1 Thessalonians. Weima argues that holiness is the most important theme of 1 Thessalonians, noting that it appears at key points throughout the letter,[97] and Gorman notes how holiness appears at key moments in 1 Thessalonians, at 3:13 and 5:23, and argues that the basic message of 1 Thessalonians is a call to holiness.[98] A similar argument for the importance of holiness can be made for 2 Thessalonians, for Paul writes about the sanctifying work of the Spirit in them at the beginning of the second thanksgiving of the letter, which leads into the second exhortatory section,[99] while the climactic return of Christ in 2 Thessalonians 1:10 results in glory in his holy people.

Holiness language is important in the Thessalonian correspondence, but its meaning needs to be explored. It needs to be recognized that holiness language has its roots in the Old Testament and the idea of separation and separateness. So, in Exodus 19:5–6, God calls Israel to be a separate, obedient, holy nation.[100] Then, within Leviticus, there are repeated calls to holiness based on the character of God, the call to be holy because God is holy.[101] Explicitly in Leviticus 20:23–26, holiness is the boundary marker

---

93. 2 Thess 1:10; 2:13.

94. But see Martin, "Circumcision in Galatia," 219–37, who links holiness to circumcision, also noting the importance of separation.

95. 1 Thess 3:13; 5:23. See also 2 Thess 1:10.

96. 1 Thess 5:26. Malherbe, *Letters to the Thessalonians*, 340–41, notes how this indicates holiness as a theme in the letter.

97. Weima, "How You Must Walk," 99–100. In Weima, *Neglected Endings*, 176–79, he argues that the expanded peace benediction at the end of the letter highlights a call to holy living.

98. Gorman, "Cruciform," 151–53.

99. See for example Malherbe, *Letters to the Thessalonians*, 358–59.

100. See Peterson, *Possessed by God*, 20. Also Weima, "How You Must Walk," 101. Compare Deuteronomy 26:18–19.

101. Lev 11:44–45; 19:2; 20:7; 22:3. Weima, "How You Must Walk," 101.

which separates Israel from the nations.¹⁰² Johnson notes how in Ezekiel 36–37 the restoration of the people is seen in a display of God's holiness.¹⁰³ Many more examples could be given, but the idea of holiness as separateness and as a defining characteristic of Israel clearly emerges from the Old Testament.¹⁰⁴ Weima notes how, surprisingly, the Spirit as a key blessing of the messianic age in Ezekiel 36–37 is applied to the Thessalonians in 1 Thessalonians 4:8.¹⁰⁵

The language of holiness and its link to separation have a number of implications for intrachurch solidarity. First, the call for purity in 1 Thessalonians 4:1–8, centered as it is on holiness language, is at one and the same time a call to be separate in terms of behavior, but also to behave in a way which protects the community from disharmony, that one brother should not take advantage of another.¹⁰⁶ The language of holiness is used to create boundaries between the community and those outside, and to define boundaries within the community. Second, the language of holiness is explicitly linked to the return of Christ as judge in 1 Thessalonians 4:6 and 5:23, placing a common expectation and standard before the community. The language of holiness serves then to further bind the ἐκκλησία together, promoting internal harmony and group identity.

The language of holiness also has two potential implications for interchurch solidarity. First Weima notes the link between holiness in sexual conduct in 1 Thessalonians 4:3–8, and at work in 4:9–12,¹⁰⁷ and notes in particular the identification of outsiders in 4:12, seeing holiness in work as a boundary marker.¹⁰⁸ I have already noted how the exhortations to brotherly love in 4:9–12 extend beyond the local church, and here we see the implications of holiness also extending beyond the local congregation, as behavior which marks out the Thessalonians as separate is displayed for the sake of the brothers in Macedonia. The implication of this is that the Thessalonians are encouraged to be interested not just in the protection and solidarity of their own ἐκκλησία, but also of other ἐκκλησίαι.

The second potential implication of holiness language for interchurch solidarity relates to the idea of God's holy people. We have already seen that

---

102. See also Weima, "How You Must Walk," 102.

103. Johnson, "Sanctification," 276–77.

104. Weima, "How You Must Walk," 102.

105. Weima, "How You Must Walk," 110–12. See also Johnson, "Sanctification," 277–78.

106. 1 Thess 4:6.

107. Weima, "How You Must Walk," 112.

108. Weima, "How You Must Walk," 117–18.

the language of holiness is drawn from OT roots, where it was applied to Israel, and therefore both Weima and Johnson argue that this marks the Thessalonians out as part of the New Israel.[109] There are two places where this usage might be discerned in 1 and 2 Thessalonians.

In 1 Thessalonians 3:13, Paul prays that the holiness of the Thessalonians will be established when Jesus returns with his holy ones. Here, the "holy ones" is a reference to Zechariah 14:5, and is generally taken as a reference to angels.[110] However, Justin King argues that the original context of Zechariah 14:5 may refer to angels or to human beings,[111] and argues that the prepositional phrase "with all his holy ones" should be read independently of "the coming of our Lord Jesus," reading instead "so that your hearts are strengthened in holiness . . . with all the saints."[112] These arguments open up the possibility that 1 Thessalonians 3:13 is a reference to human beings. However King's argument that Zechariah 14:5 remains a key text for interpreting 1 Thessalonians 4:14, so that those who have fallen asleep are the holy ones who return with God, indicating that "holy ones" is used for humans in 1 Thessalonians,[113] relies on an overlap between the Septuagint of Zechariah 14:5 and 1 Thessalonians 4:14 of ὁ θεός and αὐτός (where different prepositions are used in 1 Thessalonians 4 and Zechariah 14), and pairs ἄγω with ἥκω. I would argue that this is too little overlap between 3:13 and 4:14 to have confidence that Paul is still thinking of the holy ones when he writes 1 Thessalonians 4:14, and therefore although it might be attractive to view 1 Thessalonians 3:13 as a reference to human beings, and therefore an example of the wider use of holy people, there is insufficient evidence for it, and certainly insufficient evidence for building a case for interchurch solidarity from it.

In 2 Thessalonians 1:10, however, the Thessalonians are included among God's holy people. Paul appears here to be using language taken from the Old Testament, specifically from Psalm 88:8 LXX (89:7).[114] This language was originally applied to the heavenly council, but the parallelism

---

109. Weima, "How You Must Walk," 102–3; Johnson, "Sanctification," 276–79.

110. So, Wanamaker, *Thessalonians*, 145; Witherington, *1 and 2 Thessalonians*, 104; Green, *Thessalonians*, 181; Malherbe, *Letters to the Thessalonians*, 214. Trebilco, *Self-designations*, 123–28, surveys the usage of holy ones before the NT, arguing that its use with reference to humans is comparatively rare. However, he still argues that 1 Thessalonians 3:13 is a reference to human beings

111. King, "Paul, Zechariah," 25–27.

112. King, "Paul, Zechariah," 32–34.

113. King, "Paul, Zechariah," 35–37.

114. Wanamaker, *Thessalonians*, 230, notes the similarity between the Septuagint of Psalm 88:6 (Eng: 89:7) and 2 Thessalonians 1:10.

of 1:9–10, where a contrast is drawn between those facing eternal destruction and those who have believed, indicates that this is a reference to believers. Given the context of punishment in 2 Thessalonians 1:5–10, where Paul talks of "righteous judgement" (v. 5), repaying with affliction (v. 6), Jesus "inflicting vengeance" (v. 8), and the punishment of eternal destruction (v. 9), the idea of separation is also present. Here then we do have a clear example of the use of holy people for the Thessalonians, which has significant implications for interchurch solidarity. The Thessalonians are encouraged to be holy, and to see that they will be part of that holy people when Christ comes; they are part of something wider than their immediate context. This reality will be seen on the last day, but like the language of brotherhood, it is another way of strengthening the community against opposition, promising both ultimate vindication and present identity. It is language which suggests an understanding of the church and of ecclesial solidarity which is more than just local, and in particular an understanding of responsibility to and from churches beyond the local.

Conclusion

In this section, I have examined three areas which potentially have a bearing on intra and interchurch solidarity: the language of incorporation in Galatians, the language of brotherhood, and the language of holiness in the Thessalonian correspondence. I have noted how Paul's language of incorporation seems to be building a picture of corporate identity beyond Galatia, how Paul operates with a strong understanding of the interchurch implications of brotherly love, and how the language of holiness and holy people has implications for behavior and identity across all churches. These findings are consistent with the wider use of ἐκκλησία by Paul, seen particularly in Galatians 1:13, but also elsewhere in his earliest letters, and demonstrate the importance of interchurch solidarity for Paul from his earliest writings. In the section that follows, I will continue to examine the intra- and interchurch implications of Paul's language, turning now to examine Paul's role seen through the language of example, imitation and apostleship.

Paul's Apostolic Role

The Language of Example and Imitation

Explicitly and implicitly, the language of imitation is found frequently in the Thessalonian epistles.[115] In 1 Thessalonians, the Thessalonians are commended as imitators of Paul,[116] imitators of the churches of Judea,[117] and those who are to be imitated.[118] In addition, the description of Paul's ministry in 1 Thessalonians 2:1–12 provides an exemplar of what conduct should be imitated,[119] and the call to follow the instructions they have received from Paul in 1 Thessalonians 4:1–2 can be seen as an implicit call to further imitation. In 2 Thessalonians, Paul and his coworkers are again held up as a model to be imitated.[120] The purpose of this examination is to establish what expectations, if any, the language of imitation used in this way entails for intra and interchurch solidarity.

In order to examine this question, it is first necessary to look at the language of imitation as it is used more generally in the culture of antiquity, before examining how Paul uses the language of imitation. Much has been written about imitation in Paul and in the first-century world.[121] It is not my intention here to repeat that work, but to draw out two features of imitation in antiquity, before looking at some key features of how Paul uses imitation language.

The first feature to be noted is that imitation is generally seen as a positive practice in the ancient world.[122] Copan notes the negative connotations of mimicry highlighted by Plato,[123] but the overwhelming majority of uses refer to a positive practice.[124] To imitate another is to seek to improve

---

115. There is also imitation language in Galatians 4:12, as noted by Clarke, "Imitators," 352–53, but this is not related to mutual imitation by churches.

116. 1 Thess 1:6.

117. 1 Thess 2:14.

118. 1 Thess 1:7.

119. Clarke, "Imitators," 338–39.

120. 2 Thess 3:7, 9; see Clarke, "Imitators," 340.

121. For a recent bibliography, see Copan, *Saint Paul*, 40fn2. For a review of research through to 1999, see Dodd, *Paul's Paradigmatic 'I'*, 18–29.

122. Copan, *Saint Paul*, 53.

123. Copan, *Saint Paul*, 52.

124. Copan, *Saint Paul*, 46–53; de Boer, *Imitation*, 6–7.

character by learning from the model.¹²⁵ We can assume this general background when examining how Paul understands imitation.¹²⁶

Second, the language of imitation can be used flexibly. Copan shows how a variety of things and people can be imitated,¹²⁷ and how the language can be used for a variety of relationships: parent-child, teacher-student, leader-people.¹²⁸ In addition, whilst imitation is focused on that which is seen, there are examples from antiquity where the object seen is absent, and is therefore "seen" through literature.¹²⁹ This flexibility will become relevant when I explore Paul's use of imitation language in relation to churches.

Coming to Paul's use of the language of imitation, I will examine intrachurch solidarity in 2 Thessalonians 3:7 and 3:9 and Galatians 4:12, before turning to how imitation functions in 1 Thessalonians 1:6 and 2:14, and any implications this might have for interchurch solidarity.

Intrachurch Solidarity

In 2 Thessalonians 3:7 and 9, Paul lays before the Thessalonians an explicit example to be imitated. They are to follow the example of Paul and his companions in working hard. Clarke notes the way in which the call to imitation here supports Paul's ethical exhortations,¹³⁰ for the Thessalonians are commanded to work hard in 2 Thessalonians 3:6. Here we see the link between authority and personal example in imitation. This link is emphasized by Michaelis,¹³¹ and noted by Dodd in his survey of the study of imitation.¹³² Dodd highlights Michaelis's identification of *mimesis* as obedience to Paul's authority, and in particular his focus on that idea, at the expense of the idea of imitation as following a model or example.¹³³ He then

---

125. Copan, *Saint Paul*, 63–64; Dodd, *Paul's Paradigmatic 'I'*, 17, quoting Dio Chrysostom.

126. Copan, *Saint Paul*, 64–69; and de Boer, *Imitation*, 1–8, 24–28, and 42–50, argue that imitation was widely discussed in antiquity, and de Boer, *Imitation*, 8–13, 28–41, argues that the idea of imitation is present in the Old Testament. See also Dodd, *Paul's Paradigmatic 'I'*, 17.

127. Copan, *Saint Paul*, 46–53.

128. Copan, *Saint Paul*, 54–59.

129. Copan, *Saint Paul*, 47 on imitation of persons of antiquity; de Boer, *Imitation*, 6, on Dio Chrysostom discussing Socrates as a pupil of Homer.

130. Clarke, "Imitators," 340–41.

131. Michaelis, "μιμέομαι," 671–72, on 2 Thessalonians 3:7, 9 and Philippians 3:17.

132. Dodd, *Paul's Paradigmatic 'I'*, 18–29.

133. Dodd, *Paul's Paradigmatic 'I'*, 19–20.

explores de Boer's focus on imitation as following a personal example,[134] as well as works by others who reach similar conclusions,[135] before examining Castelli's study,[136] which he argues highlights the need for understanding imitation as emphasizing both personal example and authority.[137] Despite Dodd's reading of Castelli, it is difficult to see how Castelli's reading of Paul's imitation as "power play" can be easily synthesized with earlier work on imitation.[138] However, the understanding that when Paul calls for imitation, he is calling for an imitation of his example with a force that does not make that imitation optional,[139] seems to be in operation in 2 Thessalonians 3:7–9. Paul's call for imitation is linked to his behavior amongst them, which then has a clear implication in the passage, as part of his warning in 3:6–12 against idleness.[140] The imitation expected here is specific and not presented as optional. It also establishes a link between intrachurch solidarity and Paul's role as one who gave an example to be imitated; one of the things that should encourage the ἐκκλησία in Thessalonica to work hard for each other is the example of Paul and his coworkers.

Galatians 4:12 offers a different example, in that the language of imitation is not explicitly used; however, the Galatians are urged to become like Paul. Several features of this verse should be noted. First, there is a link between imitation and the language of brotherhood, as Paul exhorts his brothers to become like him.[141] Second, this is a call to imitate Paul's conduct in not going back to the slavery of Torah obedience.[142] Third, Paul uses the verb δέομαι here, which indicates that this comes as a request, not a command. Here we see the flexibility of Paul's use of the idea of imitation, but nevertheless the link between his behavior and that of the churches of

---

134. Dodd, *Paul's Paradigmatic 'I'*, 20–22. de Boer's *Imitation*, xii–xiii, explicitly intends to critique Michaelis.

135. Dodd, *Paul's Paradigmatic 'I'*, 22–25.

136. Castelli, *Imitating Paul*, 21–33.

137. Dodd, *Paul's Paradigmatic 'I'*, 25–29. At various points in Dodd's argument, he notes statements in Michaelis and Fiore which preserve both imitation as example and imitation as authority, but also how the emphasis of both leads in different directions.

138. Castelli's reading of Paul's call to imitation as a power play has been significantly challenged by Copan, *Saint Paul*, 181–219, the level of foundational assumptions. See also Clarke, "Imitators," 331–33.

139. It is not surprising then that imitation also features in discussions of Paul's apostleship. So Schütz, *Anatomy*, 226.

140. Malherbe, *Letters to the Thessalonians*, 450, notes the link to church discipline here.

141. Clarke, "Imitators," 352, notes the affectionate appeal to brothers here.

142. Longenecker, *Galatians*, 189, widens the imitation here to the whole of 1:13—4:11. See also Clarke, "Imitators," 352.

Galatia. However the request comes, the implication for intrachurch solidarity remains: right action is encouraged by reflecting on Paul's conduct, and imitating him.

Interchurch Solidarity

I will now examine 1 Thessalonians 1:6–7, where the Thessalonians, as they imitate Paul, are a model to others, and 1 Thessalonians 2:14, where the Thessalonians imitate the churches of Judea. Looking first at 1 Thessalonians 1:6, two related questions need to be resolved: who, and what, is being imitated? The Thessalonians are described as imitators of "us and the Lord," which can be taken to be Paul, Silvanus, and Timothy (with priority given to Paul as the principal correspondent), and the Lord Jesus. However, there are a number of things that the Thessalonians do in 1 Thessalonians 1:6–10 which cannot be a direct imitation of Jesus because they are not things that Jesus does: most notably in vv. 9–10, where the Thessalonians are described as turning from idols and waiting for the return of Christ. Thus, Michaelis denies that the language of imitation involves "true imitation" of the earthly or heavenly Lord, and focuses on mimesis as obedience.[143] Copan surveys four ways in which imitation in this verse has been understood: imitation as reception of the word,[144] as joyful reception of the word, as joyful reception of the word in the midst of tribulation,[145] and imitation of the lifestyle of the messengers.[146] Copan rejects the first three of these options in order to preserve the reality of imitation here: Christ did not receive the word, and therefore, if they are imitating Jesus, it must be in some other way.[147] Similarly, de Boer argues that the point of imitation here is the experience of afflictions,[148] and it seems reasonable to allow a more limited sense of imitation of the Lord here rather than to deny it altogether with Michaelis. A distinction does, however, need to be made between the wider sphere, within which the imitation of Paul—which can be seen in their faith, hope, and love in the Lord, and reception of the gospel in power (1:3–5)—operates—and

---

143. Michaelis, "μιμέομαι," 672–73.

144. For this understanding, see Michaelis, "μιμέομαι," 670.

145. de Boer, *Imitation*, 114–15. However, note that de Boer later widens the scope of imitation when he considers both Paul's conduct in enduring suffering (119–20) and that their imitation is of the Lord (122–23).

146. Copan, *Saint Paul*, 84–86.

147. Copan, *Saint Paul*, 85, see also Clarke, "Imitators," 334.

148. de Boer, *Imitation*, 114–15.

the much more limited sense, in which they are direct imitators of the Lord, in experiencing suffering.[149]

If the imitation of Jesus needs to be carefully delineated here, the question remains as to how the imitation of Paul, and of Silvanus and Timothy, is to be understood. The context of 1 Thessalonians 1:5 is important here, as the imitation that the Thessalonians practice is in relation to the behavior of Paul and his coworkers whilst in Thessalonica. Copan argues that Paul's use of himself as an example in 1:5,[150] the numerous references in 1 Thessalonians to how Paul and the apostolic team acted,[151] and the way in which imitation was understood in antiquity would incline Paul's hearers to take his reference here to broadly mean imitation.[152] Copan describes this as the imitation of the "lifestyle," ethos and message of Paul,[153] having already argued for this understanding of imitation in Paul and the ancient world.[154]

Once the question of who and what is to be imitated has been answered, a second question can be addressed: how are the Thessalonians to be an example to all the believers in Macedonia and Achaia (1 Thess 1:7)? Paul describes what this model entails in 1 Thessalonians 1:8–10: it is their faith in God, how they turned from idols to serve the living God, and how they await the return of Christ. The Thessalonians have imitated Paul's ethos and their ethos is to be imitated,[155] and as the focus in the letter is on living lives worthy of God, the ethical element is paramount.[156]

In 1 Thessalonians 2:14–16,[157] we see that the Thessalonians have become imitators of the churches in Judea in their suffering, and therefore similarities with 1:6 can be observed: the Thessalonians have received the word of God (2:13) in the midst of suffering. However, two new elements are added here. First, this is the imitation of ἐκκλησία by ἐκκλησία, and sec-

149. Copan, *Saint Paul*, 85–86.

150. For his detailed argument on the close relationship between vv. 5b and 6, see Copan, *Saint Paul*, 77–83.

151. On this and the preceding point, see Dodd, *Paul's Paradigmatic 'I'*, 213–14.

152. Copan, *Saint Paul*, 86. So also Clarke, "Imitators," 337–40.

153. Copan, *Saint Paul*, 104.

154. For a summary of his conclusions on this see Copan, *Saint Paul*, 70–71.

155. Clarke, "Imitators," 338.

156. Clarke, "Imitators," 339–40.

157. This passage has often been considered an interpolation, because of the comments about the Jews here and the apparent difficulty of reconciling this with Romans 9–11. However, more recent commentators have argued that it is part of the original text, and that its language is consistent with the rhetoric purpose of 1 Thessalonians: Witherington, *1 and 2 Thessalonians*, 82; Malherbe, *Letters to the Thessalonians*, 172. See also Bockmuehl, "1 Thessalonians 2:14–16," 1–31.

ond, there is the issue of distance: given the considerably greater geographical and cultural distance between these churches than between Macedonia and Achaia, it might be asked what it means for the Thessalonians to imitate the churches in Judea.

Some commentators argue that the imitation here is not conscious,[158] but that there is a simple comparison in which Paul draws parallels between the experiences of the churches in Judea and in Thessalonica.[159] To argue in this way is to argue that there is no real imitation of ἐκκλησία by ἐκκλησία in 1 Thessalonians. However, I would argue that there are two reasons why the imitation here should be seen as real, and not as a simple comparison or analogy that Paul draws.

First, de Boer argues that Paul's letters indicate that he communicated with his churches about his earlier persecution of the church, and that in 1 Thessalonians there is evidence that he talks about other churches and speaks of persecution in the context of Old Testament history, Jesus, and the spread of the gospel. Therefore, it is possible to see the Thessalonians deliberately imitating a known pattern from the Judean churches: "As opposition and persecution began to engulf them and they began to feel the pangs of suffering inflicted upon them for their new faith, what would have been more normal than to consider what other Christians had done in like circumstances?"[160] This point is reinforced by Thompson's argument that good roads, hospitality, a thirst for news of other churches, the importance of imitation and example, and the availability of letter carriers suggest that information could spread quickly.[161] de Boer points to the continued importance of the Jerusalem church in early Christianity, even for Paul,[162] and that the Jerusalem church (and by extension its sister churches in Judea) had a "mother church" role which would have been imitable,[163] and there would have been particular interest in what was happening in Jerusalem and Judea. It is then reasonable to expect that the general contours of behavior in Judea would become known in Thessalonica, and, perhaps, vice versa.[164]

---

158. See Clarke, "Imitators," 335–36, for a summary of this position. Copan, *Saint Paul*, 85. Cf. de Boer, *Imitation*, 98–103, who argues for active imitation here.

159. For example, see Bruce, *1 & 2 Thessalonians*, 45; Witherington, *1 and 2 Thessalonians*, 83; Malherbe, *Letters to the Thessalonians*, 168; Copan, *Saint Paul*, 85. de Boer, *Imitation*, 103, explores this idea before rejecting it.

160. de Boer, *Imitation*, 106, citing 1 Thessalonians 1:8–9; 2:15–16; 3:4.

161. Thompson, "Holy Internet," 49–70. On letter carriers, see Richards, *Paul and First-century*, 201–9.

162. Citing Gal 1:18; 2:1; and Rom 15:19.

163. de Boer, *Imitation*, 104.

164. If the book of Acts is accepted as a generally accurate account of the early

Second, there is evidence from the ancient world of groups imitating groups, as noted by Copan.¹⁶⁵ Notably, the examples he cites are to do with character: avoiding sloth, or following the example of runners in finishing the race and not becoming weary. These are not accidental comparisons; rather, they are encouragements to deliberate imitation, even if the runners involved are only known by reputation. Here we can observe the mediating role of Paul, who communicates the behavior of one ἐκκλησία to another. Although 1 Thessalonians 1:8–9 may contain an element of hyperbole, Paul indicates that others are also communicating between ἐκκλησία. The imitation of group by group follows the general pattern of imitation elsewhere in Paul and in the ancient world: looking at the model and seeking to learn from and emulate it. Just as Paul presents his behavior as a model to be imitated in 2 Thessalonians 3:7–9, so too the Judean churches are presented as a model of conduct.

The Thessalonians are commended for a real imitation of the Judean churches and for being a real example to other churches. In both the instances in 1 Thessalonians, the imitation relates to perseverance in the face of suffering. However, given the wider context of imitation in Paul and antiquity, imitation of ἐκκλησία by ἐκκλησία need not be limited to perseverance in suffering. Rather, imitation is participation in a shared ethos: an ethos which Paul models for the church in Thessalonica and elsewhere, which they can model for other churches, and which they can receive and imitate from other churches.

As I have indicated, there are several helpful studies which explore imitation in Paul. However, because of their focus, all these studies tend to focus on imitation within the local church, and so the interchurch dynamics of the language of imitation are frequently lost. Here I offer two implications of this survey of the use of imitation language in 1 and 2 Thessalonians for our understanding of relationships between churches.

First, the language of imitation demonstrates Paul's concern for group solidarity and mutual encouragement, not just within an ἐκκλησία, but also from ἐκκλησία to ἐκκλησία. So, Paul himself is encouraged as the recipient of this positive report about the Thessalonians.¹⁶⁶ The fact that Paul mentions the Judean Christians to the Thessalonians indicates that there is an advantage in knowing that others have experienced something similar to what they have experienced, and that they have persevered through suf-

---

church, then there is good evidence for the communication of information between churches—for example, in the events before and after Acts 15.

165. Copan, *Saint Paul*, 47–48.

166. 1 Thessalonians 1:8, taking vv. 7–10 as what motivates the thanksgiving in vv. 2–3.

fering, because it encourages group solidarity. To put this another way, it would be a loss to the Thessalonians not to have the positive example of the Judean churches to encourage them to persevere. Similarly, it is of benefit to these other believers to know what the Thessalonians have done, so that the faithfulness of the Thessalonians might be of benefit to other Christians in their region. Here we see that local churches are part of a wider grouping or community.

Second, we see some evidence here of Paul's expectation that there will be a shared ethos amongst the churches: they are those who have accepted the word of God and been willing to endure suffering because of it. The churches in view here are certainly those of the Pauline mission, explicitly the churches of Macedonian and of Achaia in 1 Thessalonians 1:7. However, the inclusion of the example of the Judean churches in 1 Thessalonians 2:14 suggests the expectation of a shared ethos across all churches. This would cohere with the idea of a shared brotherhood and a shared identity as those who are set apart for holiness, awaiting the return of Christ noted in section 3.2.

This shared ethos, demonstrated by accepting the word of God and being willing to endure suffering because of it, can also be seen in Galatians. In Galatians 2:11–14, Paul criticizes Cephas for drawing back from eating with the gentiles when "certain men" came from James (v. 12). Peter is criticized here for an unwillingness to suffer, acting out of fear of the "circumcision party" (v. 12). In this, he is followed by the rest of the Jews, including Barnabas (v. 13). Paul rebukes Cephas in v. 14 because his behavior was not in line with the truth of the gospel. Paul then encourages the Galatians to learn from the negative examples of Cephas, Barnabas, and the Jewish Christians in Antioch, whose failure to fully accept the word of God in this area would be an encouragement to the Galatians to stand firm and not to turn to a different gospel (1:6). Like the churches in Judea, the church of Antioch can serve as an example, despite not being a church of the Pauline mission.

Paul considers it of benefit to churches to imitate what others do (or should do), in reception of the gospel and in persevering through suffering. As noted in 1 Thessalonians 1:6, this imitation has wider implications. ἐκκλησίαι can strengthen ἐκκλησίαι by being good examples, by persevering, and by living out their shared ethos. Again, as we saw earlier with the language of brotherhood, this suggests a relationship that goes beyond financial support and hospitality into the much wider area of belief and general ethical behavior. The language of imitation fosters a close relationship between churches.

The Role of the Apostle

In this section, I will examine Paul's apostolic self-awareness. This will involve an examination of how apostolic authority in Paul is usually understood, recognizing the wide range of material on apostleship in Paul, but focusing on those areas which have implications for ecclesial solidarity. Then I will look more closely at apostolic authority in Galatians, particularly Galatians 1 and 2, and in 1 Thessalonians, before examining the use of parental language in 1 Thessalonians.

Apostolic Authority in Paul

Lightfoot is generally credited with originating the modem discussion of apostleship.[167] He raises questions in a number of areas, and these questions still form the basis for much of the discussion about apostleship. This discussion can usefully be examined under three headings: the question of the origin of the term apostle, issues related to the qualifications of an apostle and who qualifies, and questions related to the function of an apostle.

ORIGIN OF THE TERM "APOSTLE"

It is generally recognized that the use of the word ἀπόστολος in classical Greek and Hellenism does not provide much assistance in understanding how the term is used in the New Testament.[168] The word appears only once in the Septuagint: at 1 Kings 14:6 (a passage missing from Vaticanus), as a translation for the Hebrew שָׁלוּחַ, a passive participle taken as a noun.[169] This has caused a number of authors to argue that the New Testament usage of ἀπόστολος is based upon the Jewish institution of the שָׁלוּחַ.[170] While this view has been challenged by a number of scholars, including Schmithals,[171]

---

167. So, for example Schütz, *Anatomy*, 22–23; Schmithals, *Office*, 19.

168. So, Lightfoot, *Galatians*, 92–93, and Rengstorf, "ἀπόστολος, ἀποστολή," 407–13, although note that some argue that the usage of Herodotus is relevant. See, for example, Agnew, "Origin," 49–53, who argues that papyri indicate one authoritatively sent, similar to Christian usage.

169. Rengstorf, "ἀπόστολος, ἀποστολή," 413.

170. Rengstorf, "ἀπόστολος, ἀποστολή," 414–20, but also Lightfoot, *Galatians*, 93, and Kirk, "Apostleship since Rengstorf," 250–52.

171. Schmithals, *Office*, 98–110, rejects Rengstorf's thesis on the basis that the evidence for the institution of שָׁלוּחַ comes from after AD 70, that common Greek usage is just as plausible a background for Paul, and that שָׁלוּחַ is not used to describe Jewish missionaries. See also Schütz, *Anatomy*, 27–28.

who argues instead for a gnostic origin to the term,[172] the rejection of gnostic origins[173] and the lack of alternative parallels suggest to some that a cautious recognition of at least the conceptual parallels between ἀπόστολος and שָׁלוּחַ is possible.[174] If this link is accepted, then emphasis falls on the authority of the sent one received from the one or ones who send.[175] However, given the lack of concrete evidence here, it does not seem wise to draw too much from any link between ἀπόστολος and שָׁלוּחַ.

Another way of examining the origin of the term is to look for nonterminological parallels between the concept of apostle in the New Testament and the Old Testament. Of significance here are the parallels drawn between Paul and Old Testament prophets. Rengstorf draws attention to the parallels between Jeremiah and Paul,[176] and Kruse notes the links between Galatians 1:15–16, Jeremiah 1:5, and Isaiah 49:1b and 5.[177] Both authors recognize the link between an independent prophetic commission from God and the authority of the word which Paul delivers, although Paul defines himself as an apostle, not a prophet. Any parallel between apostle and prophet does not help with the origin of ἀπόστολος, although it might illuminate how Paul understood the term. The lack of a clear origin for the term highlights the importance of close exegesis of the New Testament for understanding apostleship, the fact that nothing can be determined from origins alone, and, as has already been demonstrated with the word ἐκκλησία, origins do not determine later usage.

Extent of and Qualifications for Apostleship

Much discussion of apostleship in the New Testament has been concerned with who can be considered an apostle and in what sense. Various authors have various lists of who can be considered an apostle,[178] and there are various theories as to how the New Testament understanding or understandings

---

172. Schmithals, *Office*, 114–230.

173. See for example Agnew, "Origin of the NT Apostle-Concept," 90.

174. Agnew, "Origin of the NT Apostle-Concept," 94.

175. Rengstorf, "ἀπόστολος, ἀποστολή," 415: "the one sent by the man is as the man himself"; Agnew, "Origin of the NT Apostle-Concept," 95, highlights the importance of prophetic vocation.

176. Rengstorf, "ἀπόστολος, ἀποστολή," 439–41.

177. Kruse, *New Testament Foundations*, 79–80. For a recent brief survey of material in this field, see Aernie, *Is Paul Also Among*, 3–7.

178. See for example Lightfoot, *Galatians*, 94–96; Schmithals, *Office*, 61–67; Best, *Essays on Ephesians*, 26–28; Clark, "Apostleship," 56–63, and Giles, "Apostles," 247.

of apostleship developed.[179] Other than to note the general agreement that Paul at least thinks of himself as an apostle in the fullest sense, it is not my intention to explore these issues here.

Of more relevance to this investigation are the qualifications of apostleship, and whether there are different types of apostle. These two areas are interrelated: if the qualifications for apostleship are considered rigorously, then some who are called apostles in the New Testament would not qualify for "full" apostleship. An examination of the views of three authors on qualifications and types of apostle demonstrates this.[180]

Kirk argues that there is only one view of apostleship in the New Testament, but that there are different forms in different circumstances. He focuses on the special call of Christ, the one apostolic mission, the message preached, and the results of the work undertaken as qualifications for apostleship.[181] Giles argues that the qualifications that Paul mentions are to have seen the risen Lord, to have brought a church into existence, to proclaim the one true gospel, and suffering in the service of Christ.[182] He distinguishes between "apostles of Christ" who have these qualifications and "apostles of the Churches," who are delegates sent from a church, and not apostles in the fullest sense.[183] Clark identifies three senses of the word apostle: those with special authority, church delegates, and itinerant missionaries and church-planters such as Andronicus and Junia.[184] Here, the first class are those who have seen the risen Lord and have received a commissioning from the Lord.[185]

While the decision as to whether there are one, two, or three principal ways in which the word "apostle" is used in the New Testament does not need resolving for the purposes of this study, it does highlight the issue of qualifications. One of the issues for investigation in this study, then, is whether Paul thought he was qualified as an apostle, what that meant, and what implication it has for ecclesial solidarity, recognizing that Paul's view

---

179. See Schültz, *Anatomy*, 22–34, who surveys literature down to 1969 with a focus on questions of authority and legitimacy, and Brown, "Apostleship in the New Testament," 474–80.

180. See also Lightfoot, *Galatians*, 97, who argues that the qualifications for apostleship are having seen the risen Christ and fruitful labors.

181. Kirk, "Apostleship since Rengstorf"; Rengstorf, "ἀπόστολος, ἀποστολή," 261–64.

182. Giles, "Apostles," 248.

183. 2 Corinthians 8:23; Philippians 2:25; Giles, "Apostles," 248.

184. Clark, "Apostleship," 62.

185. Clark, "Apostleship," 63 argues that Paul and Peter have a special place as those who lead the respective 'apostleships' or missions.

of apostleship in his earliest letters needs to be examined without relying on later material to interpret it.

The Functions of an Apostle

Schmithals lists eighteen attributes of Paul's apostleship.[186] Some of these relate to origins and qualifications, and some to Schmithals's later comparison of Paul's understanding of apostleship with gnostic understandings.[187] However, a number of functions can be isolated from Schmithals's list, which helpfully summarize the functions of an apostle, as they are usually understood. *The Apostle has a mission*: he is to preach Christ,[188] and he does not build on another's foundation.[189] He is a prophet with a teaching ministry,[190] and he glories in doing the work of God.[191] *The Apostle has authority*: crucially, this authority rests on the gospel which is proclaimed.[192] *The Apostle is an example to others*: such as the churches to which Paul writes.[193] *The Apostle suffers*.[194]

Of these functions, we have already explored Paul's role as an example to others, and as has been noted there, being an example worthy of imitation is not a uniquely apostolic role, nor is suffering for the gospel. What is potentially distinctive about an apostle is the idea that the apostle is an authoritative missionary with a God-given, gospel-focused ministry, and this will be explored here as it impacts on Paul's understanding of ecclesial solidarity.

---

186. Schmithals, *Office*, 22–55.
187. Schmithals, *Office*, 198–230.
188. Schmithals, *Office*, 22–24.
189. Schmithals, *Office*, 44–46.
190. Schmithals, *Office*, 51–53.
191. Schmithals, *Office*, 54–55.
192. Schmithals, *Office*, 40–42, see also Schütz, *Anatomy*, 40–52. Best, *Essays on Ephesians*, 36, 49, argues that Paul doesn't issue instructions based on his apostleship, and makes use of apostleship when dealing with church leaders, not congregations. However, as I have already argued, authority is explicit and implicit within apostleship, and so I do not think it is realistic to restrict Paul's apostleship as Best does.
193. Schmithals, *Office*, 42–44.
194. Schmithals, *Office*, 47–50.

Apostolic Authority in Galatians

Galatians is a letter that is greatly concerned with apostolic authority. There is the question of Paul's authority in relation to those in Jerusalem,[195] in relation to Peter,[196] and in relation to the Galatians themselves.[197] In examining plot and character in Galatians 1 to 2, Wiarda argues that this autobiographical section communicates much about Paul's apostleship,[198] and argues that apostolic defence is the primary concern of the section, with a secondary paradigmatic purpose.[199]

Paul's argument in Galatians 1 and 2 contains four key assertions about his apostleship. First, Paul asserts in Galatians 1:1 that he is an apostle by Jesus Christ and from God, and not from men. The significance of this statement for understanding Galatians has frequently been noted: Paul speaks not with an authority derived from men, but with God's authority. His message is not derivative, but rather, as a message from God, it must be obeyed.[200] Second, the message is more important than the messenger. This is expressed most clearly in Galatians 1:8: Paul has no authority to change the message,[201] but also in Paul's report of his visits to Jerusalem and in his conflict with Peter in Antioch in chapter 2, where the standing of the "pillars" or of Peter is secondary to the centrality of the truth of the gospel message.[202] Third, Paul has a particular role as apostle to the gentiles. Paul's commission received at conversion is to preach to the gentiles,[203] and he and Peter have parallel roles.[204] Fourth, Paul's understanding of his apostolic role is arguably, at least in part, prophetic. Kruse notes the links to Jeremiah 1:5 and Isaiah 49:1b and 5 in Galatians 1:15–16, and how both these Old

---

195. Gal 1:11–24.

196. Gal 1:18; 2:11–14.

197. Gal 1:6–10. Note that here I am not concerned with identifying the opponents of Paul in the letter beyond Paul's identification of them as those who preach another gospel, and his arguments against them based on his view that they have misunderstood law and grace. I will continue to use the traditional designation "Judaizers" where necessary.

198. Wiarda, "Plot and Character," 248–49.

199. Wiarda, "Plot and Character," 251. Cf. Longenecker, *Galatians*, 20; Lightfoot, *Galatians*, 65–66.

200. So, Clark, "Apostleship," 50; Martyn, *Galatians*, 94–95; Schütz, *Anatomy*, 114.

201. See for example Schütz, *Anatomy*, 122.

202. See Schütz, *Anatomy*, 135–56.

203. Galatians 1:15. See discussion in Schütz, *Anatomy*, 133–35.

204. Galatians 2:8. See Clark, "Apostleship," 52, on the two "apostleships" of Peter and Paul.

Testament passages "speak of a gentile dimension to the messenger's task."[205] Aernie also notes the link with Isaiah 49:1 here, arguing that Paul sees his ministry here as an extension of the prophetic tradition, as one called before his birth.[206] Oropeza argues for a further prophetic allusion to Habakkuk 2:2–4 in Galatians 2:2, based on later use of the passage in Galatians 3:11.[207] Paul's running in Galatians 2:2 is, for Oropeza, the running of a herald, taking the message to different places.[208] This would supply a further connection between Paul's prophetic understanding of his ministry: as apostle to the gentiles, he is a prophet to the gentiles.

While Galatians does not cover all of the four functions mentioned here, there is clearly material here about Paul's mission and authority, and these four key assertions about Paul's apostleship in Galatians are largely uncontroversial. The implications of Paul's apostolic role for his relationship with the Galatians are frequently noted. In terms of intrachurch solidarity, the fact that Paul speaks authoritatively and with a message that is more important than the messenger indicates that solidarity is ultimately based in response to the gospel of Jesus Christ, highlighting oneness in Jesus Christ despite any cultural, social, or other differences there might be, a conclusion Paul himself draws in Galatians 3:28. Paul's role as apostle to the gentiles would be of particular encouragement to gentiles in the churches of Galatia, to consider themselves fully part of the local ἐκκλησία.

The intrachurch dimension of Paul's apostolic role in Galatians is frequently noted, but his apostolic role is rarely applied beyond the relationship between Paul and the Galatians, or between Paul and individual churches. However, as apostle to the gentiles, Paul guards the gospel, not just "his" ἐκκλησίαι. Paul castigates the Galatians for turning away from the gospel, and strongly defends his independence of the Jerusalem authorities,[209] but he opposed Peter,[210] and he opposes the "Judaizers" on the basis of the incompatibility of their teaching or practice with the gospel, not on the basis of them operating illegitimately in his jurisdiction.[211] This points to an understanding of the ἐκκλησία wider than a series of local ἐκκλησίαι, which are interrelated because they are all connected to Paul. There is a presumption here that all ἐκκλησίαι should have the same gospel, irrespective

---

205. Kruse, *New Testament Foundations*, 79.
206. Aernie, *Is Paul Also Among*, 136–37.
207. Oropeza, "Running in Vain," 141–43.
208. Oropeza, "Running in Vain," 143–46.
209. Gal 1:12.
210. Gal 2:11–14.
211. Even though Galatians 2:9 could be read to suggest different jurisdictions.

of founder, and that the connections between ἐκκλησίαι are more than just interpersonal. This can be seen to fit with Paul's concerns for the behavior of the brothers, and its implication beyond the local congregation.

Apostleship in 1 Thessalonians

There is one occurrence of ἀπόστολος in the Thessalonian correspondence where Paul refers to the demands that could be made as apostle of Christ: 1 Thessalonians 2:7.[212] The reference to apostles is plural, and so some commentators include Silas and Timothy here,[213] or just Silas.[214] What is noticeable about the discussion of whether Silas and Timothy can be included is that it becomes a discussion of what Paul means here by apostles: whether he has in mind a wider or a narrower sense. Malherbe offers a different perspective, arguing that there is an epistolary plural here because of the context of Paul's labor in v. 9, which is "so personal to Paul that Silas and Timothy could not be included."[215] However, Fulton notes the absence of epistolary plurals in her examination of ancient letters from multiple senders,[216] and argues that the first person plurals in 1 Thessalonians are self-referring rather than epistolary, referring back to the actions of Paul, Silas and Timothy amongst the Thessalonians and since they left Thessalonica.[217] Rather than excluding Silas and Timothy completely, it is perhaps better to see their role in this section of the letter in a parallel to their epistolary role in the letter, as described by Fulton; they are all in some sense apostles, but Paul is the lead apostle, who speaks in the first-person singular on occasions[218] and autographs the letter.[219]

The more critical issue here is to recognize what Paul says about the relationship between the apostle(s) and the Thessalonian congregation, and here Paul alludes to the fact that he/they were entitled to make demands as apostles of Christ, but indicates that instead he behaved like a nursing mother (2:7). Given Paul's concern in 1 Thessalonians 2:1–12 to provide an example to the Thessalonians, there is perhaps a distinction to be noted here

212. Eng: 2:6.
213. Bruce, *1 & 2 Thessalonians*, 31.
214. Green, *Thessalonians*, 125–26; Witherington, *1 and 2 Thessalonians*, 80, argues that Silas may therefore be amongst the group who have seen the risen Lord.
215. Malherbe, *Letters to the Thessalonians*, 144.
216. Fulton, "Phenomenon," 189.
217. Fulton, "Phenomenon," 199–200.
218. 1 Thessalonians 2:18; 3:5 (twice); 5:27. See Fulton, "Phenomenon," 221–22.
219. 1 Thessalonians 5:27. Fulton, "Phenomenon," 202.

between the authority that Paul has as an apostle and his desire to operate in Thessalonica without making demands. Paul may not consider an appeal to his apostolic authority to be the best means to promote intrachurch solidarity in Thessalonica.

Paul as Parent in 1 Thessalonians

I have shown above how Paul's use of the language of brotherhood draws upon first-century understandings of the family, with a concern for group identity, the prevalence of fictive kinship language, and the close, reciprocal, and mutually affirming associations of "brother." In coming to examine Paul's use of parental language, a few brief observations about the first-century understanding of "father" and "mother" need to be made. Here it needs to be recognized that we are not necessarily dealing with the daily reality of family life in antiquity, but rather with a set of cultural assumptions.

Fathers were often portrayed as powerful figures in the first-century world,[220] as the head of the family, the *paterfamilias*, and the centre of the patronage structure of the wider *familia*,[221] as figures of authority, with responsibilities to the household[222] and legal authority over the women of the household.[223] The architecture of many Roman houses tended to reinforce that authority.[224] However their absolute authority can be overstated: laws regarding patrimony could give women some independence,[225] and social status was important in determining social freedom.[226] The mother was generally portrayed as active in the household, in child-rearing, and in relation to other women.[227] However, social status would have had an impact on her role: she may have had considerable independence due to her status, or experienced further restrictions because of it.[228] Certainly, the mother would have been seen as a symbol of nurturing and affection. Like other

---

220. Note that much of the evidence here is Roman, but White, "Paul and Pater Familias," 464-65, argues that Galatians 4:1-3 shows same basic structure in Greek families in the East of the empire.

221. See Osiek and Balch, *Families*, 38-40; White, "Paul and Pater Familias," 457-58. Many fathers would not have this powerful role—for example, slaves, or freedmen who relied upon their former owners for patronage.

222. White, "Paul and Pater Familias," 458-59.

223. Osiek and Balch, *Families*, 56-58.

224. White, "Paul and Pater Familias," 460-63; Osiek and Balch, *Families*, 5-35.

225. White, "Paul and Pater Familias," 458-59.

226. Osiek and Balch, *Families*, 58.

227. Osiek and Balch, *Families*, 42.

228. Osiek and Balch, *Families*, 58; White, "Paul and Pater Familias," 458.

women in the household, she was considered to be vulnerable and to need protection.[229]

In 1 Thessalonians, there are two places where parental language is used.[230] In 1 Thessalonians 2:7, the imagery is of a nursing mother with her children; in 2:11, the imagery is of a father exhorting and encouraging his children. The first-person plural is used here, probably including Silas and Timothy with Paul here,[231] and although resolving this issue is not essential to my argument here, this needs to be noted.[232] In 2:7, Paul is compared to a mother.[233] This is a metaphor of nurture[234] and, potentially, given the common first-century understandings of motherhood, of vulnerability.[235] In 2:11, Paul talks about his conduct as that of a father to his children, and Burke has shown how, based on first-century understandings of what was desirable in fatherhood, this was both a relationship of affection and authority.[236] This language is also part of the process of socialization, which we have already seen with the idea of brotherhood, as familiar family imagery is used to define and describe the relationships between Paul and the Thessalonians. Paul is the father of his converts; the one who speaks with

---

229. See Osiek and Balch, *Families*, 38–40. The kind of protection offered to women and the implicit value placed upon them would vary with social status.

230. Burke, *Family Matters*, 130–62, also adds orphan in 2:17, and see Burke, "Pauline Paternity in 1 Thessalonians," 59–80, on 1 Thessalonians 2:11–12.

231. Green, *Thessalonians*, 127, includes Silas and Timothy in 2:7, and 133–35 includes Silas and Timothy, but also focuses on Paul in 2:11. Malherbe, *Letters to the Thessalonians*, 86–89, excludes them based on the use of the epistolary plural. Bruce, *1 & 2 Thessalonians*, 36, focuses on Paul for both. Witherington, *1 and 2 Thessalonians*, 80, includes Silas and Timothy, but talks about Paul on 81.

232. As noted, an analogy can be drawn here between the role of Silas and Timothy as cosenders of the letter, where Paul remains the chief sender; whilst Silas and Timothy are parents, it is Paul's parental role which is chiefly in view. I will therefore refer to Paul's role here, recognizing that this is not intended to exclude Silas and Timothy.

233. There is considerable debate over where Paul writes νήπιοι (infant) or ἤπιοι (gentle) here. The text-critical and external evidence favours the former, with P46, the original hand of α and various other uncials, and various versions supporting this reading against an editor of α and other later uncials. See Burke, *Family Matters*, 154–57. Green, *Thessalonians*, 181, and Malherbe, *Letters to the Thessalonians*, 145, also agree on the text-critical evidence, although Malherbe describes "infants" as too difficult and prefers "gentle." νήπιοι is a difficult reading, and while it might be preferred on text-critical grounds, it is by no means universally accepted; see Bruce, *1 & 2 Thessalonians*, 29.

234. Burke, *Family Matters*, 151–54.

235. If νήπιοι (infant) is preferred, this would also imply vulnerability.

236. Burke, "Pauline Paternity," 68.

authority;[237] and the one who shows his love for his converts in his earnest desire to see them.[238]

This imagery indicates Paul's authority over the converts, his care for them, and his example of right conduct among them. Paul presents himself as one concerned with nurturing and fostering the solidarity of the church in Thessalonica.

Conclusion

In this chapter, I have examined ecclesial solidarity in Paul's earliest letters, with a particular focus on the neglected area of interchurch solidarity. I have found significant elements in these letters which indicate that Paul operates with a wider-than-local conception of the church and believes that local churches have extensive responsibilities one to another:

The meaning of ἐκκλησία: Paul uses ἐκκλησία as a reference to the local church, and ἐκκλησίαι for local churches, either a defined group or possibly for churches in general. He uses the singular ἐκκλησία with a wider-than-local reference. His usage is distinct from that noted in chapter 2.

Imagery related to ἐκκλησία: There is evidence of some sense of corporate solidarity in Christ here. In his language of brotherhood, Paul points to an ongoing relationship between churches which goes beyond financial support and hospitality—in 1 Thessalonians 4:9–12, Paul commands the church in Thessalonica to live quietly and work hard for the sake of other churches. In addition, the language of brotherhood implies strong connections, not just intrachurch but also interchurch, as the "fictive kinship" of brothers extends beyond the local church. This sense of a wider set of relationships is bolstered by the language of holy people used, where the addressees of the letters are encouraged to view themselves as part of something wider than themselves.

The language of imitation and apostleship: Paul's use of imitation language and the use of that language for churches imitating churches further reflect Paul's desire that strong connections should exist between churches in terms of a shared ethos, founded on the right response to the word of God—seen explicitly in suffering for that right response, but also implicitly extending to other behavior. Paul's authority as an apostle focuses on his authority as one who proclaims the gospel. The gospel is a message for all churches, suggesting links beyond the Pauline mission.

237. Burke, "Pauline Paternity," 74–75, who notes how in 2:6 Paul doesn't make demands of them as an apostle.

238. 1 Thessalonians 2:17–20; Burke, "Pauline Paternity," 80.

We see from his earliest letters that Paul is concerned with fostering intrachurch and interchurch solidarity, and that his concern for interchurch solidarity is much more extensive than is generally recognized.

4. The Corinthian Correspondence

Introduction

IN THIS CHAPTER, I will examine the two extant letters which Paul wrote to the church in Corinth. In both letters, Paul addresses issues in the church in Corinth which have come to his knowledge, either through letters from them or from verbal reports. These issues will be examined in the text below as they are relevant to this study; however, there are two social realities of first-century Corinth which will inform my understanding of 1 and 2 Corinthians. First, that Corinth's re-foundation as a Roman Colony is important for understanding the polity of the city and the church.[1] Second, that the Corinthian Christians came from a range of social backgrounds.[2]

Of these social realities, the first is largely uncontested, although the continued occupation of the site after the destruction of the Greek city and before the foundation of the Roman colony,[3] and the danger of overemphasizing the importance of the number of freedmen amongst the original colonists,[4] need to be noted.

The second reality is contested by some. Meggitt argues against the common identification of the Erastus of Romans 16:23 with the one who laid the pavement in Corinth, thus indicating that Erastus was not of elite status,[5] and that the Pauline churches, including Corinth, shared the bleak

---

1. Thiselton, *First Epistle*, 3–4; Fitzmyer, *First Corinthians*, 25.

2. Thiselton, *First Epistle*, 28. Four phases can be identified as to how NT scholars have understood the relative wealth or poverty of the early church. In the first phase, the majority of Christians were considered to come from the lower class (Gehring, *House Church*, 167). This assumption was then challenged by a number of authors, leading to the recognition of an "emerging consensus" that "a Pauline congregation generally reflected a fair cross-section of urban society" (Meeks, *First Urban Christians*, 73). The third phase is the challenge posed by Meggitt, and the fourth the current response.

3. Fitzmyer, *First Corinthians*, 24–25.

4. Oakes, "Contours," 32–35.

5. Meggitt, "Social Status of Erastus," 220–25. For a recent survey of the literature surrounding the identification of Erastus, see Brookins, "(In)frequency," 496–516. Brookins concludes that the name is rare in first-century Greece, and that the identification of Erastus as the one who laid the pavement in Corinth is therefore plausible.

material existence of the nonelite.[6] Meggitt seeks to demonstrate that the basic economic level of 99 percent of people in the Roman Empire, those who did not belong to the elite, was one of subsistence. Having surveyed the evidence, he concludes that the nonelite of the cities "lived brutal and frugal lives, characterized by struggle and impoverishment."[7] He then looks at the economic location of Paul and the Pauline churches and finds that "they shared in the bleak material existence that was the lot of the non-elite inhabitants of the Empire."[8] He then applies these conclusions to Corinth and other churches.[9]

However, Meggitt adopts a binary model,[10] where there is no midrange group, just 99 percent of the populace experiencing abject poverty,[11] and this model has been challenged. Longenecker argues that the binary model owes more to the rhetorical constructions of the elite and their binary values than to economic reality,[12] that Meggitt himself recognizes it as an oversimplification,[13] and that even the evidence that Meggitt uses sometimes suggests an upward mobility which he would deny.[14] Longenecker and Friesen have provided economic models which allow for midrange groups, which are neither elite nor living in abject poverty,[15] perhaps making up around 30 percent of the population.[16] Both Longenecker and Friesen then examine individuals, and place some within the Corinthian Church in this midrange grouping;[17] this would fit with 1 Corinthians 1:26, where Paul says not many were well or high-born. Paul's use of a relative

6. Meggitt, *Paul, Poverty and Survival*, 153.

7. Meggitt, *Paul, Poverty and Survival*, 73.

8. Meggitt, *Paul, Poverty and Survival*, 153.

9. Meggitt, *Paul, Poverty and Survival*, 155–78.

10. The attribution of a binary economic model to Meggitt is that of Longenecker, *Remember the Poor*, 41–42.

11. Meggitt, *Paul, Poverty and Survival*, 50–53.

12. Longenecker, *Remember the Poor*, 42–43.

13. Longenecker, *Remember the Poor*, 42, quoting Meggitt, *Paul, Poverty and Survival*, 5.

14. Longenecker, *Remember the Poor*, 42n17. Theissen, "Social Conflicts," 371–91, argues that, despite Meggitt's extensive criticisms, the conflict between the strong and the weak is "class conditioned."

15. Friesen, "Poverty in Pauline Studies," 323–61; Longenecker, *Remember the Poor*, 36–59.

16. Friesen, "Poverty in Pauline Studies," 346–47. See also Oakes, *Reading Romans*, 56–62, who argues from a survey of housing types in Pompeii that 67 percent of people are in the lowest economic category, the poor.

17. Longenecker, *Remember the Poor*, 236–46; Friesen, "Poverty in Pauline Studies," 348, 357.

term here implies that economic and social distinctions existed within the Corinthian Church.

Whilst much of the work on the social setting of the Corinthian correspondence has focused on 1 Corinthians, some have examined 2 Corinthians. There is disagreement over whether 2 Corinthians represents an intensification of existing tensions, or whether new elements, such as a new set of visiting preachers, changes the dynamic.[18] However, whether or not new arrivals can be detected, and wherever such new arrivals may have arrived from, the social issues arising from status would remain broadly the same.

Meeks surveys the social level of Pauline Christians, and concludes that, although the supreme top and bottom of the social scale are missing, there is plenty of evidence for Christians occupying the ranks in between; although later work may have further nuanced this conclusion, the conclusion itself remains sound.[19] Theissen argues that this is true of Corinth.[20] Whatever the precise figures for the different groups, and however the different economic levels are generated, the ability to distinguish between the elite and the nonelite, and then to distinguish some levels of economic and social distinction within the nonelite, does seem to be established. This general picture will be assumed in examining the social setting of the Christian community in Corinth.

Ecclesial Solidarity and the Corinthian ἐκκλησία

In examining the occurrences of ἐκκλησία in Paul's earliest letters, I noted a number of important features of ecclesial solidarity. First, in terms of intrachurch solidarity Paul uses ἐκκλησία as an identity marker for a group with an ongoing existence, rather than for a group which only exists when assembled. Second, the core identity of this group is in another: Jesus Christ. Third, I found evidence for a concern for interchurch solidarity in Paul's uses of ἐκκλησία. Paul's provincial or regional use of ἐκκλησία expressed a common bond between churches in Galatia and Judea. Paul's use of "churches of God" at 2 Thessalonians 1:4 encouraged interchurch solidarity through mutual recognition of a common relationship to Jesus Christ, and implicitly in the context of the Day of the Lord, a shared expectation for the future. In Galatians 1:13, I argued that Paul refers to the "whole church,"

---

18. On the differing views see, for example, Sumney, *Servants of Satan*, 131; Hall, *Unity*, 144–48; Horrell, *Social Ethos*, 217–18; Barnett, *Corinthian Question*, 155–77.
19. Meeks, *First Urban Christians*, 73.
20. Theissen, *Social Setting*, 106.

a transcongregational usage of the singular. I also noted how Paul's usage showed considerable divergence and movement away from Greek Literary or Septuagint usage.

In Paul's earliest letters, I examined seven references to ἐκκλησία spread over fourteen chapters. In coming to 1 Corinthians, we find twenty-two references to ἐκκλησία spread over the sixteen chapters of the book, and nine references across thirteen chapters of 2 Corinthians. We see here a greater frequency of occurrence than in the earliest letters, and of the letters in the Pauline corpus, only Ephesians shows a similar frequency of usage to 1 Corinthians;[21] therefore, the Corinthian correspondence is a significant place for exploring ἐκκλησία and ecclesial solidarity. In this section, I will examine 1 Corinthians 1:2, intrachurch solidarity, and interchurch solidarity.

Introducing Solidarity: 1 Corinthians 1:2

The first reference to church in the letters comes in 1 Corinthians 1:2, where Paul writes τῇ ἐκκλησίᾳ τοῦ θεοῦ τῇ οὔσῃ ἐν κορίωθῳ.[22] Three questions arise. First, what is Paul addressing when he addresses the ἐκκλησία in Corinth? Second, what is the significance, if any, of Paul using the designation "of God"? Third, how does the whole phrase relate to the rest of the verse?[23]

First, there are a number of indicators that multiple domestic churches made up the local church in Corinth. There is a reference in 1 Corinthians 14:23 to ἡ ἐκκλησία ὅλη coming together, which suggests meetings of the church which were not ἡ ἐκκλησία ὅλη.[24] A plausible explanation

---

21. Ephesians has nine occurrences in six chapters. Compare Colossians (four occurrences in four chapters), 1 Timothy (three in five), Philippians (two in four), and Romans (five in sixteen).

22. The same phrase appears in 2 Corinthians 1:2, and, except where noted, comments relating to 1 Corinthians 1:2 also apply to this verse.

23. There is also a textual issue here in that some manuscripts, including P46, have transposed τῇ οὔσῃ ἐν κορίωθῳ to follow "those sanctified in Christ Jesus." This might be considered the original reading on the grounds of *difficilior lectio probabilior*; however, it can be traced to the western text (Thiselton, *First Epistle*, 72–73); additionally, most find that the phraseology is too awkward, and therefore argue that the shift is the result of accidental omission and displacement (see Fitzmyer, *First Corinthians*, 125).

24. Burke, "Paul's Role as 'Father,'" 105–13; Kloha, "Trans-Congregational," 177–78, argues that for Paul there is no practical distinction between "church" as individual local congregation and "church" as multiple congregations gathering together. However, a reference to the whole ἐκκλησία here does suggest some form of distinction is made.

for the existence of factions in Corinth[25] is that Christians met in different households, such as that of Chloe (1:11), and that this led to a primary identification with the household, or with Paul, Cephas, or Apollos, rather than with ἡ ἐκκλησία ὅλη. Finally, archaeological study suggests that most Roman houses would not have been sufficient to hold the likely size of the Corinthian Church.[26] When Paul addresses the church of God in Corinth at the beginning of 1 and 2 Corinthians, he is addressing a church which sometimes meets as a local church, and which meets separately in domestic churches. As noted in chapter 1, solidarity within the local and between domestic churches that form the same local church is considered intra-church solidarity, because the local church could, and (from the evidence of 1 Corinthians) did, sometimes meet. However, intrachurch solidarity in the Corinthian correspondence covers relationships between domestic churches which meet separately as well as together, adding an additional dimension here.

Second, two reasons are commonly given for Paul's use of church of God here. It is seen either as an appropriate designation for the church, alongside saints and elect,[27] or a reminder that the church belonged to God, not their factions.[28] Both reasons appear apposite here, given that Paul addresses factions in the letter from 1:10, and reminds the Corinthians of their identity in God and Christ in various ways in 1:2. So here we see ἐκκλησία being used as an identity marker, with a reminder that that identity is in another.

Third, regarding how this phrase relates to the rest of the verse, the reference to those who are sanctified and holy will be examined more fully in the upcoming section on holiness language. The reference to "with all the ones who call upon the name of our Lord Jesus Christ in every place" does appear to be a reminder to the Corinthian Church that they are part of something translocal,[29] as their unity with all those who are called is emphasized.

25. Here I agree with the majority view that there were factions in the Corinthian Church, rather than "bickerings" (Munck, "Church Without Factions," 62–70). See Meeks, *First Urban Christians*, 75–77.

26. Murphy-O'Connor, "House-Churches," 133, estimates forty to fifty. Barnett, *Corinthian Question*, 225–27, identifies fifteen households in Corinth, each with approximately fifteen members, for a total local church of two hundred. De Vos, *Church and Community Conflicts*, estimates the number at around one hundred.

27. Conzelmann, *1 Corinthians*, 22; similarly, Fitzmyer, *First Corinthians*, 125.

28. Fee, *First Epistle*, 31; see also Thiselton, *First Epistle*, 73–74, who traces this interpretation back to Chrysostom; Garland, *1 Corinthians*, 26–27.

29. See Garland, *1 Corinthians*, 28; Stenschke, "Significance and Function of References," 217–18; Kloha, "Trans-Congregational," 179; Thiselton, *First Epistle*, 78–79.

1 Corinthians 1:2 is a good place to begin this survey, not just because it is the first occurrence of ἐκκλησία in these letters, but also because it highlights both intrachurch and interchurch solidarity. The Corinthians are to strive for unity in the ἐκκλησία of Corinth, but are also to have an awareness of a wider translocal grouping of those who call on the name of the Lord.

Intrachurch Solidarity

I will begin this section by examining 1 Corinthians 14, because here ἐκκλησία in the singular occurs seven times, and these references reveal a number of things about Paul's understanding of intrachurch solidarity in a chapter which is concerned with what kind of behavior is appropriate when the Corinthians meet together. Two features emerge from 1 Corinthians 14.

First, the ἐκκλησία is a place which should be characterized by building up. There is a repeated emphasis in these verses on the ἐκκλησία being built up (1 Cor 14:4, 5, 12), which Paul links to instructing others (1 Cor 14:19). They are to keep silent if no interpretation is available which builds up (1 Cor 14:26-28), or if to speak up in the ἐκκλησία would be shameful, not encouraging (1 Cor 14:36).[30] Paul's concern for building up can be traced back to 1 Corinthians 8:1 and the contrast between knowledge that puffs up and love that builds up, and to Paul's role as an apostle, laying the foundation on which others build (1 Cor 3:10-11).[31] When Paul talks of "building up" in 1 Corinthians 14, then, the kind of behavior that building up involves has already been established: from 1 Corinthians 3:10-11, we see that the building needs to be careful, and must be on the foundation of Jesus Christ; from 1 Corinthians 8-10, and the discussion of the weak and strong, we see that building up is focused on an "other-regard" which "requires that the practice of the strong be compromised insofar as it endangers the weak."[32] These are strong injunctions to consider corporate solidarity before individual satisfaction, which show Paul's concern with intrachurch solidarity. What emerges here in 1 Corinthians 14 is a pattern of ecclesial life, where the identity of the ἐκκλησία is expressed through behavior marked by the building up of others in the ἐκκλησία. Members of the

---

30. For a discussion of the textual issues surrounding 1 Corinthians 14:34-35, see Thiselton, *First Epistle*, 1148-50. With Thiselton, I treat the text as "almost certain." The interpretation of these verses has generated enormous material; for a recent bibliography and discussion see Thiselton, *First Epistle*, 1146-62.

31. Thiselton, *First Epistle*, 1088; Schütz, *Anatomy*, 224-25.

32. Horrell, *Solidarity and Difference*, 182.

ἐκκλησία are to modify their behavior, for the sake of the ἐκκλησία, as God is among them.[33]

Second, as well as a place for building up, the ἐκκλησία is also a place into which outsiders might come (1 Cor 14:23–5), and where the unbeliever will be convicted of sin by the congregation and will turn to and worship God. A number of implications for intrachurch solidarity follow from this passage. First, we see the ἐκκλησία acting corporately, as all who prophesy convict and examine the outsider.[34] In keeping with the context of the passage, this prophesying will be verbal, and intelligible to the outsider, who responds to what they hear from all. Second, Paul's concern with the response of outsiders who are present in the assembly creates a distinction between the ἐκκλησία and the assembly; it is possible for people to be present in the assembly, but to be outsiders and therefore not part of the ἐκκλησία. This is a distinctively Pauline usage, whether the comparison is with Greek literature[35] or with the strictures of Deuteronomy 23.[36] Again we see Paul using ἐκκλησία in an innovative way, as an ongoing identity which exists whether or not it is assembled. Third, parallels can be seen here with what has already been seen in chapter 3 in discussions of brotherhood and the language of holiness, where the ἐκκλησία has an ongoing kindred identity which is also defined as separation from outsiders, and therefore we can see Paul here operating with the same understanding of intrachurch solidarity. Fourth, Paul describes the mechanism for transferring from being an outsider to a member of the ἐκκλησία, one who worships God. As Paul has already reminded the Corinthians in 1 Corinthians 5:9–13, their separate identity from outsiders does not mean that they are to avoid all contact with them, but rather that their lives are to be marked by a distinctive pattern of behavior; others can also be saved by the foolishness of the cross (1 Cor 1:18) and become part of the ἐκκλησία. Finally, the Corinthians are reminded that God is among them (v. 25), their core identity remains in another, and the presence of God is what should mark out the ἐκκλησία.

33. This is not to preclude the exhortation to behave for the sake of Christ, following the example of Christ, or because of what Christ has done. See for example 1 Corinthians 5:7, and the later discussion on example and imitation.

34. Aernie, *Is Paul Also Among*, 105–6, 111, notes a further communal dimension here in the original context of the Isaiah 28 quotation, and the desire for restoration of the community of Israel.

35. Compare Aristophanes, *Ecclesiazusae*, where the women who shouldn't have been there had to pretend to be men, otherwise they would have had to leave. See *Eccl.* 20, 89, 270, 289, 352, 376, 490, 501, 548, 740.

36. Note the ongoing reference to these strictures in Nehemiah 13:1–3 and Philo, *Leg.* 3.8, 3.81; Philo, *Post.* 177; Philo, *Ebr.* 213; Philo, *Conf.* 144; Philo, *Migr.* 69; Philo, *Somn.* 2.184.

Similar expectations can be seen elsewhere in 1 Corinthians. In 11:18, Paul is concerned about harmonious relationships when the ἐκκλησία comes together, having heard that there are divisions among them. He wants their behavior to be marked by a concern for the other rather than replicating social norms.[37] The discussion of profaning the body and blood of Christ and of judgement in the community[38] in 1 Corinthians 11:27–33 draws particular emphasis to the ἐκκλησία as a body whose identity is in Christ. In 1 Corinthians 5:4–5, where the assembled ἐκκλησία is to enact judgement on another,[39] with the power of the Lord Jesus Christ, the emphasis falls on communal activity for the sake of the sexually immoral man, even though that means delivering him to Satan.[40]

One final example of intrachurch solidarity remains to be examined. In 1 Corinthians 6:4, Paul is suggesting that anyone within the church in Corinth would make a better judge over internal affairs than one from outside the church,[41] in the context of the issues raised by lawsuits among believers.[42] What is noticeable here is how the ἐκκλησία is encouraged to take on a role that was often fulfilled by the Greek *polis* assembly, the judgement of legal cases.[43] Clarke argues that the background to 1 Corinthians 6:1–8 is "vexatious litigation" undertaken by "men of relatively high social standing,"[44] and that Paul encourages "private arbitration."[45] I would add to his reconstruction the observation that what Paul is talking about here is not so much private arbitration as a judgement which the ἐκκλησία is

---

37. See for example Winter, *After Paul Left Corinth*, 154–58; Chow, *Patronage and Power*, 102–12.

38. For a discussion of the nature of the judgement here, see Roetzel, *Judgement in the Community*, 136–42.

39. See Roetzel, *Judgement in the Community*, 115–25. Note that ἐκκλησία is not used in this verse. However, an assembly of the ἐκκλησία is clearly in view.

40. For the purposes of this study, it is not necessary to establish the meaning of this phrase. See Thiselton, *First Epistle*, 392–400, for a discussion of these verses.

41. Taking the sentence imperatively. Thiselton, *First Epistle*, 432–33, argues for an interrogative interpretation, but also notes the indicative exclamatory interpretation, and notes that the issue is finely balanced.

42. Clarke, *Secular and Christian*, 59–60, argues that secular leadership patterns in Roman Corinth, highlighting the importance of wealth and honour, explain the predilection for law courts as a way of confirming status in 1 Corinthians 6; Chow, *Patronage and Power*, 123–30, detects powerful patrons here; Aasgaard, *Brothers and Sisters*, 220–26, argues that the specific legal situation in view is a conflict over inheritance, possibly between brothers.

43. See for example Thucydides, *History*, 2.60; Aristotle, *Pol.* 1282a.

44. Clarke, *Secular and Christian*, 71.

45. Clarke, *Secular and Christian*, 69–70. See also Aasgaard, *Brothers and Sisters*, 227–28.

better equipped to make on one of its own members than one who has no standing in the ἐκκλησία. Here we have an indication that the ἐκκλησία can sometimes operate as an alternative to the institutions of the *polis*.

Looking at intrachurch solidarity in the Corinthian correspondence as a whole, we see that ecclesial life is expressed through behavior marked by the building up of others. The ἐκκλησία has its core identity in God and Christ. There is a distinction between the ἐκκλησία and the assembly, which can include outsiders, and those outsiders should be considered as those who could become part of the ἐκκλησία. There is one occasion where the ἐκκλησία takes on a role associated with the *polis* assembly. These features of the ἐκκλησία will be further examined as imagery and the role of Paul are explored.

Interchurch Solidarity

The Corinthian correspondence contains a number of references to interchurch solidarity, and they will be examined under five subheadings: regional solidarity, normative behavior, mutual accountability, Paul and the churches, and the collective singular use of ἐκκλησία.

Regional Solidarity

Paul refers in 1 Corinthians 16:1 to the Galatian churches, in 1 Corinthians 16:19 to the churches in the province of Asia, and in 2 Corinthians 8:1 to the churches in Macedonia. While these references are to various local ἐκκλησίαι, two things should be noted. First, we see a continuation of Paul's habit of referring to groups of churches by their regional or provincial location. Second, we begin to see how Paul applies this regional designation, as in each case these churches are identified to teach the Corinthians something. In 1 Corinthians 16:1–4 and 2 Corinthians 8:1–5, the Corinthians are to follow the examples of the Galatian and Macedonian churches respectively in their giving, and in 1 Corinthians 16:19, the Corinthians receive greetings from an area with which Paul wants them to engage. In chapter 3, I noted the example of the Judean churches in 1 Thessalonians 2:14 and the exemplary role of regional churches continues in the Corinthian correspondence. Here Paul continues that emphasis, as he indicates that the church in Corinth should learn from other churches and should imitate their behavior. We can see this as a direct challenge to the Corinthian Church's emphasis on its own knowledge and competence, and their concern with their own status.[46]

Van Kooten[47] argues that Paul's discussion of churches at the provincial level points to an alternative structure of the Roman Empire and compares this to Greek supralocal assemblies. As Van Kooten himself notes, Paul does not combine the ἐκκλησίαι here into a single ἐκκλησία, and I would argue that this indicates that solidarity expressed by cooperating rather than competing local assemblies, without them being subsumed, superseded, or replaced by a "supralocal assembly," is one of the distinctive features of Paul's thought. Paul is concerned with creating a solidarity based on mutual recognition, imitation, and support, rather than one expressed through the membership of a supralocal assembly or other representative structure. Therefore, his provincial or regional usage is not the beginning of an alternative structure, but rather a way of encouraging local ἐκκλησίαι to express solidarity with other believers as widely as possible, by learning from them, imitating their behavior, and supporting them.

Normative Behavior

There are several references that encourage the Corinthians to do that which is done in other churches. 1 Corinthians 4:17 refers to what Paul teaches in every church; although the singular is used here, it refers to various local ἐκκλησίαι. In 1 Corinthians 7:17, Paul refers to a rule that he lays down in all the churches—in 1 Corinthians 11:16, to a practice which all the churches have, and in 1 Corinthians 14:33–34, to a rule which is practiced in all the churches.

It is important to establish here the scope of "all the churches." In 1 Corinthians 7:17, Paul's reference to "my rule in all the churches" indicates that the churches of the Pauline mission are in view,[48] and 1 Corinthians 4:17 is similar, as it refers to Paul's ways and what he teaches. In 1 Corinthians 11:16, Paul states that "we" do not have such a practice, nor do "the churches of God." Whatever the precise referent of "we" here, Paul distinguishes between himself/his group, and the churches, and in doing so provides a comprehensive reference for the churches of God, which "does

---

46. For various aspects of Corinthian concern for status, see Meeks, *First Urban Christians*, 73; Clarke, *Secular and Christian*, 21, 39; Winter, *After Paul Left Corinth*, 282–86.

47. Van Kooten, "Ἐκκλησία τοῦ θεοῦ," 536–37.

48. So Fitzmyer, *First Corinthians*, 307.

not allow for an exception."[49] Therefore, and consistent with Paul's earlier usage in Galatians 1:13 of "church of God" for a church he did not found, that term should be taken comprehensively. In 1 Corinthians 14:33, Paul refers to the churches of the saints. Later I will examine the language of holiness and holy people, but in chapter 3, I showed how the language of holy people was used to include the Thessalonians with all those who have believed in Jesus in 2 Thessalonians 1:10, and the same can reasonably be expected from the use of holiness language here. In addition, in both 1 Corinthians 11:16 and 14:33, it is helpful to Paul's argument if the references he makes are as comprehensive as possible, indicating that it is the Corinthians who are in the minority position.[50] Therefore, when Paul writes "all the churches" in 1 Corinthians 11 and 14, he does not just mean the churches of the Pauline mission, but all churches.

The implication of Paul's argumentation here is that the behaviors and beliefs that are normative in "the churches" should also be normative in Corinth. This can be seen clearly in 1 Corinthians 11:2-16. Paul is dealing with something that is contentious in Corinth, and in making his argument, Paul uses arguments from the creation order and men and women's relationships to God (1 Cor 11:3-12); from the Corinthians' own sense of what is right and what is in the nature of things (1 Cor 11:13-15); and from what Paul practices and what is practiced in the churches (1 Cor 11:16). There are several complex arguments here, beyond the scope of this study, but among the reasons why the Corinthians should do as Paul commands is the practice of the churches. The Corinthian Church must take account of what happens elsewhere.[51]

Mutual Accountability

As well as encouraging the Corinthians to see themselves as part of something wider than themselves, and to take account of that which is normative in all the churches, Paul also encourages the development of mutual accountability. This can be seen in the references in 2 Corinthians 8 to the views of "all the churches." In 2 Corinthians 8:18, there is an unnamed brother who is praised by all the churches, and then chosen by all the churches in

---

49. Stenschke, "Significance and Function of References," 207.

50. See Stenschke, "Significance and Function of References," 207–8; Furnish, *2 Corinthians*, 408, refers to "church discipline" in 11:16.

51. Similarly, Stenschke, "Significance and Function of References," 206; Garland, *1 Corinthians*, 304.

2 Corinthians 8:19.[52] In 2 Corinthians 8:23, there are two brothers in view, described as representatives or envoys of the churches, and in 2 Corinthians 8:24, Paul is concerned that the Corinthians behave rightly towards these representatives of the churches, so that the churches can see it.

Three observations can be made about these references. First, in the treatment of these envoys, the Corinthian ἐκκλησία has a responsibility to act in a way which other churches will approve. This has a similar impact to the call to take account of what is normative in all the churches, although here the arbiter is not Paul, as is the case in 1 Corinthians 4:17 and 7:17, but the other churches.

Second, the Corinthian Church must take account of what happens elsewhere, and what decisions other churches make; the delegates are suitable because they are chosen by the churches, and the fact that their names are not mentioned may indicate that they are not known to the Corinthians.[53] This need to take account of the decisions of others is not without limits, and certainly a commitment to the truth of the gospel[54] and holy behavior remain paramount; however, there is at least a sense here of churches taking decisions which other churches need to respect. There are similarities here to Paul's call to take account of what is normative in the churches, but the focus shifts from Paul's role to the decisions of these other churches, even though Paul is the messenger in this case. The imposition of an artificial distinction might be illuminating here: as well as respecting what is normative in other churches in matters of doctrine, the Corinthians are also to respect the wise administrative decisions of other churches.

Third, there is a tantalizing but undeveloped indication here of churches acting together. There is no clear indication of the mechanism for this, or the extent to which it happened, or what Paul's precise role was in this. However, churches in at least one region acted together, and in acting together gave their collective decisions greater authority, for in 2 Corinthians 8 and 9, one of the reasons why the Corinthians can have confidence in the collection is because of the existence of these envoys chosen by the

---

52. Harris, *Second Epistle*, 601, notes how the expression could (but need not be) restricted to the Macedonian churches, or all the churches of the Pauline mission. Even if viewed at its most restrictive, as only the Macedonian churches here and in the rest of chapter 8, there is still an indication here of churches acting together.

53. Furnish, *2 Corinthians*, 435–36, rejects this idea, on the grounds that if the man was renowned, then he would have been known to the Corinthians, and that a famous person is not introduced anonymously. However, his reconstruction assumes that the names must have been removed from the letter later, for which there is no evidence, and therefore I would agree with Harris, *Second Epistle*, 601–2, that the exclusion of the names is because they will be introduced to the Corinthians by Titus.

54. Gal 1:8.

churches, who show that this is not just an action which Paul is taking (2 Cor 8:20-1),⁵⁵ nor is it the action of a single local ἐκκλησία.⁵⁶

2 Corinthians 8-9 then indicates the development of the idea of mutual accountability between churches, where the decisions of others need to be acted on and respected, and where Paul's role as one who handles communication between the churches is somewhat relativized. Paul may be the main communication vehicle, but he is not the only one.

Paul and the Churches

There are three references in 2 Corinthians to Paul's relationship with other churches. 2 Corinthians 11:8-9 indicates that Paul received support from Macedonia, and therefore is not a reference to all churches. However, it reinforces the sense already noted in 2 Corinthians 8-9 of the Macedonian church functioning as an example to the Corinthians, and as evidence that other churches stood behind Paul's ministry.⁵⁷ In 2 Corinthians 12:13, although the other churches are not named, the Corinthians would know who Paul means, and Paul most likely has particular churches or individuals within churches who offered support in view.⁵⁸

In 2 Corinthians 11:28, in the context of his trials and tribulations, Paul talks of his concern for *all the churches*. It might be concluded here that Paul has in view churches founded by the Pauline mission.⁵⁹ However, Paul wrote Romans and Colossians to churches he did not found and spent much of his ministry collecting for the church in Jerusalem,⁶⁰ he has already referred to all the churches of God in a number of places in 1 Corinthians, and has also discussed the Jerusalem church in 2 Corinthians 8-9, and therefore there seems to be no reason to limit the force of all to just Pauline churches. In chapter 3, I noted in my discussion of 2 Thessalonians 1:4 that Paul was encouraging interchurch solidarity through the mutual recognition of

---

55. On this passage see also Stenschke, "Significance and Function of References," 210-12.

56. Perhaps indicating an implicit criticism of the Corinthian tendency to act independently of others.

57. Stenschke, "Significance and Function of References," 195-96.

58. Harris, *Second Epistle*, 757-58. Stenschke, "Significance and Function of References," 196-97, sees this as an example of Paul's standard of ministry in all churches. I would argue that, as this is a reference to Paul's ministry, then the churches where he ministered are in view, as in 1 Corinthians 4:17 and 7:17.

59. Furnish, *2 Corinthians*, 519; Witherington, *Conflict & Community*, 453.

60. Harris, *Second Epistle*, 812-13, also notes the concern Paul has for the Jewish race in Romans 9.

a common origin, and implicitly in the context of the Day of the Lord, a common experience of present and future. In the earlier discussion of 1 Corinthians 11:16 and 14:33–34, I noted that Paul had more than just the churches of the Pauline mission in view, and that the Corinthians needed to take account of what happens elsewhere; this has been further illustrated by the references in 2 Corinthians 8. Here, the reference to all the churches is more personal, and Paul is not giving an instruction. However, this reveals his concern for the collective of all churches.

The sense of solidarity with the churches that Paul expresses here is deep, as Paul contends that he shares in the weakness of others (2 Cor 11:29). Whilst there is no explicit call to imitation here, Paul is "boasting" of his behavior in 2 Corinthians 11, and therefore it is possible that Paul is presenting his concern for all the churches as a model for how the Corinthians should be concerned for all the churches, or at least indicating that the circle of care and concern should extend beyond Corinth. As well as respecting what is normative in other churches in matters of doctrine, the Corinthians are also to respect the wise administrative decisions of other churches, and to generally care about what happens in them.

Collective Singular Use of ἐκκλησία

There are a number of occurrences of the word ἐκκλησία in 1 Corinthians which are neither singular references to the local church nor plural references to multiple local churches.

In 1 Corinthians 10:32, Paul is concerned that the Corinthians should act in a way which will not cause anyone to stumble, whether Jews, Greeks, or the church of God. It is possible in the context of chapters 8–10, where Paul is concerned with the impact of one believer's behavior on another in Corinth, to argue for a reference here to the local church in Corinth.[61] However, Paul talks of three categories of people here: Jews, Greeks, and the church of God, which suggests that the church of God exists at least in some sense as a separate entity to the two groups into which humanity has been divided by Paul in this letter.[62] In addition, the immediate context of 1 Corinthians 10:23–30 refers to relations with those outside the church, and

---

61. See O'Brien, "Church," 91; also, Fee, *First Epistle*, 489n68.

62. Fitzmyer, *First Corinthians*, 403. Paul uses these two categories elsewhere in 1 Corinthians 1:22, 24 and 12:13. Thiselton, *First Epistle*, 795, notes that here the people of God are partly redefined, in contrast to the argument of 10:1–22. Meeks, *First Urban Christians*, 108 notes the distinction made between Jews, gentiles and the church of God.

so it makes the most sense to understand Jews and Greeks as a reference to Jews and Greeks outside rather than inside the church. The dispute may have arisen within the church in Corinth, but it has implications for the church conceived of in more general terms, in its relation to "the world." The behavior of the Corinthian Church is not only a local matter.[63]

In 1 Corinthians 15:9, we read how Paul persecuted the church of God. This is a very similar statement to Galatians 1:13, and seems to function in a similar way.[64] I argued there for a reference to the "whole" church. Here, I would say that "church of God" here is most naturally taken as a reference to the church conceived of as a whole, for the same reasons as given in chapter 3.

Having now examined five of the occurrences of "church of God" in the Pauline corpus, it is possible to identify a pattern. On two occasions, the church of God has been given a particular geographical referent: Corinth. However, on the occasions where a particular geographical referent is not given, I have argued that the church as a whole is in view, as in Galatians 1:13, 1 Corinthians 10:32, and 15:9. The same pattern has also been observed with "the churches of God": a geographical designation can be given, such as at 1 Thessalonians 2:14, but otherwise, as at 2 Thessalonians 1:4 and 1 Corinthians 11:16, a general reference is in view.

One reference might be seen to not fit this pattern: 1 Corinthians 11:22. In contrast to 10:32, where the wider context suggests a more generalized reference, this verse most naturally reads as having an impact on those within Corinth, and therefore the designation "church of God" may be being used here in a similar way to its use in 1:2 (and 2 Corinthians 1:2). However, given the close proximity of this verse to 10:32, where I have argued that Paul uses "church of God" in a more extended sense, and to 11:16, where the plural is used in a more general way, it seems reasonable to argue that the whole church is also in view here; as well as humiliating those who have nothing, the Corinthians are showing their disregard for the wider church by their unworthy participation in a rite designed to proclaim the Lord's death until he comes (1 Cor 11:26).[65] If this is the case, then, where a geographical referent is not specified, church or churches of God refers to the whole church.

---

63. See Stenschke, "Significance and Function of References," 206–7.

64. Fitzmyer, *First Corinthians*, 125; Fee, *First Epistle*, 734n107; Giles, *What on Earth*, 114–21.

65. Stenschke, "Significance and Function of References," 207, suggests that a wider entity may be in view here due to the body metaphors in 1 Corinthians 12:12–31. See also Kloha, "Trans-Congregational," 178.

Finally, in 1 Corinthians 12:28, we note first the immediate context: Paul is discussing the body of Christ, which we will examine a little later in this chapter. Here, Paul describes how God has appointed people with various gifts in the church as part of his discussion of the body of Christ. Without going into the detail of these gifts, at least one of them, apostles,[66] represents something that has been given not just to the Corinthian Church but to the translocal church.[67] This means that ἐκκλησία here is most naturally taken with a wider-than-local reference,[68] and that Paul, as well as using "church(es) of God" in a wider sense, can also use ἐκκλησία in this sense.

Two implications follow from this collective usage. First, Paul's usage of ἐκκλησία is a significant departure from that seen in Greek literature or the Septuagint. Second, on three of the four occasions where ἐκκλησία is used for a collective singular in 1 Corinthians, Paul's concern is that the Corinthians should take account of and modify behavior because of the "the church." This is explicit in 10:32 and 11:22, where they are called not to offend or despise the church of God, and implicit in 12:27, where they are the body of Christ but are reminded that the church is wider than Corinth. This reinforces what we have already seen in the letter about the need to take account of the ἐκκλησία beyond Corinth.

Conclusion

There are then a number of passages in the Corinthian correspondence which indicate Paul's concern for interchurch solidarity, and indicate that he uses ἐκκλησίαι provincially, and ἐκκλησία(ι) to conceive of the church as a whole. This has been disputed by a number of New Testament scholars,[69] but the cumulative effect of the evidence from 1 and 2 Corinthians, as well as that from Paul's earliest letters, suggests that while it is not the most common usage, it is nevertheless an observable one in all of Paul's letters, with several implications.

First, Paul's provincial usage, although not an attempt to create an alternative ecclesial structure, functions to encourage and challenge the local

---

66. Taking apostles as a particular group of "church founders": Thiselton, *First Epistle*, 1015; Fitzmyer, *First Corinthians*, 482.

67. The Corinthians certainly knew of such apostles, such as Cephas (1 Cor 1:12), and also of people who exercised apostolic ministry in Corinth and also elsewhere, such as Apollos (1 Cor 3:6; 16:12).

68. See Kloha, "Trans-Congregational," 178–79. For alternative views here, see Fee, *First Epistle*, 618n13; Meeks, *First Urban Christians*, 108.

69. For example, O'Brien, "Church," 92; Banks, *Paul's Idea*, 28–31, 40.

church in Corinth to express solidarity with other ἐκκλησίαι by recognizing, learning from, imitating and supporting them.

Second, Paul talks of what is normative in all the churches. This can be taken to include churches outside the Pauline mission in 1 Corinthians 11 and 14. It fosters the idea of a common identity across all churches, expressed in common beliefs and practices.

Third, there are indications in 2 Corinthians 8 and 9 of churches working together, in the appointment of the envoys and the administration of the collection. While the mechanism for this is unclear, this would further strengthen interchurch solidarity, as churches communicated and cooperated in joint ventures.

Fourth, Paul's concern for all the churches suggests a model of concern that should be followed by the Corinthians.

Fifth, I have argued that Paul conceives of the churches in 1 Corinthians 11:28, and the church of God in 1 Corinthians 15:9 and elsewhere, as a whole. Both the singular and the plural can be used in this collective way. The church of God is conceived of as something which can be persecuted (1 Cor 15:9; cf. Gal 1:13), or offended or disregarded (1 Cor 10:32; 11:16). As such, the Corinthians need to take account of the whole church when they act.

As has been noted throughout this section, the ecclesial solidarity expressed in the Corinthian correspondence shows similarities with, and builds upon, that which is expressed in Paul's earliest letters. Sometimes this is a case of ideas becoming more explicit, such as in Paul's use of church of God in 1 Corinthians. On other occasions, such as in examining the provincial use of ἐκκλησία, clarity comes from having a larger total number of occurrences to explore.

1 and 2 Corinthians show a highly developed sense of both intrachurch and interchurch solidarity. I will now explore the functioning of that solidarity in examining ἐκκλησία and imagery used for the church: holiness language, temple imagery, brotherhood, and the body.

Ἐκκλησία and Other Imagery

The Language of Holiness

In my examination of the Thessalonian correspondence, I noted the importance of holiness language, and how the language of holiness was used to create boundaries between the community and those outside, and to define boundaries within the community, as well as being explicitly linked to the return of Christ as judge. The language of holiness served to bind the ἐκκλησία together, promoting internal harmony and group identity. I also noted the idea of God's holy people, and how that is expressed in 2 Thessalonians 1:10. Similar concerns can be seen in the Corinthian correspondence.

There are a number of places where the language of holiness is used to create and reinforce boundaries. In 1 Corinthians 16:15, Paul emphasizes the serving role of the household of Stephanas, service which would strengthen the saints.[70] Trebilco notes how the idea of service within the group would reinforce group boundaries.[71] In 1 Corinthians 6:1–2, the saints are first those in Corinth, who have competence to judge civil cases, and then the saints in general, those who will judge the world. As in 1 Corinthians 14:33, the issue is separateness. Trebilco notes both the eschatological language here[72] and the "boundary-creating function"[73] of the contrast between the holy ones and unbelievers in 1 Corinthians 6:6. The behavior of the Corinthians is explicitly founded on eschatological reality; they are competent to judge in Corinth because they will judge the world, and so Paul brings together the boundaries that were to exist in Corinth and the ultimate distinction between "the saints" and "the world." Holiness language is used in 1 Corinthians to reinforce boundaries between the community and outsiders, but also to reinforce boundaries between believers and the world in general, and therefore impacts upon intra- and interchurch solidarity

Holiness language is also used to emphasize participation in a wider group. In 1 Corinthians 1:2, the recipients of the letters are addressed as saints. This could be viewed as an alternative designation for the ἐκκλησία, and I have already noted the possibility that the reference to others who call upon Jesus' name is a reminder to the Corinthian Church that they are part of something translocal. In 1 Corinthians 1:2, the emphasis falls on the common origin in Christ that the Corinthians share with all people everywhere who call on the Lord. This suggests that the Corinthians should view themselves as part of a wider group: the saints. 2 Corinthians 1:1 has a different emphasis to 1 Corinthians 1:2, the letter being addressed to the church in Corinth, and the saints in Achaia. Here "saints" is not being used for the totality of believers, as in 1 Corinthians 1:2, but it still functions to emphasize the "corporate-ness" of the Christian communities[74] to

---

70. Although I have treated this as intrachurch solidarity, Stenschke, "Significance and Function of References," 205, suggests that this service may have been wider, as it included Paul (1 Cor 16:18).

71. Trebilco, *Self-designations*, 136.

72. Trebilco, *Self-designations*, 131–32.

73. Trebilco, *Self-designations*, 135.

74. Trebilco, *Self-designations*, 130.

emphasize interchurch solidarity. This can be seen when 1 Corinthians 1:2 is compared with 2 Corinthians 13:12, where Paul uses "the saints" of an unnamed group who are "with him," which is probably a reference either to the Macedonian Christians in general, or the church in Thessalonica from where Paul writes;[75] the precise location does not need to be established for this to be a greeting from one set of saints in a region or city, to another group in a region (2 Cor 1:1). The saints are a separate group from the world, and they share a common identity.

This common identity entails different behavior. The link between this language of "the saints" and the designation of Israel as a holy people has been noted,[76] and there are a number of places where the behavioral implications of holiness are emphasized. First, the Corinthians are those who have been sanctified in Christ (1 Cor 1:2; 6:11), not those who indulge in immorality (1 Cor 6:9–10). Second, the language of cleansing is applied to leaven and the Passover in 1 Corinthians 5:6–8, as the Corinthians are exhorted to cleanse out the old leaven of sexual immorality. Third, Leviticus 26:12 and Isaiah 52:11 are applied to the Corinthians in 2 Corinthians 6:16–18, encouraging a concern with separate, holy behavior, avoiding that which is unclean. Fourth, the language of "holy people" is broadened from its application in 2 Thessalonians, where it was linked to Christ's parousia, for there are links to Christ's death in 1 Corinthians, particularly in 1 Corinthians 5:7, where Christ is the Passover Lamb. Fifth, in 1 Corinthians 14:33, the link is explicitly made here between being part of the saints and behaving in a way which is practiced by all the saints.[77]

Finally, the Jerusalem collection provides an example of how solidarity could work in practice.[78] Paul uses saints to refer to those in Jerusalem (1 Cor 16:1; 2 Cor 8:4; 9:1, 12). The emphasis here is on service of the saints in 2 Corinthians 9, but service to the saints in Jerusalem is explicitly linked to the churches of Galatia in 1 Corinthians 16:1 and the churches of Macedonia in 1 Corinthians 8:1. Churches in three different provinces support the saints in Jerusalem, demonstrating the practical application of the idea of service of the saints.

The language of "the saints" and the idea of the holy people in Paul's letters to the Corinthians has two implications for understanding interchurch

---

75. Furnish, *2 Corinthians*, 586–87. Stenschke, "Significance and Function of References," 219–20, argues that "all the saints" here is a reference to all Christians. This is possible; however, I would argue that in the letter's closing, Paul probably has in view a particular group of saints who are with him. (Cf. 1 Cor 16:19–20.)

76. See for example Trebilco, *Self-designations*, 136.

77. Trebilco, *Self-designations*, 130.

78. See also Stenschke, "Significance and Function of References," 208–9.

solidarity. First, the designation "the saints" brings together the local and the translocal in a similar way to the use of ἐκκλησία already noted: the local saints and the whole group of saints are in view in 1 Corinthians 6:1-2, just as Paul talks of both the local and the whole ἐκκλησία in these letters. I would argue that this strengthens the case I am making for Paul's early and frequent use of the designation church of God (and sometimes just church) to mean "whole church."

Second, in his use of the language of saints in 1 Corinthians, Paul predicates local behavior on the identity of the whole. Importantly, this is a present reality, not just a revelation of the saints on the last day. They will judge the world (1 Cor 6:2), but the saints now are all those who in every place call upon the name of Jesus (1 Cor 1:2). This is the same pattern as has been observed with Paul's usage of ἐκκλησία in 1 and 2 Corinthians, and is a strong assertion of interchurch solidarity, based on belonging to the same group: the saints.

Having examined holiness language, I will now examine the closely related terminology of temple in the Corinthian correspondence.

Temple Imagery

There are three passages in the Corinthian letters where Paul uses temple imagery in relation to the church or individuals: 1 Corinthians 3:16-17, 3:16-17, and 2 Corinthians 6:16-7:1.[79]

I will begin here with 1 Corinthians 6:19-20, where Paul is usually thought to be speaking of the body of each believer as a temple.[80] Holland has challenged this view, arguing that temple and body imagery are always applied to the church, not the individual, that Paul uses the definite article and the singular for the temple, and that the plurals in vv. 19-20 indicate a corporate setting for the temple here.[81] However, in arguing that all the

---

79. Paul can also use "temple" in the sense of a cultic building, as in 1 Corinthians 9:13. See Fee, *First Epistle*, 412 for the background to this term. Many argue that a physical temple and not the church is also in view in 2 Thessalonians 2:4, as the place where the man of lawlessness exalts himself; for example, Malherbe, *Letters to the Thessalonians*, 420-21; Witherington, *1 and 2 Thessalonians*, 218-220; McKelvey, *New Temple*, 135-36. For a contrary view, see Beale, *Temple and the Church's Mission*, 274-81. Either way, Paul makes no application of the temple imagery in 2 Thessalonians to the Thessalonians. Therefore, I consider it proper to begin an examination of temple imagery as applied to those to whom Paul writes, in 1 Corinthians.

80. So Minear, *Images of the Church*, 97; McKelvey, *New Temple*, 102; Thiselton, *First Epistle*, 475.

81. Holland, *Contours*, 127.

other uses of the concept of temple and body refer to the church, Holland allows one exception (John 2:19) and cites only four supporting passages (1 Cor 3:16; 6:19; 2 Cor 6:16; Rev 21:3). This is hardly sufficient evidence to say this concept is always applied to the church; if 1 Corinthians 6:19 is accepted as a reference to the individual, perhaps in some ways parallel to John 2:19, then two of the five New Testament references that link temple and body would be to individuals. His statement that "Their 'body' is *the* temple of the Holy Spirit"[82] in discussing the definite article is also misleading: 1 Corinthians 6:19 does not give the emphasis that Holland suggests. The use of the second-person plural with the singular of "body" is interesting, but without Holland's other two pieces of evidence, and with the immediate context of 1 Corinthians 6:16, where Paul uses the imagery of the marriage of a man and a woman in relation to becoming one body with a prostitute, and 1 Corinthians 6:18, where a man sins against his own body, it seems best here to take the references throughout 1 Corinthians 6:12-20 as to the body of an individual. Paul does then here talk of the individual as God's temple, and the use of the second person plural about "body" in 1 Corinthians 6:19 highlights that all of the Corinthians need to heed Paul's words. This passage then has implications primarily for the individual, and perhaps by extension for intrachurch solidarity; however, as these would be necessarily tentative, I will not examine them here.

There are then two passages to be considered here, in examining the ecclesial implications of temple imagery: 1 Corinthians 3:16-17 and 2 Corinthians 6:16—7:1.

In 1 Corinthians 3:16-17, Paul describes the Corinthians as God's temple, those in whom God's Spirit dwells. As God's temple, they are sacred, and there is a warning that God will act against anyone who destroys God's temple. It is important to see this description in the context of chapter 3, where, from v. 9, Paul talks of the Corinthians as God's building. The purpose of this imagery in 1 Corinthians 3:10-15 is to highlight Paul's role as one who lays the foundation, and that the foundation can only be Jesus Christ, for one who builds on the foundation must be careful, for the last day will reveal the quality of workmanship. The imagery shifts in v. 16 from building to temple,[83] but the warning remains: each must be careful how they build. Given that divisions in the church are again to the fore in 3:1-4 and 3:22, the warning is against those who would destroy the church with

---

82. Holland, *Contours*, 127. Emphasis original.

83. Beale, *Temple and the Church's Mission*, 245-48, argues that the temple is in view all along, based on the use of garden imagery in relation to the temple and the imagery of building with costly materials (and garden items) in 1 Kings 5-7.

their divisions.[84] What is noticeable here is that the temple most naturally refers not to the whole church, but to the church in Corinth.

Several observations can be made about this passage. First, the temple is described as the place where God's Spirit dwells, whether that temple is viewed corporately (1 Cor 3:16–17) or as an individual (1 Cor 6:19); in fact, if καί in 3:16 is explicative, as McKelvey argues, then they are the temple because of the indwelling of the Spirit.[85] Here the core identity of the church in another is stressed, with a focus on the unifying work of the Holy Spirit. In addition, a link can be made here between Paul and the Corinthians, for although he is not present with them, in 1 Corinthians 5:3–5, he describes himself as being with them in spirit, which I take with Fee and others to be a reference to Paul's actual presence amongst them in the Holy Spirit.[86] Therefore, although Paul is not present with them bodily, he is really present with them through the Spirit.

Second, the imagery of the temple in 1 Corinthians 3 is related to the idea of holiness. In 1:2, the church in Corinth is made up of those who are sanctified and called to be holy; in 3:16–7, the temple is holy by virtue of being the place where God dwells, by his Spirit. This holiness should be displayed by the Corinthians, as they know that they are God's temple and have God's Spirit. The holy temple is to be preserved, not destroyed (verse 17). Temple imagery functions then alongside holiness imagery to encourage intrachurch solidarity in Corinth, as the Corinthians should value their identity as a holy temple and seek to preserve unity.[87]

Third, the imagery of the temple emerges in the context of the construction of a building. This building will be tested on the last day, and therefore, while the imagery of the temple emphasizes what already is, there is also an implication here that this temple must continue to be built. Here Paul demonstrates his flexible use of imagery.

The second passage to be considered here is 2 Corinthians 6:14—7:1. Paul refers to a group as the temple in 2 Corinthians 6:16,[88] in the context of his injunction not to be yoked with unbelievers. The identity of this group needs to be established. McKelvey states that, although Paul "thinks of the temple image in a universal sense, the reference is primarily to the

---

84. See Thiselton, *First Epistle*, 316–17; McKelvey, *New Temple*, 98–102.

85. McKelvey, *New Temple*, 101.

86. Fee, *First Epistle*, 203–5; Thiselton, *First Epistle*, 391. See Fitzmyer, *First Corinthians*, 236, for a contrary view.

87. Compare Schnackenburg, *Church in the New Testament*, 83–85; Pickett, *Cross in Corinth*, 92–93; Thiselton, *First Epistle*, 316–17.

88. For text-critical comments on this verse, see Furnish, *2 Corinthians*, 363.

congregation at Corinth."⁸⁹ I would agree that Paul has the Corinthian congregation in view, as the people to whom his words apply; however, I would argue that the temple imagery here is universal in scope for three reasons. First, the five antitheses in vv. 14–16 deal with universal opposites, in particular the contrast between light and darkness in v. 14. Second, the quotations from the Old Testament which follow in vv. 17–18 deal in language which first applied to the whole people of God. Third, Paul includes himself here as part of the temple of the living God, whereas in 1 Corinthians 3:16, when the Corinthian Church was primarily in view, he was not included. Note that the characteristics of this universal temple emphasize the same issue as the temple in Corinth, or the temple as applied to the individual: enjoying the presence of God by being separate and distinctive to those around (2 Cor 6:16–18).⁹⁰

The use of temple imagery then draws attention to the close connection between the local and the whole. McKelvey argues that the imagery here is about the local church, but that also "the local implies the universal (just as the universal implies the local)."⁹¹ I would contend instead that temple imagery is applied to the individual, the Corinthian Church, and to all God's holy people. There is a usage here which is similar to some of the ways in which ἐκκλησία is used in this letter: the church in Corinth is the temple, but at the same time, the temple is the whole church, which is being refined and prepared for the return of Christ, who will suddenly come to his temple.⁹² In addition, in 1 Corinthians 6:19, the imagery of the temple is applied to the individual,⁹³ emphasizing the flexibility with which the imagery can be used.

Brothers

The language of brotherhood is not used as frequently in 1 and 2 Corinthians as in 1 Thessalonians, but "brothers" is still used forty-one times in 1 Corinthians, and thirteen times in 2 Corinthians.⁹⁴ Of these, twenty

---

89. McKelvey, *New Temple*, 94. Note that Furnish, *2 Corinthians*, 363, takes this as a reference to the whole people of God, based on the same identification at 1 Corinthians 3:16.

90. Harris, *Second Epistle*, 504–6.

91. McKelvey, *New Temple*, 106.

92. Mal 4:1.

93. Contra Holland, *Contours*, 127.

94. See Aasgaard, *Brothers and Sisters*, 313 for a table comparing occurrences.

occurrences in 1 Corinthians are a direct address in the plural, and three in 2 Corinthians.[95]

I have already noted in chapter 3 the importance of the idea of φιλαδελφία in antiquity. There I noted the importance of kinship structures in the ancient family to promote group identity and to denote boundaries and responsibilities (the emphasis Plutarch and others put on brotherly love) and the enduring nature of sibling relationships. I showed how brotherhood language fostered a shared identity and encouraged collective behavior in 1 and 2 Thessalonians and Galatians. In addition, in terms of interchurch solidarity, I showed how Paul uses the language of brotherhood to emphasize the relationship between the Thessalonians and himself, how "brothers" is used in Galatians to imply membership of a wider group, and how in 1 Thessalonians 4:9–12, the behavior of brothers in one place was seen to potentially impact brothers elsewhere, indicating brotherly relationships at a deeper level than financial support and hospitality.

Intrachurch Solidarity

Paul addresses the Corinthians as brothers to emphasize intrachurch solidarity, as a direct antidote to disunity. This can be seen in Paul's first usage of the terminology, in 1 Corinthians 1:10–11, where he expresses surprise or disappointment at the situation at Corinth as reported by Chloe's people, and appeals for unity. The language of brothers is appropriate as a way of promoting unity, on the assumption that families should be united.[96] The same usage to promote unity can be seen in 1 Corinthians 3:1, where Paul addresses strife (v. 3), and in 4:6.[97] The practical outworking of unity at the Lord's Supper is in view in 11:33, and in the exhortation to be subject to fellow workers and laborers (1 Cor 16:15–16).

"Brothers" is used to remind the Corinthians of their calling and identity in Christ (1 Cor 1:26), of what they were as pagans (1 Cor 12:1–2), and of what they already know about the gospel (1 Cor 15:1). Here, the language of brotherhood fosters intrachurch ecclesial solidarity, by emphasizing a

---

95. 1 Cor 1:10–11, 26; 2:1; 3:1; 4:6; 7:24, 29; 10:1; 11:33; 12:1; 14:6, 20, 26, 39; 15:1, 31, 50, 58; 16:15; 2 Cor 1:8; 8:1; 13:11. See Aasgaard, *Brothers and Sisters*, 313; Thiselton, *First Epistle*, 115n34.

96. Thiselton, *First Epistle*, 114–15, notes that there are some familial assumptions here.

97. Hellerman, *When the Church*, 78, notes the frequency of the usage of the "surrogate family model" in 1 Corinthians 1–3, citing 1:11, 26; 2:1;and 3:1. See also Trebilco, *Self-designations*, 32–33.

shared identity in God and Christ and membership of a new family.⁹⁸ A similar pattern can be seen on those occasions where Paul wants the Corinthians to know something (1 Cor 10:1; 15:50); this additional knowledge will help them in their shared identity and encourage intrachurch solidarity.

"Brothers" is used to exhort the Corinthians to right behavior. In 1 Corinthians 7:24, the brothers are exhorted to remain in the condition they were called and are reminded in v. 29 that the time is short. Paul uses brothers to address them with himself as an example (4:6), before exhorting them to be mature in their thinking (14:20), to build others up (14:26), and to desire to prophesy but not forbid tongues (14:39). I have already noted the relationship between ἐκκλησία and building up in this chapter, and here we see the close relationship between brotherly behavior and behavior in the ἐκκλησία. The language of brotherhood here serves to underline intrachurch solidarity by emphasizing the collective nature of behavior and how it should be founded in a concern for others. The exhortatory function of "brothers" can also be seen in 2 Corinthians 13:11.

There are also several occasions in 1 Corinthians 6–8 where the language of brotherhood is applied to specific situations, in terms of how one brother should treat another, and these occasions need to be examined, as they have important implications for ecclesial solidarity.

In 1 Corinthians 6:1–11, Paul deals with lawsuits among believers, and in the central section of his argument makes extensive use of the language of brotherhood.⁹⁹ I have already discussed how this section indicates the competence of the ἐκκλησία to try these cases, and the distinction made between "the saints" and "the world" in this passage. The language of brothers here adds an additional dimension, focusing on the shameful behavior of brother going to law against brother before unbelievers (6:5–6), and then arguing for a different standard of behavior, being willing to suffer wrong, rather than wronging, the brothers (6:7–8).¹⁰⁰ Aasgaard argues that brotherly language is used here to emphasize relationships within the church, and that the language of holiness is used to emphasize the distinction between "saints" and "the world."¹⁰¹ However, 1 Corinthians 6:6 directly links brothers and unbelievers, and therefore this section does not divide as neatly as Aasgaard proposes. Rather, the distinction is between what is happening in

---

98. Trebilco, *Self-designations*, 26–27.

99. See Aasgaard, *Brothers and Sisters*, 217–19 on structure of this section, and the role of "brothers" language here.

100. Aasgaard, *Brothers and Sisters*, 228–30; Trebilco, *Self-designations*, 34–35.

101. Aasgaard, *Brothers and Sisters*, 230–31.

the ἐκκλησία in Corinth, and the use of the language of "saints" in v. 2 and vv. 9–11 to refer to all believers, and to provide the eschatological focus.

In 1 Corinthians 6, Paul encourages the renunciation of rights for the sake of others. Furthermore, this concern for brothers takes place in a context which emphasizes the distinction between brothers and outsiders, where relationships within the group take precedence over those outside the group.[102] In terms of intrachurch solidarity, we see that the brothers in Corinth are to model conduct which is for the sake of the other within the church, and to be concerned for the reputation of the church with outsiders.[103]

The pattern of group relationships taking precedence over other relationships is nuanced somewhat by 1 Corinthians 7.[104] Here, there is a distinction between a brother or sister, and the unbelieving spouse (1 Cor 7:12, 15). However, divorce is not allowed just because the wife or husband is an unbeliever, but only if the unbelieving partner separates (verse 15). Furthermore, 1 Corinthians 7:14 indicates that, in some sense, the unbelieving spouse is made holy because of the believing spouse. This holiness is not salvific, as v. 16 indicates, and Deming links Paul's teaching here to a Corinthian fear of "*moral* pollution via *physical* association with non-Christians."[105] Here as elsewhere, Paul is seeking to nuance the Corinthians' attitude to outsiders. As I noted earlier in my discussion of ἐκκλησία, the separate identity that Paul indicates the Corinthians have does not mean that they are to avoid all contact with outsiders, but rather that their lives are to be marked by a separate pattern of behavior, for others can also be saved (v. 16), and become part of the ἐκκλησία. Thus, the group identity that Paul is espousing is not one of separation from the world, but engagement with it, as a holy people, a group of brothers. Existing relationships can continue and be sanctified by the involvement of a brother or sister.

In 1 Corinthians 8:7–13, Paul talks of destroying a brother (v. 12) and sinning against brothers (v. 12), in the midst of an exhortation to behave in a way which does not make a brother stumble (v. 13). The wider context here is his discussion of the weak and the strong in the context of food sacrificed

---

102. See Aasgaard, *Brothers and Sisters*, 233–35.

103. See also Hellerman, *When the Church*, 83.

104. Hellerman, *When the Church*, 91–94, argues that this passage reinforces the priority of sibling relationships by emphasizing not being bound in v. 15. However, in doing this, he does not take account of the holiness language in v. 14, and therefore misses Paul's nuancing of attitudes to outsiders.

105. Deming, *Paul on Marriage and Celibacy*, 135. Emphasis original.

to idols.[106] A number of features of Paul's argument here contribute to intrachurch solidarity.

First, Paul draws a contrast between knowledge which puffs up and love which builds up (8:1), and goes on to argue for the principle of self-renunciation, that the strong, following Paul's example, should modify their conduct for the sake of the weak (8:13),[107] even though Paul largely agrees with the theological stance of the strong.[108] I noted the importance of building up in my discussion of ἐκκλησία in 1 Corinthians 14, where the same principle of modifying conduct applied, for the sake of others in the ἐκκλησία. This passage further demonstrates Paul's use of the idea of building up to encourage solidarity, as each takes account of the needs of others and links it to familial obligation.[109]

Second, the motivation here is also Christological, for sinning against a brother for whom Christ died (8:11) is also sinning against Christ (v. 12). Here the Corinthians are reminded that their ecclesial solidarity rests in another: Jesus Christ, and particularly his death.[110]

Third, the language of brotherhood here has a unifying direction, tying together the weak and the strong,[111] and, as Aasgaard notes, by only addressing the strong here, Paul makes the strong view the weak as siblings, not as inferiors.[112] Given the issues of status already noted in Corinth, this would be a potent way of encouraging the fulfilment of obligations to ensure intrachurch solidarity.

There are then many passages where Paul is concerned with intrachurch solidarity in 1 Corinthians. It forms part of his argument for unity

---

106. Aasgaard, *Brothers and Sisters*, 178–84, notes the similarities to Romans 14:10—15:1 here, and argues for the possibility of a moral-philosophical *topos* here. He notes parallels with Plutarch.

107. See Aasgaard, *Brothers and Sisters*, 185–89, 194–97, on the likely social implications of this.

108. Horrell, *Solidarity and Difference*, 172–74, notes that it is the weak consciences of the weak which make the acts here sinful.

109. Theissen, *Social Setting*, 107, 139, argues that prevailing ethos of Pauline Christianity revealed in these conflicts is that of "love-patriarchalism," which takes social differences for granted, but by emphasizing obligations of respect and love within the Christian community, seeks to oblige the "strong" to look after the "weak." Largely in agreement with Horrell, *Social Ethos*, 195–98, 233–37, I would argue here that brotherly obligations are one of the key ways in which Paul encourages ecclesial solidarity, rather than obligations only on the strong issuing from "love-patriarchalism."

110. See Aasgaard, *Brothers and Sisters*, 192–93; Trebilco, *Self-designations*, 33–34; Horrell, *Solidarity and Difference*, 181.

111. Trebilco, *Self-designations*, 33.

112. Aasgaard, *Brothers and Sisters*, 201.

in 1 Corinthians 1–4, and forms a part of Paul's argument in each of the following sections of 1 Corinthians.[113] Paul clearly sees it as a potent metaphor in his arguments for unity and against divisions based on social status, and encourages the Corinthians to see themselves as part of a family, rather than focus on their own social position.

Interchurch Solidarity

There are four ways in which Paul uses the language of brotherhood to encourage interchurch solidarity. First, there are a number of occasions in 1 and 2 Corinthians where Paul particularly emphasizes his relationship with the Corinthians. In a sense, this is implicit in all the plurals of direct address; however, there are occasions when Paul is more explicit. Paul reminds the Corinthians of his conduct among them in 1 Corinthians 2:1, and in 2 Corinthians 1:8 he wants his brothers to know what happened to him in Asia. He reminds them of his pride in them (1 Cor 15:31) and, as in 1 Thessalonians 5:26, encourages them to greet one another with a holy kiss. Further, Paul addresses them as "my beloved brothers" in 1 Corinthians 15:58, and as "my brothers" in 1 Corinthians 11:33; 14:39, in the context of behavioral exhortations. This suggests that Paul's close relationship with them should be a further inducement to act rightly.[114] As in Paul's earliest letters, Paul seeks to maintain and further solidarity between the Corinthians and himself. Given that Paul is neither present nor a member of any of these churches, this is clearly a case of solidarity beyond the local church. However, given that the solidarity is with Paul, it is not interchurch solidarity, although it does suggest the possible applicability of brotherhood language beyond the local congregation.

Second, on a number of occasions, Paul uses "brother" as a designation,[115] and these designations show Paul's concern for interchurch solidarity. In 1 Corinthians 16:11–12 and 20, Paul refers to brothers who he is expecting, who he encouraged Apollos to travel with, and who send greetings. In each case, these are not people in the Corinthian Church. They are not further designated as brothers in another ἐκκλησία; rather, their location is indicated by the context. They are, simply, brothers. In 1 Corinthians 15:6, Paul refers to the brothers to whom Christ appeared after the

---

113. 1 Cor 5–6; 7; 8:1—11:1; 11:2—14:40; 15; 16.

114. Trebilco, *Self-designations*, 27; Aasgaard, *Brothers and Sisters*, 279–80.

115. In addition to those mentioned in this paragraph, see 1 Corinthians 1:1, Sosthenes; 1 Corinthians 16:12, Apollos; 2 Corinthians 1:1, Timothy; 2 Corinthians 2:13, Titus. Paul also refers to the physical brothers of the Lord in 1 Corinthians 9:5.

resurrection. These would have been members of the Jerusalem church, and yet they can be described as brothers to those who have probably never met them. A similar pattern can be seen in 2 Corinthians: there is a brother in 2 Corinthians 8:18, 22 and 12:18 who is from another ἐκκλησία, and brothers who are sent to the Corinthians in 9:3 and 9:5. These brothers are messengers of the churches (8:23), indicating that they are part of a network of brotherly relations involving Paul, the Corinthians, and other ἐκκλησία. In 2 Corinthians 11:9, it is brothers from Macedonia who supply Paul's needs. Finally, in 1 Corinthians 9:5, Paul refers to the apostolic right to have a sister as a wife. The reference here is clearly to a believing wife,[116] and shows "sister" being used as a general term for a believer, in the same way as brother.[117] While therefore 1 and 2 Corinthians lack the explicit teaching of 1 Thessalonians 4:11-12 on brotherly love beyond the congregation, nevertheless, the Corinthians have brothers inside and outside Corinth. Their primary responsibility may be to their brothers in Corinth, but that does not mean they can ignore or neglect their brothers elsewhere. "Brothers" can be used to encourage the Corinthians to express interchurch solidarity.

Third, in 2 Corinthians 8:1, Paul addresses the Corinthians as brothers in the context of what they need to know, in a similar way to 1 Corinthians 10:1 or 15:1. However, there is an added dimension here, for Paul then uses the example of the ἐκκλησίαι of Macedonia, whose activity in 8:2-4 shows brotherly love in practice in a strong example of other-regard, in their gift for the saints. Thus, as Paul builds his argument in 2 Corinthians 8-9 to encourage the Corinthians to give generously, one of the motivations to that giving is that they should be showing brotherly love for the saints elsewhere, just like the ἐκκλησία of Macedonia.[118] As in 1 Corinthians 6, we see the combination of the language of brothers, holiness, and ἐκκλησία. Here "the saints" is primarily a reference to the church in Jerusalem, while it is brotherly love which is to have wider implications. This shows the flexibility of Paul's language, and shows the practical outworking of interchurch brotherly solidarity.

Finally, twice in the Corinthian correspondence, Paul refers to false brothers. In 1 Corinthians 5:11, the context is a false brother in the Corinthian congregation (v. 12), and therefore one who is to be judged. However, in 2 Corinthians 11:26, the false brothers in view are a much more generalized group, which Paul appears to have encountered on a number

---

116. Trebilco, *Self-designations*, 24.

117. Most instances of brother would still be inclusive of sisters, unless the context suggests otherwise. See Trebilco, *Self-designations*, 25.

118. See also here Meeks, "Circle of Reference," 312-13.

of occasions.[119] Trebilco has noted the boundary-marking function of this language, marking boundaries within the community.[120] In terms of interchurch solidarity, we see how the need for a distinction to be made on the basis of activity within the congregation of brothers in 1 Corinthians 5:11 also applies more widely, so that a general division should be made between true and false brothers. This would encourage the Corinthians to identify themselves as part of a group, the true brothers, and would remind them of how continued membership of this group is dependent on right behavior.[121]

Paul is very concerned with intrachurch solidarity in Corinth. However, his use of brother language also shows his continued awareness and concern for interchurch solidarity; the brotherhood of believers extends beyond the boundaries of Corinth, and the members of that wider brotherhood have responsibilities to one another. A similar pattern can be observed in Paul's earliest letters, although the flexibility of Paul's language needs to be noted.

The Body

There are a large number of occurrences of σῶμα in 1 Corinthians. Many of them refer to the physical body of an individual or individuals.[122] A few references are to other kinds of body.[123] I will examine references in chapters 10–12, which refer to a corporate body.[124]

However, before examining these passages, I will note some of the features of the body metaphor in antiquity. Martin, in a study which seeks to look at the body as the Corinthians understood it,[125] argues that the

---

119. See Furnish, *2 Corinthians*, 537, who notes the possibility that this group is the same as the Judaizers of Galatians 2:4, but may be a wider group. Either way, the reference here is more general than that in 1 Corinthians 5:11.

120. Trebilco, *Self-designations*, 38. See also Aasgaard, *Brothers and Sisters*, 300–302.

121. Aasgaard argues for a "wide range" of unacceptability here (*Brothers and Sisters*, 302). Therefore, I would argue that a wide range of behavior needs to be acceptable.

122. 1 Corinthians 5:3; 6:13, 15, 16, 18, 19, 20; 7:4, 34; 9:27; 11:24, 27 (and see discussion here on v. 29); 13:3; 15:44.

123. 1 Corinthians 15:37 and 38 referring to seeds, 15:40 referring to heavenly and earthly bodies in relation to the sun, moon, and stars.

124. Holland, *Contours*, 116–17, interprets 1 Corinthians 6:18–20 corporately. However, see my comments above on the temple, and generally note that this would mark an abrupt change in 1 Corinthians 6 where the rest of the many references to body in the chapter are to the body of an individual. Holland is right to point out that some of the boundaries drawn between the individual and corporate in modern western thought are not those drawn in the ancient world.

125. Martin, *Corinthian Body*, 36–37.

Greek understanding of the body politic is an essential background for understanding what Paul writes, and that Greek *homonoia* speeches demonstrate a long tradition of using the body politic imagery to encourage concord,[126] and "a particular ideology of social control that I have called "benevolent patriarchalism."[127] Further, he argues that the human body in antiquity was a microcosm, a smaller version of the universe at large,[128] and that this understanding can be seen in assumptions about medicine, and how the outer body shows the reality of the inner body.[129] Lee reads Paul's language of the body in 1 Corinthians against a Stoic background or context,[130] and argues that body language was an essential part of the resocialization of the Christian, of explaining the "new world" which he or she had joined.[131] Lee further notes the flexible way in which the imagery of the body of Christ is used, against the background of an image which could easily move between the universe or cosmos and the state.[132] Aasgaard notes the way in which ancient authors used the body metaphor to emphasize sibling harmony,[133] noting in particular how Plutarch uses the metaphor to encourage brotherly harmony through recognition of unity in diversity.[134] Thus, in the ancient world, the body metaphor can be used *representatively*, where the body represents one or more bodies, and can be used to emphasize *unity in diversity*.

In 1 Corinthians 10:16-17, Paul identifies those who eat the bread as participating in the body of Christ, and how that participation signifies that "we are one body." In 1 Corinthians 10:16, the Lord's Supper is in view, where taking the bread and cup is seen in the context of taking the body and blood of Christ (cf. 1 Cor 11:23-26).[135] In 1 Corinthians 10:17, Paul

126. Martin, *Corinthian Body*, 38-47. See also Lee, *Paul, the Stoics*, 39-45.

127. Martin, *Corinthian Body*, 47, who argues that Paul accepts this basic structure in his use of the metaphor. Note that Lee, *Paul, the Stoics*, 145, argues against Martin here, and for an actual reversal of status in the body of Christ in the way Paul uses the metaphor.

128. Martin, *Corinthian Body*, 16. See also Lee, *Paul, the Stoics*, 45.

129. Martin, *Corinthian Body*, 16-18.

130. Lee, *Paul, the Stoics*, 23.

131. Lee, *Paul, the Stoics*, 20-21.

132. Lee, *Paul, the Stoics*, 135-36. On Stoic thought, see also Dunn, "Body of Christ," 157.

133. Aasgaard, *Brothers and Sisters*, 82-83, 85.

134. Aasgaard, *Brothers and Sisters*, 100, 102. See Plutarch, *Frat. amor.* 478d, 485f-86a.

135. I would argue that the Lord's Supper is certainly in view here, whatever the precise reference of "the cup of blessing," for which see Thiselton, *First Epistle*, 756-60.

then applies the common participation in the bread (which is the body of Christ), stating that common participation in the bread creates one body.[136] Here the body in v. 17 includes Paul, and this suggests that the body metaphor in v. 17 includes more than just the Corinthians. There are two contextual factors which support this. First, in 1 Corinthians 10:1–13, Paul makes an argument based on the experience of the whole people of Israel in the wilderness, which is then applied to the Corinthians in 10:14–21: they are to flee from idolatry (v. 14), and it is in the context of fleeing from idolatry that Paul encourages them to recognize that they are one body because they share one bread, before again calling the Corinthians to consider what happened to Israel (v. 18). This suggests a parallel between the actions of all Israel in partaking of the rock, which is Christ (vv. 3–4), and Paul's concern that the Corinthians should recognize their membership of one body as those who partake of the bread.[137] The Corinthians here are not the totality of God's people as body, but rather members of that body, a membership expressed in participation in the Lord's Supper. Second, in concluding this section of the letter in 10:23—11:1, Paul refers to giving no offense to the church of God in 10:32, and as I noted earlier, I take this to be a reference to the whole church. Thus, as members of the (whole) body of Christ, the Corinthians are to take account of the whole church.

There is another possible corporate reference in 1 Corinthians 11:29. As Thiselton notes,[138] modern scholars divide over whether the body in view here is the church, or the body of Christ. On the one hand, the immediate context of 11:24 and 27, where Christ's "sacramental" body is in view, suggests a singular reference to Christ's body; however, the language of 1 Corinthians 10:17 suggests the possibility of understanding the body here as the metaphorical body of Christ. Rather than deciding between these alternatives, it is possible to see here a reference to the body which can be taken as either or both: the Corinthians are to discern the body, and to recognize that, when partaking of the Lord's Supper, they are participating in the body and blood of Christ; therefore, they must not profane the body and blood of the Lord (11:27); at the same time, the issues of disunity which mark the Corinthians' observance of the Lord's Supper, their "despising of the church of God" (11:22), suggest that they should also be discerning the metaphorical body of Christ and taking account of the ἐκκλησία.[139] Given

---

136. Thiselton, *First Epistle*, 769. Thiselton notes that the use of one body in 10:17 contrasts with the divisions of 1:10–12.

137. See Minear, *Images of the Church*, 183–84.

138. Thiselton, *First Epistle*, 893.

139. Compare Martin, *Corinthian Body*, 194–95, who finds four meanings of body in 11:29: the elements, Christ's body to be recognized in the Eucharist as a memorial of

that I have also suggested that 11:22 may well be a reference to the whole church, and not just the local church in Corinth, we may further clarify this reference to the ἐκκλησία: the Corinthians are to discern the body of Christ in Corinth, but also the body of Christ, which is the whole church. This corresponds to the representative usage from antiquity noted here.

In both 10:17 (and then 11:29), Paul uses the imagery of the body to encourage interchurch solidarity, by noting their participation in, and encouraging them to take account of, something which is the ἐκκλησία in Corinth, but is also wider than that, and includes all believers.

The final set of metaphorical references to the body of Christ come in 1 Corinthians 12:12–31, where Paul discusses the body in the context of the right use of spiritual gifts. Paul states his main point in 12:12–13: we are many, but we, through one baptism in the Spirit, are one. He then explores what that means in terms of the parts of the body having different functions, concluding that these many parts are required to make the body function effectively.[140] Paul then argues that this means those parts which might be considered less important must be given special honor, so that there should be no division.[141] Further, Paul asserts that the body suffers and is honored together before reminding them that they are the body of Christ and part of it (1 Cor 12:27). Finally, Paul applies this model to the church in 1 Corinthians 12:28–31: not all have the same gifts, but, by implication, they are all needed for the church.

The language of body in 1 Corinthians 12 is then primarily about unity, and can be seen to complement the language of holiness and brotherhood which I have already explored in encouraging behavior which takes account of others.[142] In terms of ecclesial solidarity, then, the body metaphor is used in 1 Corinthians 12 to encourage unity through the exercise of diverse gifts. However, the question remains as to the scope and extent of the body in 1 Corinthians 12:12–31. O'Brien argues for a dual referent here: that the body of Christ is the Corinthians (v. 27), but also "a wider group including Paul and possibly others" (the "we" of v. 13),[143] and this fits with Paul's usage of "we" and "you" in the passage. However, O'Brien takes "church" as a reference to the church in Corinth here, and therefore I would argue misses an additional dimension of Paul's language: in talking of the Corinthians as the body of Christ, he wants them to keep in mind the whole body of Christ,

---

the death of Christ, the church, and the individual Christian.

140. 1 Cor 12:14–20.
141. 1 Cor 12:21–25.
142. Aasgaard, *Brothers and Sisters*, 173, 191.
143. O'Brien "Church," 106–7.

including Jews and Greeks, slaves and free (v. 13), and the whole church of God (v. 28). This conceptual broadening of the horizons of the Corinthians is something which we have seen Paul engage in throughout the letter, and in his usage of body imagery in chapters 10 and 11.

In examining 1 Corinthians 12, Lee notes the flexible way that the imagery of the body of Christ is used, against the background of an image which could easily move between the universe or cosmos and the state:[144] in 1 Corinthians 12:12–26, where Paul is talking about the body in general terms, Paul is included in the body, whereas in 1 Corinthians 12:27–30, where he deals with the issue of spiritual gifts in Corinth, he excludes himself.[145] There is then a "universal" body of Christ, of which Paul talks in 12:12–26, and a specific body of Christ in Corinth, which Paul addresses in 12:27–30.[146] Thus, when it comes to 12:24b–26 and issues of concern and suffering, Lee argues that this is about more than order in the Corinthian assembly; rather, it is a statement of eschatological reversal that defines the believers as part of something radically different,[147] and may be part of asserting that Jesus, not Caesar, is Lord.[148] Certainly, as with 10:17 and 11:16, there is a representative use of the body here, where the body of Christ means both the ἐκκλησία in Corinth, and believers more generally.

The imagery of the body in chapter 12 is then used to encourage unity within the church in Corinth, and therefore to foster intrachurch solidarity. However, it also has wider implications, for when Paul talks about the mutual suffering and mutual honoring of members or parts of the body, he is not only talking about what happens within the church in Corinth, but what happens in Corinth has a wider impact, and about what should happen in the body in general. This is also the case in 10:17 and 12:29. The importance of this for interchurch solidarity is twofold. First, in coming to the body, we have an image which is primarily used by Paul in 1 Corinthians for the sake of interchurch solidarity; in deploying this imagery, Paul seems to have been specifically concerned with interchurch solidarity. Second, the representative usage I noted above shows that "body" can be used to stand for one thing and another thing at the same time. This may indicate the usefulness of the imagery for Paul, but also helps to elucidate the relationship between intra- and interchurch solidarity, which has been occasionally visible in this study, in particular when examining the idea of

144. Lee, *Paul, the Stoics*, 135–36.
145. Lee, *Paul, the Stoics*, 133–34.
146. Lee, *Paul, the Stoics*, 134–35.
147. Lee, *Paul, the Stoics*, 148.
148. Lee, *Paul, the Stoics*, 149.

"the church of God" in Galatians 1:13 and 1 Corinthians: behavior which should be undertaken for the sake of the body of Christ or the ἐκκλησία in Corinth should also be undertaken for the sake of the body of Christ, the church of God, more generally.

Conclusion

In looking at the language of holiness, temple, brothers and the body of Christ, a trend towards encouraging the Corinthians to look beyond themselves can be observed. They are to take greater account of their own local church: they are the saints, they are brothers, they are God's holy temple, and they are the body of Christ, despite their differences and diversity. At the same time, holiness and temple language emphasizes that they are part of a wider grouping, they are reminded that they have brothers in the Lord beyond Corinth, and the Corinthian body operates in a context where all the baptized are part of one body, and so the Corinthians must also take account of the church beyond Corinth. This coheres with what we have already seen from the use of ἐκκλησία.

Apostleship and Imitation

Example and Imitation

In chapter 3, I noted how imitation language applies to relationships between churches. First, that the language of imitation demonstrates Paul's concern for group solidarity and mutual encouragement, not just within an ἐκκλησία, but also from ἐκκλησία to ἐκκλησία. And second, I noted evidence of Paul's expectation that there will be a shared ethos amongst the churches of, and beyond, the Pauline mission, as Paul considers it of benefit to churches to imitate what others do, in reception of the gospel, in persevering through suffering, and by implication more widely. Here I will explore how Paul's language of imitation and example impacts upon ecclesial solidarity in the Corinthian correspondence.

Intrachurch Solidarity: Imitate Me

There are two explicit calls to imitate Paul in 1 Corinthians: 4:16 and 11:1. In 4:16, Paul calls upon the Corinthians to "become imitators of me." He relates this call to imitation to his role as their father in Christ, through the gospel (4:15), and highlights a particular role for himself as father, as opposed to their countless guides in Christ, addressing them as his beloved children (4:14). He sends Timothy, his child, to them to remind them of his ways in Christ (4:17). He then concludes this section with a warning to the arrogant, that he will discipline them if necessary (4:18–21). Several features of this passage require further comment to understand Paul's call to imitation here and its implications for ecclesial solidarity.

First, Paul casts himself as their father,[149] and refers to them as his beloved children (4:14–15). It is on the basis of his fatherhood that he calls upon them to imitate him.[150] This fatherhood is in Christ Jesus through the gospel, and as father, Paul expects to be obeyed, and the Corinthians to imitate his example.[151] Burke argues that here Paul is acting within the normal social conventions of a father, operating for the good management of his family, willing to use force if necessary, but preferring to use persuasion.[152] The father/child dynamic here reinforces the call to imitate Paul, strengthening Paul's exhortation, and implying holistic imitation, as a child imitated the father.[153]

Second, it should be noted here that Paul is their father in Christ through the gospel (v. 15), and is sending Timothy to remind them of his ways in Christ (v. 17). Therefore, although the exhortation of v. 16 invites the Corinthians to imitate Paul, their imitation is clearly of Paul as he imitates Christ; the imitation he calls for is of his ways in Christ.[154] At the heart of Paul's call to imitation here lies the implicit imitation of Christ.[155]

Third, Timothy is cast here as a faithful child of Paul in the Lord, who will remind them of Paul's ways in Christ. Aasgaard notes here how Timothy, as a faithful child of Paul, will act on his behalf.[156] Timothy therefore

---

149. In 1 Corinthians 4:15, Paul says that they do not have "many fathers," which might imply that they do have a few—perhaps Paul and Apollos, and some others. See for example Clarke, *Serve the Community*, 219–21. Aasgaard, *Brothers and Sisters*, 131, sees a singular role for Paul here. For the purposes of this study, either is acceptable.

150. See Copan, *Saint Paul*, 117; Dodd, *Paul's Paradigmatic 'I'*, 71; Clarke, "Imitators," 343; de Boer, *Imitation*, 153.

151. See Copan, *Saint Paul*, 116, on cultural expectations of imitation.

152. Burke, "Paul's Role as 'Father,'" 105–13. For a similar argument see Aasgaard, *Brothers and Sisters*, 290; Copan, *Saint Paul*, 115–16; Clarke, "Imitators," 343–44. Castelli, *Imitating Paul*, 100–102, highlights the authoritarian tone in this passage.

153. Copan, *Saint Paul*, 123.

154. See Copan, *Saint Paul*, 120–21; Clarke, "Imitators," 346.

155. See here also Copan, *Saint Paul*, 117; Fee, *First Epistle*, 186. de Boer, *Imitation*, 152–54, notes the extensive and confident use Paul makes of imitation language to further the gospel in Corinth.

156. Aasgaard, *Brothers and Sisters*, 290.

functions as a further stimulus to imitation, both in what he will say when he comes to Corinth, but also in the behavior he models, faithfully imitating Paul.[157]

Fourth, there still remains the question of what is to be imitated here. Paul refers in v. 14 to something he has written, thus raising the expectation that the content of what needs to be imitated has already been written, and this probably includes all of 1:10—4:13.[158] In calling the Corinthians to imitate Paul, in the context of a warning of discipline (4:18-21), Paul implies that their present behavior is wrong, and he describes that behavior in 4:6-7: they are puffed up with pride.[159] In contrast, Paul portrays his own behavior as that of a servant of Christ (4:1-5), and explicitly draws attention to the example of himself and Apollos (4:6) before contrasting their puffed-up behavior with the selfless and giving lifestyle of the apostles in 4:8-13.[160] Paul cast himself as father here, and wants the Corinthians as his children to imitate his life and heed his teaching through Timothy, and therefore the imitation here is general. However, it does have a particular focus, that the Corinthians should imitate Paul in the selfless service of others in Christ, rather than being puffed up with their own interests.[161] Furthermore, this selfless service of others in Christ is patterned after Christ's own example, who experienced the weakness of the cross for the sake of others.[162]

As Paul addresses the divisions in 1 Corinthians 1-4, whatever their cause, one of the strategies he uses is to call the Corinthians to imitate his behavior. This is a strong call, presented as a father to his children, and will be further bolstered by the visit of Timothy. Furthermore, it is an imitation founded in the imitation of Christ, as Paul demonstrates weakness and folly for the sake of Christ (4:10) in his model of selfless concern for others. It is this shift in attitude that Paul believes will foster intrachurch solidarity in the Corinthian Church by healing their divisions.

Paul's second call to imitation in this letter, found in 1 Corinthians 11:1, comes at the end of the section which begins in 8:1 with a discussion of meat sacrificed to idols.[163] I have already noted the importance of the prin-

---

157. Copan, *Saint Paul*, 121-22; de Boer, *Imitation*, 147-50.

158. See Copan, *Saint Paul*, 114n32; Dodd, *Paul's Paradigmatic 'I'*, 45-48.

159. Copan, *Saint Paul*, 112-13.

160. See Copan, *Saint Paul*, 118-19; Clarke, "Imitators," 344-45. For examples of behavior to be imitated stretching back to 1:10, see Dodd, *Paul's Paradigmatic 'I'*, 49-61.

161. So also, Copan, *Saint Paul*, 124; de Boer, *Imitation*, 154.

162. In 1 Corinthians 1:17, 18, 23-25, and 2:1, Paul emphasizes Christ crucified, and the "folly" and weakness of God displayed in the cross. See Pickett, *Cross in Corinth*, 82-84.

163. Copan, *Saint Paul*, 133-34 notes the references to Paul not being a stumbling

ciple stated in 8:13 for this section, and Paul's willingness to limit himself for the sake of others.[164] In 9:1–18, he expands that principle beyond meat sacrificed to idols, to other examples of his renunciation of his rights, before again outlining his principles of conduct in 9:19–27: that his behavior is for the sake of the gospel, and therefore he disciplines himself to run with purpose.[165] Then in chapter 10, he uses Israel as an example for the Corinthians (10:11), who are to take heed (v. 12), and flee from idolatry (v. 14). This will lead them to right thinking on food sacrificed to idols (10:14–22). Paul then gives them two examples of how to behave (10:23–30), based on the principle of "building up" (v. 23) which I have already noted. In 1 Corinthians 10:3—11:1,[166] Paul gives a final instruction, which closes with his call to imitation.

There are four things to notice here. First, in v. 31, Paul draws a general example from the specific instructions about idol meat: the Corinthians should do everything for the glory of God.[167] They are not to give offense or cause anyone to stumble, but are to seek the advantage of others, that they might be saved (vv. 32–33).[168] The call to imitation in 11:1 is then a call to follow Paul's example as he behaves this way.[169] Here again we see the centrality of other-regard and behavior for the sake of others, which Paul has espoused throughout 1 Corinthians. Second, in imitating Paul, the Corinthians are imitating one who imitates Christ; both Paul and Jesus seek the advantage of others, that they might be saved,[170] and their behavior in general is to bring glory to God. As in 4:16, they are reminded that their ultimate reference point is found not in themselves or in Paul, but in Christ and God.[171] Third, I have argued that "church of God" in 10:32 should be taken as a general reference to the "whole" church, and this would indicate that, although the focus here is on intrachurch solidarity, nevertheless their other-regarding behavior is to have a wider audience. Fourth, as part of Paul's exposition of his own behavior as their example, Paul uses the example of those baptized into Moses. In doing so, he calls them to judge

---

block throughout this section. See also Clarke, "Imitators," 346.

164. Copan, *Saint Paul*, 126.
165. Copan, *Saint Paul*, 128.
166. Copan, *Saint Paul*, 130–31, on the structure here.
167. Copan, *Saint Paul*, 131.
168. Copan, *Saint Paul*, 132–33.
169. Copan, *Saint Paul*, 135–37.
170. See Copan, *Saint Paul*, 139–42, on which parts of Christ's life Paul might be referring to.
171. See de Boer, *Imitation*, 51–58.

for themselves what he says (10:15). Whilst they are not being called into judgement on Paul's words,[172] they are being called to exercise wisdom and discernment, to follow Paul's argument and to see how it applies in their situation.[173] Thus, imitation should be seen here as a process which the community participates in together.[174]

1 Corinthians 4:16 and 11:1 show how the language of imitation supports intrachurch solidarity in the Corinthian Correspondence. The Corinthians are to foster intrachurch solidarity in following Paul's example by making other-regard central to their behavior, rather than self-interest. In doing so, they are imitating Christ, and seeking to glorify God.

Interchurch Solidarity: Norms and Examples

Addressing interchurch solidarity in relation to imitation in the Corinthian correspondence requires giving attention to three areas: following good examples, the language of normative behavior, and the collection for Jerusalem.

Following Good Examples

Twice the Corinthians are exhorted to imitate Paul. However, there are also others that they should learn from. They are also to take note of the examples of Timothy[175] and Apollos.[176] Timothy comes as a representative of Paul, and therefore imitation of Timothy could be counted as a substitute imitation of Paul.[177] However, to include Apollos here must represent an element of risk, given the issues Paul highlights in 1 Corinthians 1:10–17, despite Paul's desire to show that he and Apollos worked together. Here is one who has an independent ministry (which Paul himself acknowledges in 1 Corinthians 16:12), who nevertheless is an example.

In 2 Corinthians 8 and 9, Paul makes use of several examples. In 2 Corinthians 8:16–24, Paul talks about those he is sending to Corinth: Titus

---

172. So Fee, *First Epistle*, 464–65.

173. Copan, *Saint Paul*, 137.

174. Compare Verhey, "Able to Instruct One Another," 149–51, who describes the churches as "communities of moral deliberation," and Samra, *Being Conformed*, 136–52.

175. 1 Cor 4:17.

176. 1 Cor 3:5, 9, 4:1. Whilst there is no explicit call to imitation of Apollos until 4:6, he is included with Paul as an example of conduct, and therefore is to be imitated. See Clarke, "Imitators," 345.

177. See for example Copan, *Saint Paul*, 119–120.

and two brothers. The first brother is praised by all the churches and has been chosen by the churches to carry the offering (2 Cor 8:18–19). The second brother is described as eager and one who has been tested (2 Cor 8:22). Both are representatives of the churches and an honor to Christ (2 Cor 8:23). I have already discussed the use of ἐκκλησία in this passage, but here we see two men who conduct themselves in an exemplary way, presented to the Corinthians as men to be honored. Here the Corinthians can learn from those who belong to other churches.

There are also events that they should learn from. In 1 Corinthians 10:11, Paul refers to the wilderness wanderings he has described in 10:1–10 as being an example and warning for those on whom the fulfillment of the ages has come.[178] The failure of a previous generation to remain faithful to God stands as an example of how the Corinthians should resist temptation (1 Cor 10:11–13), and a group separated from the Corinthians by time, space, and in many cases race, is nevertheless an appropriate example. The Corinthians can learn how to behave now from a group in the past.[179] The fact that all those who passed through the sea (10:1) are in view here is significant, as here we see the idea of a people of God whose conduct is relevant for the ἐκκλησία in Corinth. As well as encouraging solidarity within Corinth, in conjunction with the use of body in 10:16 and ἐκκλησία of God in 10:32, this language suggests a solidarity beyond Corinth.

The Corinthians can also learn from other churches. So, in 2 Corinthians 8:1–5, Paul lays before the Corinthians the example of the Macedonian churches, an example they are to follow in giving generously. This example remains present in this section of 2 Corinthians, as Paul wishes to compare the earnestness of the Corinthians with others,[180] while in 9:1–5 the views of the Macedonian believers are again referenced to encourage the Corinthians to give generously. Note here that the behavior to be imitated is similar to that which Paul modeled: giving of self for the sake of others. Stenschke also notes here how generosity in one church produces thanksgiving in another, furthering interchurch solidarity through mutual affection.[181]

Therefore, in the Corinthian correspondence, we see a similar pattern to that observed in 1 Thessalonians, where other churches are used as examples.[182] We also see Paul operating with a network of imitation that is not

---

178. See also 1 Corinthians 10:6; Clarke, "Imitators," 346.

179. See Copan, *Saint Paul*, 47–48, for examples of imitation of people from the past from the Greek literature.

180. 2 Cor 8:8.

181. Stenschke, "Significance and Function of References," 213–14.

182. 1 Thess 2:13–16.

just between the church to whom he writes and Paul. It involves other individuals and groups, past and present. This suggests the continuing relevance of the belief and behavior of individuals and churches one to another. The Corinthians are to take account of the behavior of others, both behavior to be emulated and behavior to be avoided. Along with ἐκκλησία, holy people, temple, brother, and body, the language of imitation is then used to foster interchurch solidarity, as the Corinthians are part of a network of churches who share a common identity as God's holy people, who are to behave with brotherly love towards one another, and who are, and are part of, the body of Christ. A critical element of that behavior is highlighted by imitation language, the call to other-regard.

What is Normative in all the Churches

There are several places in 1 Corinthians where Paul explicitly refers to what happens in all the churches. These instances shed light on interchurch relationships.

In 4:17 Paul sends Timothy to remind the Corinthians what he teaches in all the churches. Timothy is thus sent as a representative of the Corinthians' father Paul, and the imitation of Christ through Paul to which he calls the Corinthians is what he teaches everywhere. There are a number of views of what Paul means by this phrase. Dodd notes here that Paul is an example to his churches,[183] and sees his use of "all the churches" here as way of emphasizing his authority.[184] Copan notes the link between life and teaching.[185] Thiselton sees here both reassurance, in that no more will be required of them than of other Christian groups, and a concern that Paul's teaching is consistent.[186] All of these contentions may well be true; however, more attention here needs to be given to the basic question: why are other churches relevant here, when the Corinthians are being called to imitate Paul's example? I would argue that here Paul reveals that he expects a norm of behavior from all churches, and that churches are accountable for their deviation from that norm. They are accountable to Paul,[187] and

---

183. Dodd, *Paul's Paradigmatic 'I'*, 71

184. Dodd, *Paul's Paradigmatic 'I'*, 72. See also Fee, *First Epistle*, 189: they are the ones embarking on a "maverick course." Castelli, *Imitating Paul*, 110, is concerned about power relationships here.

185. Copan, *Saint Paul*, 121–22. See also de Boer, *Imitation*, 147–52, for a discussion of the relationship between life and teaching.

186. Thiselton, *First Epistle*, 375–76.

187. As one who holds them to account in Christ.

his letters show that he holds them to account. However, the network of imitation which I just noted also suggests that churches are accountable to one another for their behavior. There is a standard of teaching which Paul assumes will be the same across all his churches.[188] Even where churches, or even some in Corinth, might have other fathers, they still have a shared ethos. This ethos is defined in 1 Corinthians 4:16 as following Paul's ways in Christ, but in the context of the network of imitation at work in these letters more generally, it can be broadened to a general Christological solidarity.

There are other examples of a similar argument elsewhere in 1 Corinthians. So, in 7:17, Paul states that his teaching in marriage is the same in all the churches, and not peculiar to Corinth, as a reminder to them that their situation is not unique.[189] Here and in 1 Corinthians 7:10 there are appeals to dominical teaching: as Paul reminds his readers in 1 Corinthians 15:3, he writes to them of what he has received. In fact, Paul is keen to distinguish in this section of the letter between his own example and teaching, and how they might wish to follow it in remaining single, and that which is commanded by the Lord.[190] The call in 1 Corinthians 7:17 comes from the Lord, and God and is a rule in all the churches. Again, we see the appeal to a shared Father and a shared ethos. Paul also appeals to what is common practice in the churches. In 11:16, Paul closes his teaching on head coverings by appealing to a common practice in the churches of God, and in 14:33–34 he commands the silence of women in the church, as in all the churches. All these examples may appear to have little to do with corporate solidarity. However, if one of the issues in Corinth was, as some suggest, the behavior of those who considered themselves free of earthly ties,[191] then these injunctions in 1 Corinthians 7 and 11 remain part of the general counsel to self-limitation for the sake of others.

One final example can be given here of the link between churches and imitation, the relationship between 1 Corinthians 10:23 and 11:1. 11:1 is the second instance where the Corinthians are explicitly told to imitate Paul, and where that imitation is linked very directly to the imitation of Christ.[192] What is sometimes not noticed, however, is the close link between the call to imitate in 11:33, and how the conduct described in 10:31–33 is related

188. Stenschke, "Significance and Function of References," 206.

189. Thiselton, *First Epistle*, 550; Fee, *First Epistle*, 311.

190. See Dodd, *Paul's Paradigmatic 'I'*, 90–95 on personal example here.

191. On 11:2–16, see Finney, "Honour, Head-coverings," 31–58, who argues that Paul calls for certain behavior based on honour and shame, out of a concern for the community.

192. For a discussion of the implications of this for the Corinthians, see Dodd, *Paul's Paradigmatic 'I'*, 110–14, and Copan, *Saint Paul*, 124–42.

to giving no offence to the church of God. As I have already argued above, the most likely referent of church of God in 10:32 is the "whole" church, and therefore Paul's call to imitation here is to behavior considered beyond the boundaries of the local church. In addition, as Copan notes, the call to imitate here is to follow Paul's example, "not to cause anyone, believer or non-believer, to falter in their relationship to God."[193] Here we have explicit confirmation of that which has been implied throughout 1 Corinthians, that the behavior of the Corinthian Church must take account of other churches.

What happens elsewhere is in some sense normative for what happens in Corinth in terms of behavior: they have an obligation to take account of what happens in other churches,[194] and Paul expects that they should be prepared to follow the good examples, and avoid the bad ones of those other churches. Here, Paul is making explicit what is implicit in 1:2: the Corinthians must take account of something beyond themselves, and that what they do in their church matters beyond their church.

The Jerusalem Collection

In 1 Corinthians 16:1-4, the Corinthians are to do what Paul told the Galatians to do, and together they will join in a common enterprise for the sake of God's people in Jerusalem.[195] Here again we see other churches being used as an example for the Corinthians. However, the significance of 1 Corinthians 16 for interchurch solidarity is that here, Paul gives the Corinthians the opportunity to participate in the network of modeling to which I have already referred. They are to make a collection (v. 2), but they are also to provide representatives to take their gift to Jerusalem (v. 3), demonstrating that they too can engage in behavior which is imitable.

This motivation can also be seen in 2 Corinthians 8:8-15. In 2 Corinthians 8:7, Paul exhorts the Corinthians to excel in the grace of giving and provides a twin rationale for their activity: that others may know their love is genuine (v. 8), and the example of Christ's self-giving (v. 9). Therefore, the Corinthians should finish the work they have started (8:10-12). Importantly, the financial implication of the principle of self-giving for the sake of others is stated in vv. 13-14: fairness resulting from abundance supplying the needy. The Corinthians then are to give generously because

---

193. Copan, *Saint Paul*, 139.

194. As we saw earlier, this is probably a wider group of churches, including Jerusalem.

195. For detailed reconstruction of the events here, see for example Downs, *Offering*, 42-53, or Georgi, *Remembering the Poor*, 49-109.

they have abundance, but also because they are following the example of Christ, and so that their conduct can be seen by others. In fact, as 9:1–5 shows, their conduct should be imitable, for Paul has been boasting about them in Macedonia (9:1–2) and does not want the Corinthians or himself to suffer humiliation if the boasting proves to be in vain (9:3–5). Paul then closes his section on giving in 2 Corinthians 8–9 by reminding the Corinthians of how their attitude to giving impacts upon their relationship to God (9:6–15), highlighting how the saints in Jerusalem will glorify God because of the actions and beliefs of the Corinthians (9:12–15).

The Corinthians are expected to participate in that which benefits God's people beyond Corinth. Not only are they to be mindful of interchurch solidarity when they act, but they are also to foster interchurch solidarity by their actions.

Conclusion

By using the language of imitation and example as he does, Paul makes it clear to the Corinthians that they are part of something translocal, and that what happens elsewhere should have an influence on them, whether as conduct to be emulated, or avoided. They also have the opportunity, through the collection, to influence what happens elsewhere in a positive way. All this makes explicit what is implicit in 1:2; that they need to take account of what happens beyond Corinth.

The Role of the Apostle

In this final section, I will explore how Paul comes as an apostle to the Corinthians. We have already looked at Paul as father and as one who should be imitated. Here we turn to the language of apostleship.

In chapter 3, I noted that the discussion of apostleship is often a discussion of origins of the term, which I argued were unclear, of the extent and qualifications for apostleship, and of the functions of an apostle. I argued that in Galatians, Paul's use of apostleship language implied an ongoing relationship with the churches he founded, and also the sense of a wider grouping of churches, whether founded by Paul or not. I found similar indications of an ongoing relationship in 1 Thessalonians.

There are several passages in 1 and 2 Corinthians which indicate some of Paul's thinking on qualifications of an apostle. The first of these comes in 1 Corinthians 1:1, where Paul describes himself as an apostle by the will of God.[196] While this description is not as sharp a contrast as that drawn in Galatians 1:1 between being an apostle through Christ and God, rather than through man, it nevertheless indicates Paul's understanding of the divine origin of apostleship;[197] this is something to which people are called. Another qualification emerges in 1 Corinthians 9:1 and 15:7–9: having seen the (risen) Lord. Noticeable here is how Paul treats this as an already accepted qualification, which the Corinthians will not dispute. Finally, in 1 Corinthians 9:2 and 2 Corinthians 12:12, a third qualification emerges: Paul's apostleship to the Corinthians is shown by his work amongst the Corinthians (9:2), and by the signs and wonders which accompanied his ministry (2 Cor 12:12).

The presence of these apostolic qualifications without comment in the Corinthian correspondence suggests a shared understanding of apostleship between Paul and the Corinthians. This shared understanding is confirmed by what can be seen in 1 and 2 Corinthians about the extent of apostleship. In these letters, Paul both includes and excludes people from the apostolic group.

To begin with the exclusions: in 1 Corinthians 1:1 and 2 Corinthians 1:2, Paul describes himself as an apostle, but excludes his cosender in each case (Sosthenes and Timothy respectively).[198] In 2 Corinthians 11:5 and 23, Paul equates super apostles and false apostles, and in 12:11–12, he contrasts super apostles and true apostles. It is not necessary here to distinguish the precise identity of the super apostles;[199] rather, to observe that Paul makes a distinction: some are apostles, presumably because they have the necessary qualifications,[200] and some are not.

In coming to the inclusions, there is one occasion in 1 Corinthians 4:9 where the apostles appear as a particular but undefined group, "us apostles."[201] Paul seems to be assuming that the Corinthians would have some idea of whom he is talking about. Later on, in 1 Corinthians, the group is more clearly defined, so in 1 Corinthians 9:5–6, the apostolic grouping appears to include other apostles, brothers of the Lord, Cephas,

---

196. See also 2 Cor 1:1.

197. Schmithals, *Office*, 24–30, sees a link here. So also Thiselton, *First Epistle*, 68.

198. See Clark, "Apostleship," 57, for a discussion of the exclusion of Timothy.

199. For a discussion of their identity, see for example Furnish, *2 Corinthians*, 502–5.

200. See Schmithals, *Office*, 21–57, on the characteristics of the Pauline apostolate.

201. Clark, "Apostleship," 58, excludes Apollos from the designation of "us apostles" on the grounds that he did not experience suffering, and was not a church planter, arguing instead that Paul has "a class in mind rather than any particular individuals" here.

and Barnabas as apostolic;[202] in 1 Corinthians 15:5–8, Paul distinguishes Cephas, the twelve, five hundred brothers, James, and all the apostles, and then includes himself as the least of the apostles. It is not necessary for an analysis of ecclesial solidarity to determine precisely who is and who is not an apostle, but rather to observe that apostle is used by Paul to distinguish a limited group, and a group which is treated by Paul as largely uncontroversial in his letter to the Corinthians. This is perhaps confirmed by the fact that, in challenging the factional elements in Corinth who are saying that they follow Cephas (1 Cor 1:12), Paul is happy to accept that Cephas might be an influence, because he is an apostle.

There is one passage, 2 Corinthians 8:23, where Paul uses apostle in a different way, to talk of "apostles of the churches." The context here indicates that this reference is to particular individuals being given a particular and limited task in relation to the offering to Jerusalem, and that a generalized apostleship is not in view.

Paul comes as part of a wider group of apostles. Paul talks in 1 Corinthians 12:28–29 about how God has appointed apostles in the church. We have already seen how this is a reference to an ἐκκλησία wider than the church in Corinth, and we do not need to agree the precise boundaries of this group in order to see that they are a limited group of individuals with a particular calling,[203] even if Paul acknowledges in 1 Corinthians 9:2 that while his apostleship could be defined more narrowly, it would at least apply to the Corinthians. This same wider group is in view in 1 Corinthians 4:9: those who will be publicly displayed in the procession.[204]

In Galatians, Paul may be at pains to point out that his message did not originate from the Jerusalem apostles,[205] but that does not mean he denies their apostleship. Paul belongs to the wider group of apostles, and when he addresses them, he addresses them as a member of that group, even if, as he points out in 1 Corinthians 15:9, he does not deserve his status. He may be the least of the apostles, but he is an apostle nonetheless.[206]

---

202. Clark, "Apostleship," 56–57, notes that Paul extends the title to Barnabas even though, according to Acts 15:39, their ministries have taken different paths.

203. Thiselton, *First Epistle*, 1015.

204. Thiselton, *First Epistle*, 359, "authentic apostles."

205. Gal 1–2.

206. And so, in 1 Corinthians 9:1–6, he has the right to sustenance, and a role; 9:2 implies that he is not an apostle everywhere; 1 Corinthians 11:23 and 15:7–9 show the role of Paul and the other apostles in the passing on of agreed truth. All this needs to be taken with Paul's concern in 1 Corinthians 3–4 that he and Apollos and others be seen as servants (1 Cor 3:5, 9; 4:1); see Clarke, "Imitators," 345.

Again, we see here the wider reality of the church in action; there are different apostles, and yet all come with an apostolic message which, in 1 Corinthians, is the same.[207] This apostolic message is the gospel, the message of the cross, for Paul's call to be an apostle in 1 Corinthians 1:1 is related to his commission to preach the gospel in 1:17; the central question of division in the church that Paul poses, assuming a negative answer, is about Christ (1:13), and the apostles have become fools and are exhibited for Christ's sake (4:9–10). There is a church beyond Corinth, which, through Paul, speaks to the Corinthian Church, speaks with authority, and speaks with a common message of the cross.

Conclusions

Here I will summarize what 1 and 2 Corinthians indicate about ecclesial solidarity. In looking at Paul's use of the word ἐκκλησία we see that, with regard to intrachurch solidarity, ecclesial life is expressed through behavior marked by brotherly love, by an active regard for holiness, and by the building up of others. The ἐκκλησία has its core identity in God and Christ. Interchurch solidarity is highlighted by the provincial usage of church, which encourages and challenges the local church in Corinth to express solidarity with other ἐκκλησίαι by learning from and imitating them, by Paul's view of what is normative in all the churches, which fosters the idea of a common identity across all churches, expressed in common beliefs and practices, by indications in 2 Corinthians 8–9 that churches communicated and cooperated in joint ventures, and by Paul's usage of "church(es) of God" for the whole church, which indicates that the Corinthians are to take account of the church of God more generally, and in their beliefs and actions, they should have both intra- and interchurch solidarity in view.

In examining the language of holiness, temple, brothers, and the body of Christ, a trend towards encouraging the Corinthians to look beyond themselves can be observed. They are to take greater account of their own local church: they are the saints, they are brothers, they are God's holy temple, and they are the body of Christ, despite their differences and diversity. At the same time, holiness and temple language emphasizes that they are part of a wider grouping—they are reminded that they have brothers in the Lord beyond Corinth, and the Corinthian body operates in a context where all the baptized are part of one body, and so the Corinthians must also take account of the church beyond Corinth.

---

207. There may be those in Corinth who follow Cephas (1 Cor 1:12), but there is no suggestion in the letter that Paul criticizes him.

Paul's use of the language of imitation in 1 and 2 Corinthians reinforces both the need to practice other-regard in the church in Corinth, and also the idea that the Corinthians are part of something translocal, and that what happens elsewhere should have an influence on them. In addition, they have the opportunity, through the collection, to influence what happens elsewhere in a positive way. Finally, the language of apostleship as used by Paul in 1 and 2 Corinthians reinforces Paul's legitimate authority as one who has been called by God, but also indicates the existence of an at least semi-defined group of apostles who have wide authority over "the church," conceived of translocally. There is a church beyond Corinth, which, through Paul, speaks to the Corinthian Church, speaks with authority, and speaks with a common message of the cross.

In 1 and 2 Corinthians, then, we see a highly developed pattern of ecclesial solidarity, which is centered on other-regard after the example of Christ, and which is to be worked out in practice both in the local church in Corinth and in relationships, beliefs, and behaviors, in a shared ethos, with the saints, the brothers, and the whole church.

5. Romans and Philippians

IN CHAPTERS 3 AND 4, I have examined five of Paul's letters and noticed a number of common themes relating to the usage of ἐκκλησία, to imagery related to ἐκκλησία, and to imitation and apostleship. In examining Romans and Philippians, I will explore whether those common themes are also present in these two letters, and any variations or differences of expression and usage.

Approaching Romans

I will examine aspects of the setting of Philippians in this chapter. However, given the extensive literature that exists on the setting and purpose of Romans, I will comment on it briefly here. Following Longenecker, the disputed issues do not relate to author, integrity, or occasion and date,[1] but rather to addressees and purpose.[2] In relation to these two areas, there are three issues relevant to this investigation. First, how did the addressees relate to other churches outside Rome? Second, how did domestic churches relate to one another? Third, what is the relationship, if any, between the purpose of the letter and ecclesial solidarity?

First, Longenecker notes how the question of addressees has been a disputed area, due to the identification of Jewish and gentile features in the letter, which have caused different scholars to argue for gentile Christians or Jewish Christians as the addressees.[3] Longenecker offers a possible solution: arguing that Christianity at Rome has a distinctly Jewish character, with strong connections to the Jerusalem church,[4] and therefore the primary question is not one of ethnicity, but of theological and social orientation. Given the concern of this study with relationships between churches, I will examine this thesis at appropriate points in this chapter.

1. Longenecker, *Introducing Romans*, 3–51.
2. Longenecker, *Introducing Romans*, 55–166.
3. Longenecker, *Introducing Romans*, 74–78.
4. Longenecker, *Introducing Romans*, 79–84.

Second, the existence of multiple domestic churches in Rome, without a centralized meeting place or organization is generally recognized,[5] although the setting for these churches is more difficult to establish. According the definitions I have adopted for this study, these domestic churches can be considered part of one local church, within Rome. However, this identification might be questioned if the domestic churches never met together, and so I will consider this terminological issue in the conclusion of this chapter.

Third, whilst discussion of the addressees of the letter has tended to focus on whether Jewish Christians or gentile Christians are the main recipients, discussion of the purpose of the letter has been much more wide-ranging, with a distinction between those who find the purpose in circumstances in Paul's own life, and those who find that it was written primarily to deal with issues in the church in Rome.[6] In seeking to resolve this issue, Longenecker argues, based on his understanding of the addressees, and his reading of the epistolary frame,[7] that the two main purposes of Romans are to give the Christians of Rome a spiritual gift, an understanding of Paul's gospel to the gentiles, and to seek assistance with the Spanish mission, with three subsidiary purposes: to define against misrepresentation of his message, to offer counsel on the strong/weak dispute (14:1—15:13), and to offer counsel on dealing with civil authorities (13:1-7).[8]

I will be broadly following Longenecker's reconstruction of the main purposes of the letter, based as it is on issues in the church in Rome. In terms of subsidiary purposes, Longenecker argues that only 13:1-7 and 14:1—15:13 are directly addressed to the Roman situation,[9] with chapter 12 and 13:8-14 being general exhortations, where Paul sets out his characteristic ethical teaching.[10] However, Oakes has shown how Romans 12 could have had a number of specific applications to a possible Roman house church.[11] I will note any points where more can be said as to subsidiary purposes from chapters 12 to 15, in relation to ecclesial solidarity.

---

5. Longenecker, *Introducing Romans*, 84–85; Gehring, *House Church*, 144–47; Adams, *Earliest Christian Meeting Places*, 30–33. Lampe, "Roman Christians," 229–30.

6. For a summary of these positions, see Longenecker, *Introducing Romans*, 93–128.

7. Longenecker, *Introducing Romans*, 133–47. On the epistolary opening, see O'Brien, *Introductory Thanksgivings*, 224–29. On the letter ending, see Weima, *Neglected Endings*, 215–30.

8. Longenecker, *Introducing Romans*, 157–59.

9. Longenecker, *Introducing Romans*, 421–22, 432–36.

10. Longenecker, *Introducing Romans*, 428–32.

11. Oakes, *Reading Romans*, 98–126. See also Jewett, *Romans*, 724–25.

Ecclesial Solidarity and ἐκκλησία

In chapters 3 and 4, I noted how Paul uses ἐκκλησία to encourage intrachurch solidarity. He uses ἐκκλησία as an identity marker for a group with an ongoing existence, whose core identity is in another. He encourages those within the local ἐκκλησία to build one another up, and ecclesial life is to be marked by brotherly love and an active regard for holiness.

I also argued that Paul uses ἐκκλησία to encourage interchurch solidarity in a number of ways. First, Paul uses ἐκκλησία regionally, which encourages a common identity for churches in Galatia, Macedonia, Jerusalem and elsewhere, involving learning from each other. Second, he indicates that what happens in these churches should also happen in Corinth, encouraging recognition of solidarity at the level of behavior beyond the local church, expressing common identity in beliefs and practices. Third, Paul's treatment of the churches as a whole, including churches he did not found, suggests some kind of solidarity across all churches. Fourth, Paul's usage of "church of God" for the "whole church" at Galatians 1:13, 1 Corinthians 10:32; 11:16; 15:9, and the use of "church" for the "whole church" at 1 Corinthians 12:28, indicates that in all their ecclesial activity, those in Galatia and Corinth needed to take account of the church both local and whole. Therefore, the building up, brotherly love, and concern for holiness which should mark their conduct in the local church should be extended to the whole church.

In examining 1 and 2 Corinthians, I explored thirty-one references to ἐκκλησία spread across twenty-nine chapters. In coming to Romans and Philippians, there are seven references in twenty chapters. Noticeable here is the comparative infrequency of the use of ἐκκλησία, particularly in Romans, where all five uses occur in chapter 16.

Some have noted an omission here: unlike in his earlier letters, Paul does not address the Romans as ἐκκλησία or ἐκκλησίαι in his letter opening. Various reasons are offered for this omission. Klein argues that the Roman church is not a proper church, and therefore Paul does not address it as one.[12] There is a suggestion that Paul uses the language of saints here, because the church was divided.[13] Others suggest that the church was divided, and didn't meet as a local church, and therefore Paul did not call the Romans as a whole ἐκκλησία.[14] Finally, Sanday and Headlam detect a progression in Paul's thought from the local unit to the body of believers.[15]

12. Klein, "Paul's Purpose," 29–43.
13. Kruse, *Romans*, 53–54; Jewett, "Ecumenical Theology," 94–97.
14. Gehring, *House Church*, 146. Similarly, Burke, *Adopted into God's Family*, 160; Moo, *Romans*, 54; Banks, *Paul's Idea*, 34.
15. Sanday and Headlam, *Romans*, 15.

Klein's contention can be easily dismissed, as Paul does describe those in Rome as saints, language intimately related to that of ἐκκλησία in 1 Corinthians 1:2 and elsewhere, and a clear indication of the reality of their faith. Also, a simple progression in Paul's thought here from the local to the "whole" can be ruled out, as the letters I have examined so far have shown significant reflection on the "whole." The other two reasons stated are, in a sense, two sides of the same argument: Paul avoids ἐκκλησία because they didn't meet together, and instead uses saints to try and bring them together. Certainly, the applicability of saints as language including all believers can be granted, and will be explored further in the section on holiness. However, ἐκκλησία does not appear in the opening of Philippians, and there is no suggestion there that the Philippians did not constitute a church. Rather, the omission here, or rather the choice of an alternative form of address, indicates flexibility in Paul's language.

Of the five occurrences of ἐκκλησία in Romans 16, one is a reference to a domestic church in Rome, the church meeting in the house of Prisca and Aquila (v. 5). This is similar to usage found elsewhere for domestic churches, such as in 1 Corinthians. Twice in Romans 16, Paul refers to a church outside Rome, in Cenchreae, near Corinth (v. 1),[16] and in Gaius's house, in Corinth (v. 23). I take Romans 16:1 to be a reference to a local church in Cenchreae (which probably represented the only domestic church in that location), as Paul distinguishes Cenchreae from Corinth by mentioning Cenchreae by name (Corinth is not named in Romans 16:23).

The meaning of ὅλης τῆς ἐκκλησίας in Romans 16:23 has been debated. Jewett argues that it does not mean the whole local church in Corinth, but rather is a reference to Gaius's reputation for hospitality.[17] However, Kruse argues that Gaius provides the venue when the domestic churches meet together as one.[18] Gehring cites Origen as patristic evidence in support of this view,[19] and notes that 1 Corinthians 14:23 assumes a meeting of ἡ ἐκκλησία ὅλη, and that the accommodation of a church of perhaps ninety members is possible in Gaius's house.[20] Whilst it might be attractive in terms of interchurch solidarity to view this reference to "whole" as having "an 'ecumenical' scope,"[21] it seems most likely that this is a reference to the

---

16. See Jewett, *Romans*, 943–44 on the likely origins of this church.

17. Jewett, *Romans*, 980–81.

18. Kruse, *Romans*, 584. Note that the language here is similar to 1 Corinthians 14:23.

19. Gehring, *House Church*, 139. Origen, *PG*14. 1289c.

20. Gehring, *House Church*, 139–40.

21. Jewett, *Romans*, 981.

local church in Corinth. Here, then, Paul commends a member[22] of a local church, and sends greeting from the host of a local church, which would encourage interchurch communication and solidarity.

Twice in Romans 16, Paul refers to groups of churches using the plural: the churches of the gentiles in v. 4, and all the churches in v. 16. Churches of the gentiles is generally taken as a reference to predominantly gentile churches in Ephesus, Rome, and Corinth who have benefitted from Prisca and Aquila's activity.[23] Jewett notes the unifying effect of this language, and suggests that here there is an implicit invitation to the "Roman house churches" to support Paul's mission and receive similar thanks.[24] Whether or not this argument can be sustained, the self-giving activity of Prisca and Aquila for the churches emphasizes interchurch solidarity, as members of one church are willing to act for the sake of others.[25]

The reference to "all the churches of Christ" in v. 16 is unique in Paul's letters.[26] Jewett suggests here that the greetings in 16:21-23 indicate the presence of representatives of other churches in Corinth when Paul writes, and therefore that "all the church of Christ" indicates their presence, but also suggest that Paul has consulted about the Spanish mission with his other churches;[27] certainly at a practical level this view is attractive, as he would likely only be able to send greetings from "his" churches which he had visited. However, I would argue that Paul's language needs to be taken to include all churches for two reasons. First, there is a desire here to view Paul as passing on actual greetings. However, in sending greetings from all his churches, Paul is unlikely to have physical representatives from all of them present with him, nor will all of them have given him specific greetings for the Roman church, therefore "all" here contains an element of generalization. Second, in the discussion of 1 and 2 Corinthians, I noted how, when Paul refers to "all the churches" or "every church," he includes churches outside the Pauline mission. It is reasonable then to see the same dynamic here, where "all" reminds the Romans of their inclusion not just within a

22. For a recent discussion of the role of Phoebe, see Perry, "Phoebe of Cenchreae," 9–36.

23. So, Moo, *Romans*, 920; Kruse, *Romans*, 560.

24. Jewett, *Romans*, 958.

25. Stenschke, "Significance and Function of References," 200, highlights how cooperation with the widely appreciated Prisca and Aquila also sheds positive light on Paul.

26. Although note how Schmidt, "ἐκκλησία," 507, relates this phrase to 1 Thessalonians 2:14 and Galatians 1:22.

27. See Jewett, *Romans*, 976–77, who also argues that Paul wants to show that he has official backing for his venture.

Pauline mission, but within a group which encompasses all the churches. The interchurch solidarity that these greetings entail, then, is not just a Pauline interchurch solidarity, but a solidarity with the whole church.[28] We see here the same collective tendency as in 1 Corinthians, and a desire by Paul to have the Roman church join with all the churches, encouraging mutuality and independence, and a common identity, after the example of Prisca and Aquila.[29]

It may also be possible to detect here a desire to emphasize solidarity between Jerusalem as one of "all" the churches and those churches founded by Paul, if the Roman believers had a strong affiliation with Jerusalem.

The word ἐκκλησία occurs twice in Philippians. In Philippians 4:15, Paul uses "church" with a local reference, to refer to the church of the Philippians.[30] This local church may, if Acts 16 is taken as a reliable record, and if the plural officers in Philippians 1:1 indicate multiple gatherings, have been made up of two or more domestic churches.[31] However, as noted in my discussion of 1 Corinthians 14:23, multiple domestic churches still made up one local church. There is also no suggestion here of local churches meeting separately as a permanent arrangement, as may have been the case in Rome.

In Philippians 3:6, in the midst of his exposition of his reasons for confidence in the flesh in 3:4b–6, Paul mentions his zeal, persecuting the church. I would argue that this is a reference to the whole church. The arguments made in chapter 3 against limiting the reference in Galatians 1:13, where Paul persecutes the church of God, to the Jerusalem church would apply here. In addition, it is hard to imagine how the church of Philippi, more distant in space and time from the events described than those in Galatia, would have heard this as just a reference to the church in Jerusalem unless Paul specified that is what he meant. Also, I have noted the usage of "church of God" in 1 Corinthians, and the usage of "church" in 1 Corinthians 12:28 to indicate the whole church, and we see a further example of that usage here.

In these two references to ἐκκλησία in the letter, Philippians does not add anything new, but is consistent with Paul's earlier usage, as Paul uses ἐκκλησία to refer to the local church and to a wider entity, encouraging both

---

28. Stenschke, "Significance and Function of References," 217, notes the link here to what is known of the Romans in Romans 1:8.

29. Jewett, *Romans*, 954–58, argues that Paul is encouraging a view of mutuality and dependence between gentiles and Jewish Christians, whilst seeking support for his trip to Spain.

30. So, O'Brien, *Philippians*, 533; Fee, *Philippians*, 442; Reumann, *Philippians*, 661.

31. See Gehring, *House Church*, 131–32. Others argue for one small church: De Vos, *Church and Community Conflicts*, 250–61; Oakes, *Philippians*, 70–76.

intra- and interchurch solidarity. This is a similar pattern to that noted in Romans, where the focus is on intrachurch solidarity and unity, but where interchurch solidarity is also encouraged.

Ἐκκλησία and imagery

In this section, I will explore five images and metaphors used for the church. Three of these have already been explored in chapters 3 and 4: holy people, body, and brothers. Two are new: the language of friendship and partnership, and the idea of heavenly citizenship in Philippians.

Brothers

We have seen how brotherhood language encourages intrachurch solidarity by fostering a shared identity: encouraging collective behavior in 1 and 2 Thessalonians and Galatians, and encouraging the Corinthians to see themselves as part of a family, rather than focus on their own social position. In addition, in terms of interchurch solidarity, I showed how Paul uses the language of brotherhood to emphasize the relationship between the Thessalonians and himself, how "brothers" is used in Galatians to imply membership of a wider group, and how, in 1 Thessalonians 4:9–12, the behavior of brothers in one place was seen to impact on brothers elsewhere, indicating brotherly relationships at a deeper level than financial support and hospitality. Paul's use of brother language in 1 and 2 Corinthians demonstrates how the brotherhood of believers extends beyond the boundaries of Corinth.

Many of the references to brothers in Philippians and Romans are similar to those already examined in chapters 3 and 4. Paul addresses the Romans as his brothers ten times,[32] and six times in Philippians.[33] Here we see a similar pattern in Paul's use of direct address: a concern with knowledge, as Paul reminds his readers of what should be common knowledge,[34] or of their status,[35] and emphasizes something he wants them to know or understand;[36] a strengthening of the personal relationship between Paul and those to whom he writes, as he informs them of his concerns and practices,[37]

---

32. Rom 1:13; 7:1, 4; 8:12; 10:1; 11:25; 12:1; 15:14, 30; 16:17.
33. Phil 1:12; 3:1, 13, 17; 4:1, 8.
34. Rom 7:1
35. Rom 7:4; 8:12.
36. Rom 1:13; 11:25; Phil 1:12.
37. Rom 10:1; Phil 3:13.

or of his attitude towards them;[38] and exhortation to right conduct,[39] or to imitate him.[40] A similar pattern can be seen in Paul's use of "brothers" as a designation. Four individuals are named as brother or sister in these letters,[41] and Paul also uses brothers to refer to members of one of the domestic churches in Rome,[42] and, in Philippians, to believers in Rome more generally.[43] Brotherly language is then used to foster intrachurch solidarity, as Paul reminds them of what they share and of their close relationship to one another and to Paul. It is also used to encourage interchurch solidarity, with the recognition of brothers in other places.

There are, however, a number of uses of brotherhood language that require further comment. First, Paul uses the term once for members of the Jewish race at Romans 9:3, a unique usage for Paul,[44] and one which highlights both the flexibility of the term and also the need to interpret it contextually.

Second, in Romans 8:29, Jesus is the firstborn among many brothers. This language might be taken to suggest that the brotherhood that all believers enjoy is founded on their common brotherhood with Christ, and this would be a potent way of developing the interchurch implications of the imagery. However, Aasgaard argues that here Paul is "only very reservedly" paralleling Jesus as son and the Christians as children, as Jesus is the firstborn to be emulated;[45] is named as son, not brother; and because Paul does not apply the idea of Christ and believers as siblings.[46] These reservations are reasonable, considering the context of the passage, which focuses on metaphors of sonship (v. 18) and children of God (v. 21), and shows a primary concern for the eschatological destiny of believers.[47] Whatever potential implications for ecclesial solidarity there might be in Paul's statement in Romans 8:29, they are not developed here.

Third, in Romans 12:10, Paul makes use of the idea of φιλαδελφία, as he did in 1 Thessalonians 4:9–12. There, φιλαδελφία had implications

38. Rom 15:14; Phil 4:1, "my brothers."
39. Rom 12:1; 15:30; 16:17; Phil 3:1, "my brothers"; 4:8.
40. Phil 3:17.
41. Rom 16:1, Phoebe; 16:15, sister of Nereus; 16:23, Quartus; Phil 2:25, Epharoditus.
42. Rom 16:14.
43. Phil 1:14; 4:21.
44. See Aasgaard, *Brothers and Sisters*, 313–14.
45. On the origin of firstborn language and its implications here, see Aasgaard, *Brothers and Sisters*, 142–43; Burke, *Adopted into God's Family*, 191–93.
46. Aasgaard, *Brothers and Sisters*, 145–49.
47. See also Aasgaard, *Brothers and Sisters*, 138–41.

beyond Thessalonica, as I explored in chapter 3. In Romans 12:9-13, however, the focus is on the local church, on love shown towards one another, not on outsiders,[48] and not on implications for churches elsewhere, taking "saints" in 12:13 as saints within Rome.[49] Differing situations in Rome and Thessalonica mean that Paul applies his language in a different way,[50] and here in Romans 12:10 that application is to intrachurch solidarity.

Fourth, in chapter 14, the term is used five times to discuss how brothers should and should not treat one another,[51] in a section of the letter dealing with the "weak" and the "strong" (Rom 14:1—15:13). There are similarities between this passage and 1 Corinthians 8:1—11:1, although the precise issues in Romans 14-15 are harder to determine.[52] In 1 Corinthians 8, there is a contrast between love and knowledge; a focus on the need to build others up; a Christological motivation; and the language of brotherhood is used to unify the weak and strong. Romans 14 is similar.[53] In 14:15, the one who grieves his brother by what he eats is no longer "walking in love," and Paul exhorts him not to "destroy" his brother. In 14:13, he is not to hinder his brother, and in 14:21, he is not to cause his brother to stumble by what he eats. Whilst the contrast here is not knowledge and love, there is a clear contrast between love, which builds others up (14:19), and that which destroys or causes others to stumble. The Christological motivation comes in 14:15: do not destroy the one for whom Christ died; instead, serve Christ (v. 18). The unifying implications of this section can perhaps be most clearly seen in 14:19, where the building up is of one another. There are also additional elements in Romans 14:1—15:13, the call to welcome which first appears in 14:1, and the restriction on judgement. The call to welcome may well have implications for divisions between domestic churches in Rome,[54] and the call not to despise or pass judgment on a brother has some similarities to Paul's exhortation in 1 Corinthians 6:1-11. What is noticeable in Romans 14:10-12, however, is how the call not to judge is linked to the universal judgement before the judgement seat of God, and therefore links the idea of brother to a universal grouping. Thus, whilst Romans 14:1—15:13 as a whole is directed towards intrachurch solidarity, and probably to solidar-

---

48. On the focus of brotherly love in this section see Aasgaard, *Brothers and Sisters*, 170–76.

49. Jewett, *Romans*, 764; Moo, *Romans*, 780; Kruse, *Romans*, 479.

50. Aasgaard, *Brothers and Sisters*, 176–77.

51. Rom 14:10 (twice), 13, 15, 21.

52. For a recent summary of possible issues, see Aasgaard, *Brothers and Sisters*, 202–6.

53. On this section in general, see Aasgaard, *Brothers and Sisters*, 206–11.

54. See for example Aasgaard, *Brothers and Sisters*, 209–10.

ity between the various domestic churches in Rome, fostering solidarity by encouraging mutual love, up-building and respect, there is one element in these verses which is suggestive of the existence of a wider "brotherhood" of believers.

Finally, it should be noted that in Romans 16:15 the term "saints" is used for members of a domestic church, in parallel to "brothers" in v. 14. The implications of this usage will be explored below, but here the parallel with "brothers" is noted.

What is noticeable about the use of the language of brothers in Philippians and Romans is that it is almost exclusively directed towards intra-church solidarity. There are some points where an awareness of a wider brotherhood seems likely, but the focus is on solidarity within the local church.

The Language of Partnership

Philippians is often seen as a friendship letter, and some argue that the language of friendship and the mutual obligations of friendship are key to understanding the letter. Sampley argues that the relationship between Paul and the Philippians can be characterized as a consensual *societas*,[55] a voluntary agreement between two parties for a shared goal: that Philippians 4:10-20 function as Paul's receipt for the financial support he has received;[56] that in Philippians Paul is not the apostle writing to the Philippian church, but one partner writing to another;[57] and that the language of *phronein*, being of the same mind, serves to call the Philippians back to their common commitment with Paul to sharing the gospel.[58]

Two questions follow from this observation. First, is kinship language being replaced by friendship language in Philippians? I would argue not, for two reasons. First, as Fitzgerald notes, kinship and friendship language are closely related: friendship language can be used as "a complement and a substitute for kinship language."[59] Second, as Witherington notes, building on the work of Alexander, Cicero would distinguish between friendship let-

55. Sampley, *Pauline Partnership*, 77-100.
56. Sampley, *Pauline Partnership*, 52-60.
57. Sampley, *Pauline Partnership*, 60-62.
58. Sampley, *Pauline Partnership*, 62-70. Note that there are other proposals for the purpose of the letter which do not focus here: Oakes, *Philippians*, 89-96; Witherington, *Philippians*, 11-15. For a summary of setting proposals, see Copan, *Saint Paul*, 143-48. These various proposals suggest that caution should be shown in making the letter solely about the mutual obligations of friendship.
59. Fitzgerald, "Paul and Friendship," 332.

ters and family letters, and that Philippians, if it must be characterized as an epistolary type, belongs to the latter category: it is a family letter.[60]

The second question is of more significance for this study: what are the implications of the language of friendship and partnership for ecclesial solidarity? Witherington notes that the formal language of friendship, *philos* and *philia*, is not used in the letter, but rather the language of partnership, κοινωνία.[61] Before examining usage in Philippians, it will be helpful to briefly survey usage elsewhere.

Κοινωνία refers to fellowship with Christ in 1 Corinthians 1:9, and in a related way to draw a contrast between partnership with Christ and with demons in 1 Corinthians 10.[62] Similarly it refers to fellowship with the Holy Spirit (2 Cor 13:13). It can refer to fellowship between Paul and the Jerusalem pillars,[63] and between Paul and Timothy,[64] for a shared experience of sufferings and comfort between Paul and the Corinthians,[65] and the verb refers to pupils sharing good things with their teachers.[66] There is also an exhortation not to partner with unbelievers at 2 Corinthians 6:4. These instances show that κοινωνία can be used in a similar way to the language of brotherhood, encouraging a mutual regard which would foster ecclesial solidarity, and emphasizing the close relationship believers enjoy with Christ. Finally, κοινωνία is used in reference to the Jerusalem collection, in 2 Corinthians 8:4; 9:13; and Romans 15:26,[67] suggesting that the language of sharing is also appropriate to interchurch relationships.

Coming then to Philippians, four "sharings" or participations are mentioned: in the gospel (1:5), in the Spirit (2:1), in the sufferings of Christ (3:10), and in partnership in giving and receiving (4:14-15). In chapter 2, Paul is encouraging the Philippians to learn from Christ's example of humility (2:1-11), and in 3:1-11, to have the right perspective on their sufferings, for the sake of Christ. These two passages have implications for intrachurch solidarity, drawing the Philippians together in unity as followers of Christ. Various suggestions have been made for the content of the partnership in the gospel in 1:5, and it is generally taken as being "broader than just financial

---

60. Witherington, *Philippians*, 20; Alexander, "Hellenistic Letter-Forms," 232–46.
61. Witherington, *Philippians*, 18.
62. 1 Cor 10:16 (twice), 18, 20.
63. Gal 2:9.
64. 2 Cor 8:23.
65. 2 Cor 1:7.
66. Gal 6:6.
67. The verbal form is also used in reference to the collection in Romans 12:13.

contributions to Paul."[68] Witherington highlights four: financial support,[69] prayer, suffering for the gospel, and defending their faith,[70] and this can be partly confirmed by a comparison with Philippians 4:14–15, which highlights financial support, but also sharing in afflictions. Whatever the precise nature of the partnership was beyond financial support, the use of partnership here might have implications for interchurch solidarity, in that we see the Philippians sharing in a concern for the progress of the gospel beyond their immediate locality. However, in the context of the letter, these implications are not developed, and the focus remains on the partnership between Paul and the Philippians.

Saints and Holy People

In my examination of the Thessalonian correspondence, I noted the importance of holiness language, and how the language of holiness was used to create boundaries between the community and those outside, and to define boundaries within the community, as well as being explicitly linked to the return of Christ as judge. The language of holiness served, then, to further bind the ἐκκλησία together, promoting internal harmony and group identity. I also noted the idea of God's holy people, and how that is expressed in 2 Thessalonians 1:10. From the Corinthian correspondence, I noted how the designation "the saints" brings together the local and the whole in a similar way to the use of ἐκκλησία: for example, the local saints and the whole group of saints are in view in 1 Corinthians 6; and how Paul predicates local behavior on the basis of the identity of the whole is, again, the same pattern as observed with Paul's usage of ἐκκλησία in 1 and 2 Corinthians. The Corinthian correspondence then demonstrates a strong assertion of interchurch solidarity, based on belonging to the same group: the saints.

In Romans, Paul addresses the saints, the holy people, eight times.[71] Three of these are references to the saints in Jerusalem (15:25–26, 31), and are linked to the collection.[72] This is Paul's service for the saints, but it is also one in which Macedonia and Achaia have participated. In chapter 4, I noted that Paul uses the Jerusalem collection to encourage the Corinthians to act for the sake of God's people in Jerusalem, engaging in behavior which

68. Reumann, *Philippians*, 151; O'Brien, *Introductory Thanksgivings*, 25.

69. See also Phil 4:10–20; 1 Thess 4:10; 2 Cor 11:9.

70. Witherington, *Philippians*, 57. O'Brien, *Philippians*, 61–62, argues that this should not to be taken passively as belief in the gospel.

71. Rom 1:7; 8:27; 12:13; 15:25–26, 31; 16:2, 15.

72. See for example Downs, *Offering*, 58–60.

is imitable, and fostering interchurch solidarity by their actions. Here in Romans 15, Paul indicates that the purpose of the collection is to relieve the poor (Rom 15:26), but that he also hopes it will foster interchurch solidarity between Jew and gentile (Rom 15:27, 31).[73] The completion of the collection is also linked to Paul's desire to travel to Spain via Rome (15:28). Here we see the use of saints to distinguish one group of believers (those in Jerusalem), but in a way which encourages solidarity with others.[74] The Romans are being encouraged in their solidarity with the saints in Jerusalem, but also encouraged to develop their solidarity with the churches founded by Paul, and with the church that will be founded in Spain.

Paul uses "saints" in reference to the believers in Rome. I have already noted the local direction of Paul's argument in Romans 12:9–13, and I take "saints" in 12:13 as a reference to the local church in Rome offering hospitality.[75] I have also noted the parallel placement of brothers/saints in Romans 16:14–15, showing how saints and brothers can be used as equivalent terms for members of a domestic church in Rome. Thus, "saints" is applied to the local church and the domestic church. The letter is written to the saints in Rome (1:7). I take this to be a reference to all the Christians in Rome,[76] and it seems to be used instead of ἐκκλησία for the "whole church" in Rome. I have argued above that this is best seen as stylistic variation, rather than a deliberate avoidance of ἐκκλησία. Perhaps it can be seen in parallel to the language of 2 Corinthians 1:2, where Paul writes to the saints in Achaia. Paul's use of saints here in Romans 1:7, and perhaps also in 12:13 and 16:15, can be seen to be a way of accessing some of the wider connotations of the language, which I noted in relation to 1 Corinthians 1:2 and 2 Corinthians 1:2, and which I will also note below.

There are two places in Romans where Paul uses "saints" for all believers. Saints is used once, at Romans 8:27, for all those for whom the Spirit intercedes. In the context of Paul's argument in Romans 8, where he focuses on how all creation waits for the revealing of the sons of God and redemption (8:19–25), this reference is best understood as being to all believers.

73. Horrell, *Solidarity and Difference*, 234–35.

74. Stenschke, "Significance and Function of References," 215–16.

75. Stenschke, "Significance and Function of References," 205, sees hospitality here as indicating more than "strictly local needs." Nevertheless, the focus in on activity for the saints who are in Rome.

76. Contra Jewett, *Romans*, 114, who argues that where the term is specified as a group of Christians, it means Jewish Christians. For this he can adduce four references: three from Romans 15, and one in 1 Corinthians 16:1. I think it is too much of a stretch from these two sets of references to argue that the Roman recipients would have understood this to be a technical term for Jewish Christians when used of a particular group in the church. See also 2 Corinthians 1:2.

In regard to Romans 16:2, a number of commentators note here the implication that Phoebe is to be offered hospitality and support befitting her position and activity on behalf of believers.[77] However, I would also argue that the saints in general are in view here, first because in Romans 8:27, Paul has already used "saints" in a universal sense, and second because of the context of Romans 16:1–2. Phoebe comes from one church to another to receive hospitality and support, and this happens in the context of 15:22–33, where Paul emphasizes his support of the saints in Jerusalem, along with the saints in Achaia and Macedonia, hoping that his service is acceptable. Thus, the support that Phoebe should receive is paralleled with the service to the saints in Jerusalem, such that the need to act in a way which is acceptable to the saints is indicated—not just in Rome, but more generally.[78]

In Romans, then, "saints" can be used for a domestic church, for the local church in Rome or elsewhere, and for believers in general. This flexibility mirrors that already noted in the use of ἐκκλησία. It is a term which encourages intrachurch solidarity by reminding the Romans of their identity as God's holy people, but also encourages interchurch solidarity by indicating that the holy people include saints in other places as well and can be considered as a whole.

Philippians is written to the saints in Christ Jesus at Philippi (Phil 1:1). As in Romans, Paul writes to the saints and does not designate them here as the church. There are also similarities with 1 and 2 Corinthians, where Paul addresses the church of God in Corinth and the saints in Achaia. There is an implicit recognition of interchurch solidarity here, for in referring to the saints who are at Philippi, Paul implies the existence of saints elsewhere, and therefore that the Philippians are part of something wider than themselves. In Philippians 4:21–22, Paul links saints and brothers; every saint is to be greeted, and the brothers and the saints send greetings. This is most likely a reference to the saints in Philippi and with Paul.[79] In Philippians, then, Paul applies the language of saints to intrachurch and interchurch solidarity, although he does not apply the language beyond the recognition of membership of this group of "holy ones."

---

77. Jewett, *Romans*, 945; Kruse, *Romans*, 555; Moo, *Romans*, 915.

78. See Stenschke, "Significance and Function of References," 205–6.

79. Stenschke, "Significance and Function of References," 220, notes possible references here to a wider group of saints beyond the addressees and those with Paul.

Body

I noted how body language is used in 1 Corinthians 10–12 with a focus on interchurch solidarity, and how the body can be used to stand for one thing and another thing at the same time. I suggested that this may indicate the usefulness of the imagery for Paul in helping to elucidate the relationship between intra- and interchurch solidarity: behavior which should be undertaken for the sake of the body of Christ or the ἐκκλησία in Corinth should also be undertaken for the sake of the body of Christ, the church of God, more generally.

In Philippians, σῶμα is used for Paul's body,[80] and the body which will be transformed to be like Christ's resurrected body.[81] In Romans, σῶμα is used to refer to physical human bodies on a number of occasions,[82] or to the physical body of Christ.[83] It is used, explicitly and implicitly, in contrast to the new life of the Spirit.[84] It is also used metaphorically in Romans 12:4–5 to refer to the church. There are similarities here with 1 Corinthians 12, in the emphasis on one body with many members (1 Cor 12:12, 14), in the different functions of members of the body (1 Cor 12:15–19), and in the emphasis on mutuality and solidarity (1 Cor 12:24–5).[85] However there are also differences in wording: In 1 Corinthians 12:27, Paul describes the Corinthians, as the body *of* Christ, and members of *it*; in Romans 12:5, there is one body *in* Christ, and members of *one another*.[86] The difference between body of Christ and one body in Christ can be seen as stylistic, and an indication that Paul's usage of body of Christ is metaphorical; they are a body which relates to Christ. Similarly, the thought of members being of one another in the sense of caring for and having the interests of others at heart is present in 1 Corinthians 12. These similarities and differences highlight the focus of the metaphor in Romans 12:4–5: it is used to encourage corporate solidarity within the local church in Rome[87] by encouraging them to recognize their fundamental unity, one with another, in Christ. The surrounding exhortations in Romans 12:3–13 indicate the issues here: the

---

80. Phil 1:20.
81. Phil 3:21.
82. Rom 1:24; 4:19; 6:12; 8:23, 12:1.
83. Rom 7:4.
84. Rom 6:6, body of sin; 7:24, body of death; 8:10–11, 13, 23.
85. Dunn, "Body of Christ," 149.
86. Dunn, "Body of Christ," 151.

87. For the likely issues in Rome, see for example Jewett, *Romans*, 743–44; Oakes, *Reading Romans*, 98–126, on how this language would have been heard by his reconstructed Roman craftworker church.

need to think rightly of oneself without arrogance (v. 3),[88] to use God-given gifts to serve one another (v. 6–8), in conduct marked by brotherly love, and serving the saints (v. 9–13), and so here as in 1 Corinthians 12, other-regard is key. The Roman believers, wherever they gather in Rome, are to view themselves as fundamentally a unity in Christ, whose gifts are to be used to build one another up.

The focus, then, of σῶμα in Romans 12:4–5 appears to be on the local church in Rome.[89] However, I noted in 1 Corinthians 12 that when Paul wanted to talk particularly of the body of Christ in Corinth, he addressed them as you (1 Cor 12:27). In Romans 12:4–5, Paul continues to use the first-person plural, including himself with the Romans in one body in Christ; this might be considered particularly noteworthy, as this is a church which Paul has never visited. Therefore, although the primary application of Romans 12:1–13 is to the local church in Rome, there is a sense of a wider body here.[90] The body of Christ is not used to address interchurch solidarity here, although it is used to address solidarity between domestic churches in Rome.

Overall, the use of "body" in Romans shows similarities with 1 Corinthians, but a difference of emphasis is the former's much briefer presentation, which focuses on intrachurch solidarity. The focus on corporate solidarity in Rome suggests that this is more than generalized exhortation,[91] but rather a deliberate focus on a particular issue in Rome: unity and solidarity in the local church. "Body" is not used metaphorically in Philippians.

Citizens of Heaven

The final image I want to consider is the language of πολίτευμα in Philippians 3:20, and the related call to "live as citizens" in Philippians 1:27. The first issue that presents itself in Philippians 3:20 is how best to translate πολίτευμα. Following Witherington and others,[92] commonwealth is probably the best translation here. Then 3:20–21 needs to be taken in the context of the passage as a whole; Lincoln notes the opposition to Paul in 3:1–19,[93] and how Paul's

---

88. Clarke, *Serve the Community*, 189–91, identifies issues of social status here and in 12:16, 13:1–7, and chapter 16.

89. Moo, *Romans*, 763.

90. See Oakes, *Reading Romans*, 102.

91. As argued by Longenecker, *Introducing Romans*, 421–22.

92. Witherington, *Philippians*, 216. See also Lincoln, *Paradise*, 97–101.

93. Lincoln, *Paradise*, 89–97.

language here forms a counter-claim to the claims of Paul's opponents.[94] However, Witherington suggests that the primary target of the language here is those who value Roman citizenship.[95] It is not critical to determine the precise opponents, but to recognize the direction of the language: the Philippians belong to something much larger and greater than themselves, a "higher and prior commonwealth."[96] They are, according to Philippians 1:27, to live as citizens worthy of the gospel of Christ, and here Paul directs them to a citizenship not in Philippi, but as 3:20 makes clear, in heaven.[97] As Witherington notes, this citizenship is an alternative to that offered by Caesar, although he argues against a direct critique of the empire here.[98]

Oakes notes that Philippi, whilst probably having a majority Greek population, was nevertheless a Roman city, where inscriptions in Latin language dominated, and where close links with the emperor were cultivated from the time of the battle outside the city in 42 BC and the founding of the Roman colony.[99] We can perhaps see here the particular applicability of Paul's language, which he does not develop elsewhere. It is at this point that the imagery used in Philippians comes closest to the pattern that has emerged from Paul's letters so far: a consciousness that they are part of something bigger which comes through most explicitly in Philippians in the idea of membership of a heavenly commonwealth.

Imitation and Apostleship

Example and Imitation

In chapter 3, I noted how imitation language applies to relationships between churches. First, that the language of imitation demonstrates Paul's concern with group solidarity and mutual encouragement, not just within an ἐκκλησία, but also from ἐκκλησία to ἐκκλησία. And then, second, we saw evidence of Paul's expectation that there will be a shared ethos amongst the churches of, and beyond, the Pauline mission, as Paul considers it of

---

94. Lincoln, *Paradise*, 97–101.
95. Witherington, *Philippians*, 216–17.
96. Witherington, *Philippians*, 217.
97. Copan, *Saint Paul*, 158, notes the parallels between 1:27 and 3:20—4:3 in the call to stand and strive together, and the structural importance of these passages within the letter.
98. Witherington, *Philippians*, 100–102.
99. Oakes, *Philippians*, 5–14.

benefit to churches to imitate what others do, in reception of the gospel, in persevering through suffering, and by implication more widely.

In chapter 4, I noted how the Corinthians were to foster intrachurch solidarity in following Paul's example, by making other-regard central to their behavior, rather than self-interest. In doing so, they are imitating Christ, and seeking to glorify God. By using the language of imitation and example as he does, Paul makes it clear to the Corinthians that they are part of something translocal, and that what happens elsewhere should have an influence on them, whether as conduct to be emulated or avoided. They also have the opportunity, through the collection, to influence what happens elsewhere in a positive way.

In Romans, there is no explicit call by Paul to imitate him, and this is understandable, as Paul has not shared his life with them.[100] However, there are a number of places where imitation is encouraged. In Romans 1, Paul hopes that he and the saints in Rome will mutually encourage one another (Rom 1:13), and commends the fact that their faith is reported all over the world (Rom 1:8).[101] Romans 1:8–15 moves from their example of faith, for which Paul gives thanks (v. 8), through Paul's prayer report (vv. 9–10), to a desire for mutual encouragement (vv. 11–12). Whilst the focus in Romans 1:13–15 is on Paul's activity and his desire to reap a harvest, the desire for mutual encouragement here indicates that, as well as presenting himself as an implicit example for imitation, Paul views the Roman believers as those who are to be imitated. Although Paul's commendation of their faith is not as explicit as 1 Thessalonians 1:6–10, where the way in which the Thessalonians are an example for those in Macedonia and Achaia is explicated, the faith of the Romans can still be taken to include both belief in the gospel and behavior resulting from that belief, in line with Paul's thought elsewhere. Paul wants them to imitate and be imitated, and Romans 1:8–15 indicates that this imitation will reach beyond the local church in Rome.

In Romans 6:17, there is a possible recognition that they have imitated others in becoming obedient to Christ,[102] if the "standard of teaching" here is taken to indicate an agreed-upon early Christian consensus, as was noted in chapter 4 regarding the references to "all the churches" in 1 Corinthians, or Paul's teaching in all the churches in 1 Corinthians 4:17. The additional element here would be the idea that this standard of teaching does not only originate with Paul, appropriate for a church which Paul did not found.

100. So, Clarke, "Imitators," 353.

101. See also Rom 16:19.

102. Understanding τύπος as following personal examples, for this see de Boer, *Imitation*, 21.

In chapter 16, individuals are commended, particularly Phoebe in Romans 16:1-2, but also the various people greeted in Romans 16:3-16.[103] Paul wants them to imitate and be imitated, and Romans 1:8 indicates that this imitation will reach beyond the local church in Rome. There are also indications in Romans of the need to imitate Christ in Romans 15:1-3, where the call not to please self is linked to the fact that Christ did not please himself.[104] Here again we see the focus on Christ as the example of other-regard, which is the behavior the Corinthians were also called to imitate.

There are two occasions within Philippians where imitation of Paul is explicitly encouraged: Philippians 3:17 and 4:9. However, the idea of imitation is present throughout the letter, as Paul presents himself (1:12-26; 3:4-16; 4:10-13), Christ (2:5-11), and others[105] as examples to the Philippians.[106] Thus, when Paul calls the Philippians to join together in imitating him in Philippians 3:17,[107] he has already provided the context for understanding his call. Philippians 4:9 is more explicit, calling for an imitation of what has been heard, received, learned, and seen from Paul.[108] These calls to imitation have a number of implications for ecclesial solidarity.

First, the call to imitation in 3:17 should be primarily related to its immediate context: Paul's example in 3:4-14.[109] In Philippians 3:4-14,[110] Paul's focus is on the surpassing value of knowing Christ and how he has turned aside from other things of value in order to follow Christ.[111] Therefore, when Paul calls the Philippians to imitate him, they are to imitate him as he seeks to follow Christ, which will involve sharing in his sufferings (v. 10). Paul is to be imitated, as he follows and imitates Christ. Both elements of this are important, for Paul presents himself both as one who imitates Christ and also one who follows Christ and receives the benefits of salvation

---

103. Note here Chester, "Pauline Communities," 113, who sees Romans 16 as a practical outworking of Paul's desire to see mutually supportive communities.

104. See Clarke, "Imitators," 353; de Boer, *Imitation*, 62, 158. Jervis, "Becoming like God," 151-55, argues for a wider pattern of conformity to Christ in the letter, but Romans 15:1-3 remains the most explicit call to imitation.

105. Timothy and Epaphroditus are positive examples in 2:19-30, and there are negative examples in 3:17-21 and 4:1-3.

106. For a sample structure which seeks to show the relationship between instruction and example in this letter, see Copan, *Saint Paul*, 152.

107. For this translation, see Copan, *Saint Paul*, 160-61. On the potential subtleties of Paul's usage, see de Boer, *Imitation*, 177-79.

108. Copan, *Saint Paul*, 178-80, on imitation of Paul's teaching and his Christ-orientated life.

109. See Copan, *Saint Paul*, 161-64.

110. See Hawthorne, "Imitation," 173-74, on parallels between 3:4-11 and 2:5-11.

111. See de Boer, *Imitation*, 183-84.

from him by faith (3:8–11). Furthermore, the explicit call to imitate Christ in 2:5–11,[112] in demonstrating humility and care for the interests of others (2:3–4),[113] shows that Paul's concern is with cultivating the right attitude amongst the Philippians, an attitude which is focused on another: Jesus Christ. He is, explicitly and implicitly, the ultimate model, and unity (2:2) in the church in Philippi is to be found in imitating and following him. This unity will be achieved through other-regard, looking first to the needs of others (2:3). Ecclesial solidarity is found in the person and work of Christ, who is the ultimate example of other-regard.

Second, there is a significant focus in the letter on intrachurch solidarity. I have already noted how Christ's example of humility is related to unity, and this call to unity is addressed to the church in Philippi (2:1–4). The call to Euodia and Syntyche to agree[114] in 4:2–3, sandwiched between the two explicit calls to imitation in 3:17 and 4:9, can also be seen as an application of the call to imitate Christ, and also to imitate all that is worthy in what Paul has done (4:8–9).

Third, the call to imitation in 3:17 also involves following other examples. The group of those to be imitated here would include the examples Paul has already given in the letter: Timothy and Epaphroditus.[115] Whilst Epaphroditus is a member of the Philippian church, Timothy and Paul both represent examples from outside Philippi. Imitation, then, as well as being of Christ, can be of others from outside the church in Philippi, all those who walk in the right way. Here we see the Philippians being encouraged to understand themselves as part of a wider grouping. In chapter 4, I noted how the Corinthians needed to take account of what other churches are doing, and here we see a similar idea at the level of individuals expressed in reference to imitation.

Fourth, a wider frame of reference for imitation is also suggested by the link between imitation and heavenly citizenship. The call to behave as citizens of the gospel in 1:27 follows Paul's example of his conduct in 1:12–26, and the call to remember heavenly citizenship in 3:20, in contrast to those whose minds are set on earthly things (3:18–19), follows the call to imitation in 3:17. In both cases, the application of the imitation involves a call to stand firm (1:27; 4:1). Following Paul's example, then, at least in

---

112. See Hawthorne, "Imitation," 166–72, on the appropriateness of imitating Christ from these verses.

113. Clarke, "Imitators," 349–50.

114. See Hawthorne, "Imitation," 176.

115. Copan, *Saint Paul*, 164–67; Hawthorne, "Imitation," 177; de Boer, *Imitation*, 182–83.

part, involves standing firm as one whose citizenship is in heaven, with a consciousness that they are part of something bigger.

In Romans and Philippians, then, we see similar patterns to those observed elsewhere. Imitation is primarily applied to intrachurch relationships, but there are indications of a wider application to interchurch solidarity. It is perhaps also in Philippians that the link between imitation and other-regard, as found in the example of Christ, is made most explicit. The language of imitation indicates that at the heart of ecclesial solidarity lies an other-regard founded on the life and work of Christ.

Apostleship

In chapter 3, I argued that Paul's use of apostleship language implied an ongoing relationship with the churches he founded, and also the sense of a wider grouping of churches, whether founded by Paul or not. In chapter 4, we saw the wider reality of the church in action: there are different apostles, and yet all come with an apostolic message which is the gospel, the message of the cross, and there is a church beyond Corinth, which, through Paul, speaks to the Corinthian Church, speaks with authority, and speaks with a common message of the cross.

Paul does not refer to himself as an apostle in Philippians, referring to himself as a slave/servant in 1:1, and this is most likely because this fits his purposes in writing the letter, encouraging the Philippians to follow Christ's example of humble self-giving.[116] He does, however, refer to Epaphroditus as ἀπόστολον in Philippians 2:25, and this is most likely a reference to his role as a messenger from the Philippians, and is similar in usage to 2 Corinthians 8:23.[117] Paul refers to himself as an apostle twice in Romans. In Romans 1:1, he is an apostle set apart for the gospel, and that apostleship (v. 5) is for the sake of all the nations, and includes those in Rome. Here, Paul's apostleship means that he has the authority to address the Romans, even though this is not a church he founded; and, as in the earlier letters, that authority is linked to a specific call to preach the gospel (1:1). Paul gives a longer summary of the content of the message of the gospel (1:2–4) at the start of the letter, which may be a way of further establishing his credentials. In Romans 11:13, Paul acknowledges his role as apostle to the gentiles, in the context of his discussion of Jewish salvation in Romans 9–11. Here again we see how that apostolic role clearly included many (perhaps the majority) within

---

116. Hawthorne, "Imitation," 172–3. See also de Boer, *Imitation*, 184–86 on Paul's stance in this letter contra Michaelis.

117. See Witherington, *Philippians*, 174; Schmithals, *Office*, 60–61.

the Roman church. Finally, in Romans 16:7, Paul refers to a wider group of apostles.[118] Here we see a similar pattern to that which was observed in chapter 4. Paul also sees himself as a representative of other churches in his role as emissary for the Jerusalem collection (Rom 15:28).

In Romans, there is a similar pattern to elsewhere in Paul's letters: Paul comes as an apostle, whose authority rests in preaching the common message of the cross, one of a larger group of apostles, but with a particular role to the gentiles.

Conclusion

In the use of ἐκκλησία in Philippians and Romans, we see a focus on intrachurch solidarity and unity, but also an acknowledgement and encouragement of interchurch solidarity. I have noted a number of places in Romans where Paul is concerned with unity in Rome and have described this as intrachurch solidarity. However, I noted earlier that if the domestic churches in Rome never met together, this designation may need to be questioned. Two observations follow. First, if the churches in Rome did not meet together, these appeals for ecclesial solidarity are strengthened, and can be considered a more significant purpose of the letter. Second, it is possible to redefine these relationships as interchurch solidarity. However, the amount of the hortatory section of the letter which is concerned with solidarity in Rome (Rom 12:3-8 on the body; 14:1—15:13 on the strong and the weak) suggests that Paul believes there should be considerable shared fellowship, even if that does not extend to the "whole church" meeting together, as in Corinth, and therefore the designation "intrachurch solidarity" should be retained, whilst recognizing the limitations of a strict intra/inter distinction.

In Paul's use of imagery, we see that the language of brothers in Philippians and Romans is almost exclusively directed towards intrachurch solidarity. There are some points where an awareness of a wider brotherhood seems likely, but the focus is on solidarity within the local church. In Philippians, Paul applies the language of saints to intrachurch solidarity. In Romans, "saints" can be used for a domestic church, the local church in Rome or elsewhere, and for believers in general. The flexibility mirrors that already noted in the use of ἐκκλησία. It is a term which encourages intrachurch solidarity by reminding the Romans of their identity as God's holy people, but also encourages interchurch solidarity by indicating that

---

118. See Jewett, *Romans*, 961–4, for a discussion of the gender of Junia and the likely origin of Andronicus and Junia. How and whether these two are to be included amongst the apostles is not a critical issue for this study.

holy people includes saints in other places as well, and can be considered as a whole. The focus of σῶμα in Romans is on the local church in Rome, suggesting a particular concern with intrachurch solidarity in Rome, although Paul's use of the first-person plural gives the sense of wider body. In Philippians, the language of heavenly commonwealth comes closest to the pattern that has emerged from Paul's letters so far: a consciousness that they are part of something bigger, which comes through most explicitly in Philippians in the idea of membership of a heavenly commonwealth. Thus, whilst the imagery in these letters is largely directed towards intrachurch solidarity, the focus does not entirely shift away from interchurch solidarity.

In imitation and apostleship in Romans and Philippians, we see similar patterns to those observed elsewhere. Imitation is primarily applied to intrachurch relationships, but there are indications of a wider application to interchurch solidarity. It is perhaps also in Philippians that the link between imitation and other-regard, as found in the example of Christ, is made most explicit. In Romans, Paul comes as an apostle, whose authority rests in preaching the common message of the cross, one of a larger group of apostles, but with a particular role to the gentiles.

6. Colossians and Ephesians

IN THIS CHAPTER, I will examine the letters to the Ephesians and Colossians. If these letters are considered to have been written by Paul,[1] then they would be roughly contemporaneous with Philippians.[2] However, as noted in chapter 1, I have chosen to treat these letters in a separate chapter, as they are generally considered to have a more developed ecclesiology.[3]

Ecclesial Solidarity and ἐκκλησία

In chapters 3 to 5, I have argued that ἐκκλησία is used to encourage intrachurch solidarity by promoting a common identity in Christ, which is expressed in brotherly behavior which builds up and has an active regard for holiness. I have also noted how interchurch solidarity receives much more attention from Paul than is commonly acknowledged, through two aspects of Paul's writing. First, in Paul's tendency to group ἐκκλησίαι together, whether provincially as ἐκκλησίαι of God or as the ἐκκλησία of God, irrespective of whether or not Paul founded the ἐκκλησία. Second, through Paul's use of the language of "all the churches," particularly in the Corinthian correspondence, which indicates a recognition of solidarity at the level of behavior beyond the local church, expressing common identity in beliefs and practices. I have also noted how the focus on intra or interchurch solidarity varies by letter. In coming to Ephesians and Colossians, I will explore how intra- and interchurch solidarity are expressed in these letters, looking first at the idea of a heavenly church, and then examining each letter in turn.

---

1. I will use "Paul" as a convenient term for the author(s) of these letters throughout this chapter.

2. See for example recent discussions in Moo, *Colossians*, 41–46, who dates Colossians to AD 60–61, and Hoehner, *Ephesians*, 92–97, who dates Ephesians to AD 60–62.

3. Dunn, *Theology*, 540–41, provides a good summary of this position, where the use of ἐκκλησία in Colossians and Ephesians is a development from Paul's position, but not a dramatic one. An argument for greater ecclesiological development between Paul's earlier letters and Colossians and Ephesians is made in MacDonald, *Pauline Churches*, 86–122.

Ἐκκλησία: Heavenly or Universal?

There are four occurrences of ἐκκλησία in Colossians,[4] and nine in Ephesians.[5] All of the occurrences are singular, and eleven are generally considered to have a wider or "more universal" reference.[6] However, O'Brien argues that the wider usage of ἐκκλησία in Colossians and Ephesians, rather than being a reference to the universal church, is a reference to the heavenly church.[7] He argues that, in Greek, ἐκκλησία means an assembly that existed only when assembled, not an organization or society,[8] that Paul uses ἐκκλησία for an actual assembly and ἐκκλησίαι for assemblies or churches in 1 Thessalonians, and that this usage is seen in Paul's other letters.[9] He notes possible exceptions to this usage, but argues that they are not actually exceptions: in 1 Corinthians 4:17, ἐκκλησία should be translated "every church";[10] 1 Corinthians 10:32 is generic and possibly localized;[11] and in Galatians 1:13, the church in Jerusalem is in view, or possibly individual gatherings where arrests were made.[12] Then, he argues that in Colossians 1:18 and 1:24, the root meaning of gathering or assembly needs to be preserved, and therefore a scattered, universal church cannot be in view here;[13] instead, the heavenly context of Colossians 1:8 and 1:24, and of Ephesians 2:5–6, indicate that the heavenly church is in view—God's people as presently gathered around Christ, who enjoy fellowship with him.[14] He describes the language here as figurative and metaphorical.[15] He acknowledges that the relationship between the earthly and heavenly assemblies is not discussed in the New

---

4. Col 1:18, 24; 4:15–16.

5. Eph 1:23; 3:10, 21; 5:23–25, 27, 29, 32.

6. All except Colossians 4:15–16. According to Best, "the whole group of Christians in all parts of the world" (*Ephesians*, 623). Hoehner, *Ephesians*, 287.

7. Whilst I trace O'Brien's arguments here, see also similar arguments in Banks, *Paul's Idea*, 27–31, 37–46. Lyons "Church and Holiness," 238–39.

8. O'Brien, *Colossians*, 57–58; O'Brien, "Church," 90; Banks, *Paul's Idea*, 27–28.

9. O'Brien, *Colossians*, 59; O'Brien, "Church," 91; Banks, *Paul's Idea*, 29. O'Brien, *Colossians*, 59.

10. O'Brien, *Colossians*, 59; O'Brien, "Church," 91–92; Banks, *Paul's Idea*, 30.

11. O'Brien, *Colossians*, 59; O'Brien, "Church," 92.

12. O'Brien, *Colossians*, 59–60; Banks, *Paul's Idea*, 30.

13. O'Brien, *Colossians*, 60; O'Brien, *Letter to the Ephesians*, 146n220; O'Brien, "Church," 93.

14. O'Brien, *Colossians*, 60–61; O'Brien, "Church," 93–94.

15. O'Brien, *Ephesians*, 25–26, 147.

Testament, but argues that the earthly should be seen not as merely parts of the heavenly, but as earthly manifestations of the heavenly assembly.[16]

Commentators have sometimes noted O'Brien's arguments.[17] However, direct engagement with them has been largely neglected. One exception to this is Kevin Giles, who argues that O'Brien makes two errors in his understanding.[18] First, by assuming that ἐκκλησία means assembly, and second by arguing that it is only possible to speak of "the church" when ἐκκλησία is used.[19] Giles suggests instead that ἐκκλησία is not the best starting point for understanding church, positing rather a "church concept" of "the Christian community,"[20] stating that "it is our argument that the concept of 'the Christian community' is the reality implied by the more developed uses of the word ekklesia/church, this expression profoundly captures the essence of our communal existence in Christ, and all other ecclesiological terms and metaphors can be subsumed under this one category."[21] By rejecting ἐκκλησία as the starting point, and by proceeding from the developed concept back into the NT, I believe that Giles's approach does not allow sufficient engagement with O'Brien's arguments. Therefore, although I am largely in agreement with Giles's two critiques of O'Brien, I have sought in this thesis to provide a more thorough exegetical examination of terminology to argue for a translocal use of ἐκκλησία which is not the heavenly church.

I have argued in chapter 2 that the Greek literary and Septuagint usage of ἐκκλησία is more flexible than O'Brien allows, is influenced by context, and should not be a limitation on Paul's usage. Therefore, whilst ἐκκλησία is primarily used outside the NT for an assembly as it assembles, this cannot dictate its meaning in the NT. In chapter 3, I noted how, in 1 Thessalonians and Galatians, ἐκκλησία is used in a way which implies translocal connections and interchurch solidarity, and in chapter 4 I argued for a number of places in the Corinthian correspondence where there are singular collective usages of ἐκκλησία which are not in a heavenly context and references to the heavenly church, but rather to the translocal church, as well as noting in chapter 5 a similar reference in Philippians. I have also argued that ἐκκλησία

---

16. O'Brien, "Church," 97.
17. See Moo, *Colossians*, 127; Hoehner, *Ephesians*, 111.
18. See Giles, *What on Earth*, 127–30, who traces this view back to Knox/Robinson, for which see chapters 1 and 2. See also, for example, Knox, *Sent By Jesus*, 19: "[Christians'] heavenly existence is their real existence and the heavenly assembly of which they are part is the real assembly, ecclesia or church, of which the local assemblies are the earthly and transitory counterparts or expressions."
19. Giles, *What on Earth*, 128–29.
20. Giles, *What on Earth*, 15–19.
21. Giles, *What on Earth*, 18.

needs to be examined in conjunction with other terminology for the church in order to understand Paul's usage, and in particular to understand his approach to ecclesial solidarity,[22] but that that investigation needs to begin with and continue to relate to how Paul uses ἐκκλησία. Therefore, I would argue that the idea of the heavenly ἐκκλησία is not a necessary implication of Paul's use of ἐκκλησία for a group that is unable to assemble. However, I would also argue that the terminology of universal ἐκκλησία should also be avoided, due to its later theological connotations,[23] and that "whole" ἐκκλησία remains the best description for the ἐκκλησία viewed translocally.

I will explore each of the thirteen occurrences of ἐκκλησία in these two letters, and their implications for ecclesial solidarity.

Colossians

Two of the four references to ἐκκλησία in Colossians are to local churches. Colossians 4:15 refers to a domestic church meeting in the house of Nympha,[24] and Colossians 4:16 refers to the church of the Laodiceans. Both occurrences are in the final section of the letter, as Paul sends greetings to various individuals and groups. As elsewhere in the Pauline corpus, these references function to encourage mutual recognition between churches in different places. The call to have Colossians read to the Laodiceans is a reminder that Paul's teaching is the same in all the churches, and suggests a mechanism whereby Paul's letters were distributed on that basis.

Colossians 1:18 is a collective singular reference to the wider ἐκκλησία, and needs to be seen in the context of Colossians 1.[25] Paul's thanksgiving in Colossians 1:3–8 and prayer report in 1:9–14 climax with a declaration in Colossians 1:13–14 of status, expressed in terms of a transfer of kingdoms from darkness to light (v. 13) and redemption/forgiveness of sins (v. 14).[26]

---

22. See also Stenschke, "Significance and Function of References," 188–89, who focuses on believers, saints, and brothers as terminology which can illuminate translocal relationships.

23. For example, Turretin, *Institutes*, 3:8.

24. For a recent discussion of the identity of Nympha, see Sumney, *Colossians*, 278–79.

25. Compare Sumney, *Colossians*, 71–72, who argues for a different application of the language of church here from 1 Corinthians 12 where intracommunity relations were in view.

26. Sumney, *Colossians*, 30–31, argues that the introductory thanksgiving and prayer extends from 1:3–23, but notes the sections given here. Compare O'Brien, *Introductory Thanksgivings*, 71–75, who takes the thanksgiving period to be 1:3–14, but also the need to recognize that the thanksgiving period passes into a hymn.

Then, various things are asserted of Christ in Colossians 1:15–20, before the assertions are applied to the Colossians in 1:21–23.[27] Paul's statement in 1:18 that Christ is the head of the body, of the ἐκκλησία, should be seen in the context of reassuring the Colossians of their status, as those who belong to the kingdom of God's Son (v. 13) and have been reconciled by his death (v. 22).

The reassurance given to the Colossians here has been variously described. There is a recognition that a close relationship is expressed here,[28] that in some sense the Colossians share in Christ's dignity and position,[29] and that Christ has a particular role in caring for the church as his body, which Barth links to Colossians 2:19, and how the head protects, provides, and gives growth.[30] The reassurance provided here is reassurance of identity in Christ, and of the protection and provision which Christ provides.[31] However, I would argue for two reasons that there is an additional element of reassurance here which is overlooked: that of being part of a grouping that is wider than Colossae. First, Paul writes of his ministry in 1:23, a reminder that, although the language here has a cosmic scope, it is directly related to earthly realities, such as the reality of the wider church beyond Colossae. Second, in chapters 3 to 5 of this book, I have argued that ἐκκλησία can be used in the collective singular for an identifiable physical grouping, a grouping not best described by either the terminology of heavenly or universal, but rather by the designation "whole church." Certainly, the focus here is on identity with Jesus Christ, but this verse may also function as a reminder of relations between churches, all of whom share this identity in Christ.

In Colossians 1:24, Paul describes an activity undertaken for his body, ὅ ἐστιν ἡ ἐκκλησία. A number of interpretive difficulties have been identified in this verse, principally in seeking to understand how Paul fills up what is lacking in Christ's afflictions.[32] Sumney notes that the most common

27. Sumney, *Colossians*, 80.
28. Bruce, *Epistles to the Colossians*, 69–71.
29. Sumney, *Colossians*, 73.
30. Barth and Blanke, *Colossians*, 206. See also Moo, *Colossians*, 128. Dunn, *Colossians*, 96, notes that significant claims are made for the church here.
31. Further examples of how this passage works to reassure the Colossians of their status in Christ can be seen in Knowles, "Christ in You," 186. Arnold, *Colossian Syncretism*, 259–60, argues that Paul is encouraging the Colossians to rely only on Christ for salvation and not an additional philosophy.
32. For a recent survey of the options here, see Sumney, "I Fill Up," 664–80. Spivey, "Colossians 1:24 and the Suffering Church," 43–62, argues that these sufferings are part of Paul's apostolic mission, but apply to the whole church, and therefore that suffering can be considered a fifth mark of the church. However, the focus in Colossians 1:24 is on something that Paul does, in contrast with the plurals used in vv. 3 and 9. See also

interpretation of the sufferings here is that they are something like the messianic woes pictured in much apocalyptic literature,[33] and this may well provide the best explanation; certainly Paul's sufferings are not salvific, as this would contradict the statements made in Colossians 1. Sumney helpfully focuses on the rhetorical function of the sufferings here, and proposes that Paul's sufferings function to demonstrate his trustworthiness to the Colossians.[34] He argues that Paul's suffering is mimetic, and serves as an implicit example to the Colossians to maintain the teaching advocated in the letter.[35] Important here is the parallel between Paul suffering for the sake of the Colossians and his suffering for the sake of Christ's body.[36] This parallel draws attention to the connection between what Paul does for them and for the whole church. Here the Colossians are encouraged to see themselves as one of the beneficiaries of Paul's apostolic mission, and therefore part of the ἐκκλησία for which Paul suffers.

In Colossians 1:18, I noted how the focus was on how the whole ἐκκλησία relates to Christ, although I also argued for a possible reminder of interchurch relationships. In Colossians 1:24, Paul's focus is on the purpose of his apostolic mission, but the argument develops in a way which encourages the Colossians to see themselves as part of the wider ἐκκλησία. In Colossians, Paul continues to use ἐκκλησία for the local church, but also for the whole church; with a primary focus on the church's identity in Christ, but where there is an implicit encouragement to view themselves as part of the wider church.

Ephesians

All nine references to ἐκκλησία in Ephesians are collective singular references to the whole church, a fact that has frequently been noted. However, attention needs to be given to how these references function in the letter, and how they encourage ecclesial solidarity.

In Ephesians 1:22–23, Paul describes how God has put all things under Christ's feet, and how he is given as head of all things to the ἐκκλησία, which is his body. Two issues in v. 22 need to be resolved. First, the precise meaning of head in v. 22 has received considerable attention, with considerable

---

O'Brien, *Colossians*, 75–76; Best, *One Body*, 130–36.

33. Sumney, *Colossians*, 100. For the apocalyptic view, see O'Brien, *Colossians*, 77–80.

34. Sumney, *Colossians*, 100–101; Sumney, "I fill Up," 666.

35. Sumney, *Colossians*, 101; Sumney, "I fill Up," 669–72.

36. Sumney, *Colossians*, 101–2. O'Brien, *Colossians*, 76–7.

discussion as to whether source or authority is the meaning here.[37] As Best notes,[38] Christ is depicted as ruler in Ephesians 1:22, and therefore in the immediate context, it is hard to escape a headship over the cosmos which implies rule and authority.[39] Second, Christ's headship here is not said to be directly over the ἐκκλησία, but over all things τῇ ἐκκλησίᾳ. Taking δίδωμι as "to give" rather than "to appoint" here yields an understanding whereby Christ is given to the ἐκκλησία,[40] emphasizing God's graciousness, but also working in a similar way to Colossians 1:18, to reassure the Ephesians of their status in Christ, the one who rules all things.

These verses need to be examined in the context of Ephesians 1 in order to understand how ἐκκλησία is being used here. In Ephesians 1:3–14, Paul describes the blessings that the Ephesians have received in Christ. Whilst this section of the epistle is difficult to structure, Paul moves in vv. 3–10 from a description of God's work in Christ to the application of that work to the lives of the Ephesians in vv. 11–14.[41] The passage moves from eternal election and predestination (v. 4) through redemption in Christ's blood (v. 7) to consummation and fulfilment (vv. 9–10). This overarching, eternal perspective is then related to Paul's addressees in vv. 11–14. Paul moves in Ephesians 1:15–23 to thanksgiving and prayer, where the intercessory prayer report (vv. 16b–19) focuses on what the Ephesians need to know, which is explicated in vv. 20–23.[42] When Paul states that Christ is the head of all things "to the church," he is passing on information about Christ which he believes the addressees need to know, just as they need to know of the blessings they have received in 1:3–14. Paul's words would act to reassure the Ephesians of the supremacy of Christ,[43] and how that supremacy is for the church, and therefore the language of the whole ἐκκλησία is used

---

37. See for example Barth, *Ephesians 1–3*, 183–92; Arnold "Jesus Christ: 'Head,'" 350–66.

38. Best, *Ephesians*, 196. See also Lincoln, *Ephesians*, 70; O'Brien, *Ephesians*, 148; Hoehner, *Ephesians*, 292. Fowl, *Ephesians*, 62–63, emphasizes both rule and organic connection between Christ and the church.

39. Arnold, *Power and Magic*, 158–65, notes the focus here on the authority of Christ.

40. So, Fowl, *Ephesians*, 63; Hoehner, *Ephesians*, 289; Lincoln, *Ephesians*, 66–67; Best, *Ephesians*, 182; O'Brien, *Ephesians*, 145. Cf. Barth, *Ephesians 1–3*, 157–58.

41. So, O'Brien, *Ephesians*, 92; Also Fowl, *Ephesians*, 34. See also Lincoln, *Ephesians*, 15–16.

42. For the structure of this passage, recognizing the move from thanksgiving, through a prayer report to the content of the thanksgiving, see O'Brien, *Ephesians*, 124; Lincoln, *Ephesians*, 47; Hoehner, *Ephesians*, 247, 252–53.

43. Arnold, *Power and Magic*, 167.

here with a particular focus on the relationship of the ἐκκλησία to Christ. The Ephesians are encouraged to remember who they are in Christ.

In Ephesians 3:10, Paul declares that the manifold wisdom of God is being made known to the "heavenly powers" through the ἐκκλησία, and in Ephesians 3:21, glory is to be given to God in the ἐκκλησία and in Christ Jesus. The manifold wisdom here in v. 10 is related to the revelation of the μυστήριον of v. 9. Caragounis argues that μυστήριον is used in two related senses in Ephesians. In 1:9-10, it is used for the inscrutable plan of God, which leads to the goal of summing up all things in Christ (1:10), whereas in Ephesians 3:2-13, it refers to the inclusion of the gentiles, v. 6, part of the process of summing up all things, which is being revealed to the powers (vv. 9-10).[44] Thus, what is being made known through the ἐκκλησία is God's plan for gentile inclusion.[45]

A key question here is how that plan is made known. Some argue that the revelation is through the existence of the church, not any particular activity,[46] whilst others, although acknowledging the lack of specifics here, would argue that some activity of the church is involved.[47] I would argue that there are a number of reasons for thinking that the activity of the "whole" church is involved. First, Hoehner argues that the use of the preposition διά, rather than ἐν, indicates that God's wisdom should be displayed by what the church does, rather than its mere existence.[48] Second, the revelation of the mystery is related to Paul's preaching as an apostle to the gentiles in v. 8, not just his existence, and it is reasonable to expect a similar thought in v. 10. Third, in 3:14-19, Paul prays that they would know the love of Christ, and be filled with the fullness of God, indicating activity which is ongoing,[49] having resumed the argument he left off in v. 1. This resumption highlights the importance of 2:20-22 and Paul's use of metaphors, which

---

44. Caragounis, *Ephesian Mysterion*, 112-13, 139-42. Hoehner, *Ephesians*, 428-34 prefers to confine the mystery here in Ephesians 3 to the fact that both believing Jews and gentiles become one new entity: Christians. He focuses on the newness of the church and the revealing of God's plan which was not known before, but which is now revealed. However, this does not appear to take sufficient account of 1:9-10, particularly given the foundational nature of 1:3-10 for the letter.

45. Which has also been a concern in 2:11-22, and fits with Paul's references to his role regarding the gentiles in 3:1 and 8.

46. O'Brien, *Ephesians*, 247-48; Lincoln, *Ephesians*, 186-87; Best, *Ephesians*, 325.

47. Fowl, *Ephesians*, 112; Barth, *Ephesians 1-3*, 364-65.

48. Hoehner, *Ephesians*, 460.

49. In 1:23, the church, the body of Christ, is described as his fullness; here in 3:19, Paul prays that believers will be filled by all the fullness of God. The church, believers, are then at one and the same time the fullness of Christ, and something which needs to be filled with all the fullness of God.

indicate that the Ephesian Christians are a building because of the unifying work of Christ (2:13–19), but are also a temple under construction (v. 22). Therefore, throughout this section of the letter, there is a focus on what has been achieved, but also on what is still being achieved, and I would argue that this pattern can also be seen in 3:10. Finally, the exhortations beginning in 4:1 and extending through the second half of the letter highlight that unity exists, but it also needs to be actively maintained.[50]

The ἐκκλησία, then, is the place where God's mystery is revealed, both by the existence of the '"whole" church as the place where Jews and gentiles are united in one new man (2:15), but also by the activity of the church. I would argue that the activity that Paul has in mind here is the activity described in chapters 4 to 6 of Ephesians, because of the continued focus on unity in these chapters. In Ephesians 3:21, Paul prays that God will receive glory in the ἐκκλησία and in Christ Jesus, before beginning 4:1 with an exhortation to walk worthily. There is a continued focus on unity in Ephesians 4:1—6:9:[51] in the use of ἑνότης in 4:1-16 as both reality and goal in 4:3 and 4:13; in the exhortations in 4:25–32 focusing on activity which is for οἰκοδομή (v. 29), encouraging kindness towards one another (v. 32), as those who are members of one another (v. 25); in the call to imitate God together in 5:1; and in the call for mutual encouragement (v. 19) and submission (v. 21) in 5:15—6:9.

Taking Ephesians 3:10 and 21 in their wider context shows that the whole church makes known the manifold wisdom of God, by its existence, and by its activity. I have argued that the activity involved here is that described in Ephesians 4:1—6:9, and this has important implications for ecclesial solidarity. First, there is a strong assertion here of the established fact of ecclesial solidarity: the whole church is a witness because of the Jew and gentile unity which has been achieved in Christ, and therefore the whole church has an established solidarity in Christ. Second, there is a strong link made between the established solidarity of the whole church and activity which takes place in the local ἐκκλησία, as seen in 4:1—6:9. Living worthy of the calling (4:1) entails behavior which will take place in the local ἐκκλησία. Here Paul applies the established fact of translocal solidarity to the local situation of the Ephesian ἐκκλησία to encourage unity and solidarity.

---

50. See Barth, *Ephesians 1–3*, 364–65. Mouton, *Reading*, 78–79, provides a summary of the many metaphors, particularly in the second half of the letter, which refer to the "New Ethos" of the church, highlighting the need to maintain unity in the community.

51. See Hoehner, *Ephesians*, 500, on the structure of this section.

The final six references to ἐκκλησία in Ephesians[52] all occur in Paul's exhortation to wives and husbands in Ephesians 5:22-33. Many treat this section of Ephesians as the beginning of a *Haustafel*, essentially divorced from what precedes. That is not possible grammatically, because of the dependence of 5:22 on 5:21.[53] However, there is a shift here from exhortations which relate to the whole community, to exhortations which relate to some within the community, although almost all, if not all, members of the community will be addressed at some point in 5:22—6:9. The twin themes of the previous passage, maintaining unity and proclaiming Christ, continue into this section, as what submission means in certain relationships is examined.

A number of writers have helpfully highlighted the structure of this passage, and how it shifts between addressing wives and husbands and demonstrating the relationship between Christ and the ἐκκλησία.[54] Wives are addressed first (vv. 22-24) and then husbands twice (vv. 25-28a, vv. 28b-31), before concluding statements in 5:32-33.[55] Sampley also notes how the passage shifts between address to readers and rehearsal of God's activity, which in turn leads to an address to readers, and so on.[56] I will therefore examine this passage in three sections: vv. 22-24, 25-27, and 28-33.

In 5:22-24, Paul calls wives to submit to husbands, and draws an analogy between wives and husbands and the ἐκκλησία and Christ. Christ and the husband are both head, and the ἐκκλησία and wives are to submit, although Christ is uniquely the savior (v. 23), which introduces an important disjunction: the analogy between Christ and the husband is not exact. Dawes identifies headship as a metaphor related to the "body model"[57]

---

52. Eph 5:23-25, 27, 29, 32.

53. Some have read the call to "mutual submission" in 5:21 as determinative for what follows, or as creating a tension with what follows. See for example Dawes, *Body in Question*, 212-15, 227-28; Sampley, *And the Two*, 117. Lincoln, *Ephesians*, 365-66. However, O'Brien, *Ephesians*, 399-404, argues that submission describes not a symmetrical relationship, but an ordered one, and that what submission means in v. 21 can only be seen when v. 22 is examined. Given the careful structure of the letter so far, it seems strange that Paul, or any other author, would fail to note a contradiction here, or that he would make the interpretation of the passage so unclear as to allow mutual submission to override what would otherwise be the most obvious interpretation of 5:22-33. Nor is it satisfactory to highlight a tension if another interpretation is possible, as is the case here. Therefore, if submission in v. 21 is part of the general exhortation to maintain unity and proclaim Christ in 4:17—5:21, then its use in 5:22-33 will be an application of that in specific situations.

54. See for example Sampley, *And the Two*, 114-47; Dawes, *Body in Question*, 81-109.

55. Dawes, *Body in Question*, 91-107.

56. Sampley, *And the Two*, 11-12.

57. Dawes, *Body in Question*, 122-24.

due to the close juxtaposition of related terms, and argues for a contextual meaning of authority rather than source.[58]

These four relationships are further considered in 5:25–28b. Husbands are exhorted to love their wives after the model of Christ. Then, in vv. 25b–27, Christ's activity for the ἐκκλησία is described before this activity is applied to husbands in v. 28a. This passage has received a great deal of attention, as Sampley's survey of the *hieros gamos*, or divine marriage, shows.[59] As Sampley has argued, the background to the passage is Ezekiel 16, where the focus falls on all that God has done for his bride Jerusalem.[60] This serves to provide husbands with a model for how to love their wives, whilst at the same time underlining the extent of Christ's care for the ἐκκλησία, and although Ephesians does not use bride-of-Christ imagery for the ἐκκλησία, the allusions to Ezekiel 16 underline the closeness of relationship between Christ and his ἐκκλησία.

In addition, Dawes notes that the reference to body in v. 28a is a reference to a literal body,[61] but recalls the imagery of v. 23. Husbands ought to love their wives as their own bodies; Christ loves his body, the ἐκκλησία. The correspondences here are not exact, in that Christ's activity for the ἐκκλησία, saving and presenting pure, are not replicated by the husband.[62] In addition, the wife is not the husband's body, but should be loved like his body.

The picture is further developed in 5:28b–33. This section begins where the other ends: he who loves his wife loves himself. Next there is an argument from common sense: everyone cares for their bodies, cherishing and nourishing them.[63] The argument then shifts to a reference to Christ's care for the ἐκκλησία. In v. 30, the argument undergoes another shift, as all are members of the body of Christ, cutting across the previous distinctions between husbands and wives. This is then underlined with the quotation of Genesis 2:24 in v. 31, prepared for by the reference to flesh in v. 28,[64] which dramatically demonstrates the close association between Christ and his ἐκκλησία, which has been building through the passage.

58. Dawes, *Body in Question*, 134–37.
59. Sampley, *And the Two*, 34–51.
60. Sampley, *And the Two*, 40–41.
61. Dawes, *Body in Question*, 152–54
62. Lincoln, *Ephesians*, 370.
63. O'Brien, *Ephesians*, 427–28 notes the appropriateness of this language for marriage.
64. O'Brien, *Ephesians*, 429; Lincoln, *Ephesians*, 380.

The mystery of v. 32 is the close relationship between Christ and the ἐκκλησία. However, as O'Brien argues, human marriage is not excluded here, because it speaks of the relationship between Christ and the ἐκκλησία.[65] Finally, v. 33 repeats the exhortation to love wives, and for wives to fear husbands, thus drawing v. 21 into an inclusion, where Paul talks of the fear of Christ.

Notice here that the twin exhortations to wives and husbands are addressed to those within a local congregation, as can be seen by the plurals in vv. 22 and 25, and yet, at the same time, v. 33 generalizes the statements already made in terms of love and fear. In addition, the relationship between individual wives and husbands is related to the relationship between Christ and his ἐκκλησία, his body, and it is then husband and wife together who are classified as members of Christ's body.

Furthermore, the use of μυστήριον in 5:22 links back to the language of μυστήριον used in Ephesians 3 for how the whole ἐκκλησία demonstrates to the powers, both by its existence and its actions, the plan of God. When the marriage relationship functions properly, it demonstrates something of the unity between Christ and his ἐκκλησία, and is therefore part of this declaration to the powers of the will of God to bring all things under the feet of Christ. The marriage relationship serves as a picture of Christ's relationship with his ἐκκλησία. As unity is maintained in the church through this properly ordered relationship, the plan of God in Christ is proclaimed to the powers.

There are two implications of this passage for our understanding of ecclesial solidarity. First, this section serves to underline Christ's sacrificial love for his church, and the dependence of the church on Christ. Ecclesial solidarity is rooted in Christ. Second, the maintenance of submission and love within a marital relationship is an issue of local church solidarity, as the solidarity in Christ of the whole ἐκκλησία is applied to marital relationships within the local ἐκκλησία; however, at the same time, the maintenance of appropriate marital relationships within the local ἐκκλησία can be seen as a witness to the reality of Christ's relationship with the church, and thus part of the revelation to the powers of Ephesians 3:10. Therefore, rather than seeing this passage as an application of the translocal to the local, I would see it rather as an example of behavior in the local ἐκκλησία being predicated on a translocal reality, which then expresses that translocal reality in concrete terms.

---

65. O'Brien, *Ephesians*, 430–35, provides a summary of the interpretative options. See also Lincoln, *Ephesians*, 381; Sampley, *And the Two*, 90–96; Hoehner, *Ephesians*, 775–81.

Conclusion

Having examined the use of ἐκκλησία in Colossians and Ephesians, a number of conclusions can be drawn. First, Colossians shows the continued local usage of ἐκκλησία. Second, Colossians 1:18 and Ephesians 1:23 show the idea of the wider ἐκκλησία being used to encourage the church in Colossae and Ephesus respectively. Third, Colossians 1:24 shows the wider ἐκκλησία being used as an encouragement to those in the local ἐκκλησία in Colossae to persevere. Fourth, Ephesians 3:10 and 3:21 show how the reality of the wider ἐκκλησία, and particularly what that wider reality expresses, is used to encourage unity and solidarity in the local ἐκκλησία. Finally, Ephesians 5 demonstrates a similar usage to Ephesians 3, but with an indication of how marriage relationships within the local ἐκκλησία express the wider reality. There are then significant similarities here with what has already been observed in chapters 3 to 5, but also considerable differences of expression.

Imagery

Brothers and Family Imagery

Compared to the other letters surveyed here, there are comparatively few references to brothers in Colossians and Ephesians. Horrell argues that this indicates a move in Colossians and Ephesians from Paul's language of brothers, with its emphasis on relations among brothers, to a desire to give ethical instruction, "according to their position within the household,"[66] indicative of a shift from egalitarian to hierarchical structures.[67] However, Darko notes the extensive use of kinship language in Ephesians,[68] and the use of brothers in a context of deep affection in 6:21–24,[69] whilst a number of authors note that the language of brothers is not necessarily egalitarian.[70] Furthermore, I have noted how "brothers" is only one of the ways in which Paul expresses his concern for solidarity, and that other imagery and the language of imitation also have ethical implications. Nevertheless, the comparative infrequency of the usage here is noticeable.

---

66. Horrell, "From ἀδελφοί to οἶκος θεοῦ," 304–6.

67. Horrell, "From ἀδελφοί to οἶκος θεοῦ," 310.

68. Darko, *No Longer Living*, 101–5.

69. Darko, *No Longer Living*, 104n181. Darco is also critical of Horrell's method, shifting from examining fictive language in the undisputed letters to examining admonitions on household relations in Colossians and Ephesians.

70. Clarke, "Equality or Mutuality," 164; Aasgaard, *Brothers and Sisters*, 91.

Four times Paul refers to another Christian as a brother, referring to Timothy in Colossians 1:1,[71] Tychicus in Colossians 4:7[72] and Ephesians 6:21, and Onesimus in Colossians 4:9.[73] As elsewhere, these references function to remind the Colossians and Ephesians of their solidarity with other believers,[74] indicate close relationship (beloved), and demonstrate the kind of behavior which is appropriate for a brother (faithful).

In Colossians 1:2, Paul writes to the saints and faithful brothers in Christ at Colossae. Dunn notes the addition of faithful here to the usual designation brothers, arguing that it reinforces the primary appeal of the letter.[75] Here we see the designation brothers used for the believing community at Colossae, in a way which highlights their fictive kinship.

In Ephesians 6:23, Paul also writes to the brothers. His use of the third-person address here is unusual and has been taken to indicate that this is a general or circular letter, or a letter that will be circulated,[76] or as a deliberate, more general reference to a wider audience.[77] I would argue that both a local and translocal reference is in view here in Ephesians 6:23-24. Whilst the construction is unusual, it follows the commendation of Tychicus in 6:21-22, as the one who will maintain and foster a close relationship between Paul and the Ephesians, and therefore I take the primary reference for brothers in 6:23 to be to those in Ephesus. As Best notes, "brothers" is used here to indicate a relationship between author and recipients,[78] and therefore 6:23 fosters solidarity between Paul and the Ephesians, who are brothers, and whose brotherly relations will be encouraged by the beloved brother Tychicus. The wider reference comes in 6:24: the use of "all" here, and the reference to "in immortality" or "forever" suggest a more generalized group, and given how 6:23-24 reflects the opening benediction of

---

71. Timothy is described as a brother rather than an apostle in Colossians 1:1. Barth, *Colossians*, 138-39, argues that Paul is marking out a colleague/coworker here, and that the avoidance of the term apostle for Timothy is not about hierarchy, but salvation history. See also Dunn, *Colossians*, 47-48.

72. Barth, *Colossians*, 476-77, argues that Paul wants to emphasize here that Tychicus is also a minister.

73. Dunn, *Colossians*, 272-73, notes how Onesimus and Tychicus are ranked similarly in the language used of them here.

74. So Darko, *No Longer*, 103; Aasgaard, "Role Ethics," 513.

75. Dunn, *Colossians*, 49.

76. O'Brien, Ephesians, 493, argues for a circular letter, and therefore that the "brothers" are members of various churches. Similarly, Hoehner, *Ephesians*, 873. Compare Lincoln, *Ephesians*, 465; Trebilco, *Self-designations*, 46, who argues that brothers indicates a wide circle of readers not known to the author.

77. Fowl, *Ephesians*, 212; Lincoln, *Ephesians*, 465.

78. Best, *Ephesians*, 618.

Ephesians 1:2,[79] this group can be seen to parallel brothers in 6:23.[80] Paul writes to a defined group of brothers in Ephesus, but recognizes them as part of the wider grouping of Ephesians 6:24, and implicitly encourages them to do the same and to express solidarity with that wider group.

In Colossians 4:15, Paul uses brothers to refer to a group other than the addressees, sending greetings to the brothers at Laodicea. In the same context, Paul refers to this group as the ἐκκλησία of the Laodiceans (v. 16), indicating an identity between the two groups.[81] Dunn argues that Paul is encouraging the Colossians to send their own greetings to the Laodiceans here.[82] However, it is more likely that Paul is asking them to send his greetings, as this section of the letter conveys greetings from Paul and those with him.[83] Given that Paul mentions a letter to the church in Laodicea in 4:16, some have questioned why Paul wants the Colossians to greet the Laodiceans. Here, the most obvious answer is probably the correct one: he wants to encourage fellowship between the ἐκκλησία in Colossae and the ἐκκλησία in Laodicea.[84] In Colossians 2:1, Paul shares his struggle for those at Laodicea and Colossae, and for others who have not seen him face to face. As Stenschke notes, Paul's desire is to see these believers knit together "locally and translocally."[85] In 4:13, Paul has noted Epaphras's work in Colossae, Laodicea, and Hierapolis. As well as being close geographically, Paul is encouraging these ἐκκλησίαι to see themselves as closely aligned, not just in their relationship to Paul and Epaphras,[86] and sees direct communication between those who recognized each other as brothers as the best means to that end. Here we see a practical application of the intrachurch solidarity that "brothers" expresses here and elsewhere in Paul's letters: those who are brothers should maximize their brotherly relations with other brothers.

Overall, there are comparatively few references to brotherly language in Ephesians and Colossians, and much of what I have argued is indicated

---

79. Lincoln, *Ephesians*, 465; O'Brien, Ephesians, 492.

80. Muddiman, *Ephesians*, 299, notes the link with "all who love the Lord Jesus" in 6:24.

81. Moo, *Colossians*, 348–49; O'Brien, *Colossians*, 256.

82. Dunn, *Colossians*, 284.

83. O'Brien, *Colossians*, 256; Moo, Colossians, 348n64, noting usage in Romans.

84. Moo, *Colossians*, 349; tentatively O'Brien, *Colossians*, 256.

85. Stenschke, "Significance and Function of References," 199.

86. Stenschke, "Significance and Function of References," 199, suggests that Epaphras might be the human agent for uniting churches in the Lycos Valley. Whilst recognizing Epaphras's role here, I would argue that Paul is probably encouraging existing relationships between these churches, and that Epaphras is therefore one agent among many.

about interchurch solidarity is implicit rather than explicit. However, there are indications of a continued concern for interchurch solidarity, particularly in Colossians 4:15 and Ephesians 6:23-24.

Holy People

In chapters 3 to 5, I have argued that holiness language is used to create and define boundaries for the community to promote internal harmony and group identity. I have argued that the designation "saints" brings together the local and the whole in a similar way to the use of ἐκκλησία, and that it can be a strong assertion of interchurch solidarity, based on belonging to the same group.

Paul uses saints in Colossians and Ephesians to refer to a wider-than-local grouping which includes, but is not limited to, those in Ephesus and Colossae. This can be seen by his use of saints in Ephesians 3:8, where he compares himself to all the saints; for the comparison to work, the widest grouping needs to be in view, and in Ephesians 1:15 and Colossians 1:4, the believers show love for all the saints.[87]

Holiness language is used to designate what they are and what they should be. It is used to relate the present and future condition of the saints in Ephesus and Colossae and beyond to the work of Christ. In Ephesians 1:4, believers are chosen before the foundation of the world to be holy in Christ; in Ephesians 1:18, the saints are described as God's glorious inheritance.[88] In Colossians 1:12, the Colossians will share in the inheritance of the saints.[89] In Colossians 1:22, Christ's death has reconciled believers to God so that they can be presented holy and blameless; a similar usage is found in Ephesians 5:27.

In Ephesians 2:19, Paul addresses his readers as fellow citizens with the saints;[90] they are together members of the one new man described in

87. On Ephesians 1:15, see for example Heil, *Ephesians*, 79-80; Lincoln, *Ephesians*, 55; Muddiman, *Ephesians*, 83-84; Stenschke, "Significance and Function of References," 204. On Colossians 1:4 see Moo, *Colossians*, 85; Dunn, *Colossians*, 58; O'Brien, *Colossians*, 11.

88. With Hoehner, *Ephesians*, 267, taking saints as human beings, noting the description of believers as inheritance in Ephesians 1:11. See also Fowl, *Ephesians*, 59; O'Brien, *Ephesians*, 135. Amongst those who believe this is a reference to angels are Trebilco, *Self-designations*, 148, and Best, *Ephesians*, 168.

89. Taking saints as human beings with O'Brien, *Colossians*, 26; Dunn, *Colossians*, 76-77; Moo, *Colossians*, 101-2.

90. Trebilco, *Self-designations*, 148, argues for angels here; Best, *Ephesians*, 27, for angels and glorified believers. However, Paul's unusual usage here is easily explained, as exclusive designation here relates to the argument in 2:11-22, where those who were

Ephesians 2:15.[91] Holiness is a state which has been promised before the foundation of the world, and achieved in Jesus Christ, but which will be fully realized once Christ returns. Ephesians 2 illustrates the complementary spatial and temporal perspectives at work here: 2:1–10 addresses the salvation the Ephesians have received in spatial categories, for they are now seated in the heavenly places with Jesus Christ (v. 6), and 2:11–22 emphasizes the temporal aspect, how those who were strangers and aliens (v. 12) are now fellow citizens (v. 19).[92] The Ephesians are part of a holy people, which offers reassurance about their status in Christ, and encourages them to view themselves as part of a larger whole.

The saints are also recipients of knowledge. In Colossians 1:26, the mystery has been revealed to the saints, and in Ephesians 3:18–19, Paul prays that they may comprehend the love of Christ with all the saints. Finally, in Ephesians 4:12, the saints are those who are equipped for ministry, which is further defined as building up the body of Christ. "Saints" is used to encourage activity to build up the body of Christ; as well as being the holy people, the saints are to actively build up others.

The saints are commended for behavior which demonstrates their holiness in Ephesians 1:15 and Colossians 1:4. In both cases, the behavior is love for all the saints. As elsewhere in Paul's letters, that love is demonstrated by patience and other-regard (Eph 4:2), and is the supreme virtue which binds everything together (Col 4:12–14). They are also encouraged to behave in a way which will benefit the saints in Ephesians 6:18, praying for the saints. In both letters, the recipients are being encouraged to continue to express solidarity with other saints, a solidarity beyond the local ἐκκλησία.

The saints are exhorted to behavior which demonstrates their holiness. In Ephesians 5:3, they are to avoid sexual immorality, impurity, and covetousness, as this is improper behavior for saints. "Saints" is best understood here as a reference to all believers,[93] and indicates the existence, at least for Paul, of a general understanding of what behavior is and is not acceptable for all believers, a shared ethos across all the churches.[94]

---

once separate from Israel have now been brought into God's household (see Hoehner, *Ephesians*, 392–93).

91. See Lyons, "Church and Holiness," 243. Lyons argues that the reference in Ephesians 2:19 is to a heavenly assembly including angels. However, the exclusion of the gentiles, which is reversed here, is described in historical terms in 2:11–13; the reversal that comes about in 2:19 is inclusion with the Jews.

92. For a discussion of spatial and temporal perspectives in the letter, see Lyons, "Church and Holiness," 239–42.

93. Hoehner, *Ephesians*, 654.

94. Similarly, Stenschke, "Significance and Function of References," 208.

Two final observations can be made about the use of "saints" in Colossians and Ephesians. First, both letters are addressed to the saints, in Ephesus and Colossae respectively.⁹⁵ In Colossians, these saints are further defined as faithful brothers; in Ephesians, they are faithful.⁹⁶ Philippians 1:1 also has "saints" as the primary description of the addressees in the greeting, and it is included in the address of Romans alongside the beloved of God.⁹⁷ A comparison can be drawn here with 1 Thessalonians, 2 Thessalonians, and Galatians, which are addressed to the ἐκκλησία or ἐκκλησίαι, and the Corinthian correspondence: 1 Corinthians is addressed to the ἐκκλησία in Corinth, who are called to be saints,⁹⁸ and 2 Corinthians to the ἐκκλησία in Corinth, and the saints in Achaia.⁹⁹ Caution needs to be exercised here because of the small sample size, but there does appear to be across these nine letters a discernible shift from the use of ἐκκλησία as the primary address to the use of saints.

Any suggestion as to why this is the case needs to be tentative. Paul's use of ἐκκλησία elsewhere in these letters, particularly in Ephesians, rules out the idea that saints has replaced ἐκκλησία as Paul's preferred terminology, and the change does not follow a pattern, which could be used to imply anything about authorship. Two aspects of the language of saints may have been useful to Paul in designating the addressees: the implication already noted that the saints are set apart, and are to be holy,¹⁰⁰ and the wider sense that the term implicitly carries of a people, even though here the saints are designated as being in Colossae and Ephesus.

Second, I noted earlier the comparative infrequency of the term "brothers" in Colossians and Ephesians. Here, I would note the comparative frequency of the term "saints" used as a designation for believers in Colossians and Ephesians, particularly in Ephesians: believers are designated as saints nine times in Ephesians,¹⁰¹ and three times in Colossians, in letters

---

95. Eph 1:1, Col 1:2.

96. See Hoehner, *Ephesians*, 144–48; Muddiman, *Ephesians*, 59–62; Best, *Essays on Ephesians*, 1–24, on the omission or inclusion of in Ephesus here. Best's reservations about the inclusion of "saints" in Ephesus relate to his view of the letter as a general letter. However, if this argument is not followed, then the external and internal evidence which Hoehner presents make inclusion of "saints" in Ephesus more likely, and therefore, however else this letter circulated, it was written first to Ephesus.

97. Rom 1:7.

98. 1 Cor 1:2.

99. 2 Cor 1:1.

100. See Trebilco, *Self-designations*, 147.

101. Trebilco, *Self-designations*, 122, notes seven occurrences, arguing that Ephesians 1:18 and 2:19 refer to angels.

with a combined length of ten chapters. In Paul's earliest letters, the term appears only once in fourteen chapters.[102] In the Corinthian correspondence, it is found eleven times, in twenty-nine chapters, [103] and there are eleven occurrences in Romans and Philippians in twenty chapters.[104] It might cautiously be argued, then, that there is a general increase in the frequency of saints used as a designation for believers through Paul's letters to churches, and this may explain, in part, the absence of the language of brothers, not from any rejection of the terminology of fictive kinship, but because, as has already been noted, there is an overlap in how these designations are used.[105]

The language of holy people is then comparatively prominent in these two letters, and serves to encourage interchurch solidarity through the recognition of the membership of a wider grouping, and through the encouragement of a shared ethos for those who are designated saints, which is expressed locally and more widely.

Temple

In 1 and 2 Corinthians, I noted how temple imagery functioned to highlight the close connection between the local and the whole. I noted flexibility, as temple imagery is applied to the individual, the Corinthian Church, and to all God's holy people. Temple language is found in Ephesians 2:20–22, and a number of features of this passage highlight how Paul uses this image to emphasize interchurch solidarity.

First, Ephesians 2:20–22 comes at the end of the section of the letter dealing with the reconciliation of Jews and gentiles in Christ (2:11–22). Ephesians 1:19 refers to the strangers and aliens of v. 12 and describes the change in status from strangers and aliens to citizens, and members of God's household. This shift in imagery serves to introduce vv. 20–22. Thus, the context here is reconciliation of Jew and gentile in Christ, indicating that the temple in view here is a temple which includes all believers.[106]

---

102. 2 Thessalonians 1:10. Trebilco, *Self-designations*, 128, lists 1 Thessalonians 3:13 here as well; see chapter 3.

103. 1 Cor 1:2; 6:1–2; 14:33; 16:1, 15; 2 Cor 1:1; 8:4; 9:1, 12; 13:12. Trebilco, *Self-designations*, 128.

104. Rom 1:7; 8:17; 12:13; 15:25–26, 31; 16:2, 15; Phil 1:1; 4:21–22. Trebilco, *Self-designations*, 128. Note that the frequency in Philippians is the same as that in Colossians.

105. See for example Colossians 1:2, saints and faithful brothers.

106. On the importance of this context, see McKelvey, *New Temple*, 108–11. O'Brien, "Church," 101–2, argues that the temple in view here is heavenly, because those without hope are now fellow citizens with the angels, noting that even if this interpretation is

Second, Christ is described as the cornerstone here,[107] in whom the building is built. This emphasizes Christ's role as the source of the temple and its growth.[108] The temple which refers to all believers is also the temple which relies on Christ for stability, coherence and growth.

Third, the οἶκος root is used six times in vv. 19-22,[109] highlighting the way in which temple language is linked to the household of God (v. 19) which has been built (v. 20), and then to a dwelling place for God, which is being built (v. 22). Also, there is a parallel between v. 21 and v. 22,[110] indicating that in Christ the whole structure (you) is joined together spiritually, and grows into a holy temple in the Lord, into a dwelling place for God. As well as making it clear that the Ephesians are part of the holy temple (v. 22), this building imagery serves to emphasize both the existing reality of that which is built and the ongoing necessity and reality of continual building. This has significant implications for ecclesial solidarity, indicating that the Ephesians are the recipients of an already-existing ecclesial solidarity, which extends to include all Jewish and gentile believers, who are fellow saints and members of the household of God. At the same time, that ecclesial solidarity is being achieved, with the implication that further action will be required to continue to build this holy temple, preparing the way to walk worthy of the life to which we have been called (Eph 4:1). Thus, while McKelvey is right to note the doctrinal emphasis of this passage compared to the more overtly ethical emphasis of 1 and 2 Corinthians,[111] this passage is not without significant ethical implications, as the Ephesians are to live in a way which builds the temple.

---

rejected, then the other contextual indicators in vv. 17-18 and 20-22 indicate a heavenly context ("Church," 309n42). However, there is nothing in these verses that necessitates a heavenly context. O'Brien also suggests in *Ephesians*, 211, that Ephesians 2:6 is an indicator of a heavenly context here. However, I have already noted how 2:1-10 and 2:11-22 form parallel arguments, meaning that there is no reason to suppose that the heavenly context of 2:6 need still be in operation here. See also Giles, *What on Earth*, 136-38, who argues for the temple as a worldwide Christian community. It may ultimately be more satisfactory to see the temple here not as either a heavenly or an earthly reality, but as a metaphorical description of Jew and gentile solidarity, which has implications for the church in Ephesus.

107. See McKelvey, *New Temple*, 114, 195-204, on cornerstone rather than capstone here. The translation capstone would not make much difference to the imagery here, as the emphasis would still be on growth in unity in Christ.

108. McKelvey, *New Temple*, 115-16.

109. O'Brien, *Ephesians*, 211n234.

110. O'Brien, *Ephesians*, 220; McKelvey, *New Temple*, 116-17.

111. McKelvey, *New Temple*, 108.

The focus of temple language in Ephesians 2:20 is on the translocal, rather than the local, as Jews and gentiles are reconciled to Christ in one new man. However, the translocal reality which is the temple has implications for the ἐκκλησία in Ephesus, as a motivator to walk worthily.

Body

I have noted how the idea of the body of Christ is used in 1 Corinthians 10–12 with a focus on interchurch solidarity, and how in Romans 12:4–5 the focus was on solidarity within the local church in Rome. I have also noted how the body can be used to stand for one thing and another at the same time. I suggested that this may indicate the usefulness of the imagery for Paul in helping to elucidate the relationship between intra- and interchurch solidarity.

Ephesians and Colossians contain two references to a human body,[112] and a number of references to the body of Christ.[113] Some of these references are to the physical body of Christ.[114] There are also a number of references to the body of Christ used metaphorically, which I will examine under three subheadings: ἐκκλησία as body, one body, and head and body,[115] noting the frequency of body metaphors, particularly in Ephesians.[116]

---

112. Col 2:23; Eph 5:28.

113. One possible reference not discussed because is it uncertain is Colossians 2:17. Here, body can be translated "substance" to reflect the contrast with the shadow of things to come (O'Brien, *Colossians*, 139–41). However, it is also possible to see here a reference to the body of Christ as reality, in contrast to the "shadow" festivals of those passing judgement (Sumney, *Colossians*, 151–53). Moo, *Colossians*, 223–24 and Dunn, *Colossians*, 177, note a possible reference to the church. If this is the case, then the reference to the body of Christ would serve as further reassurance to the Colossians that they are the body of Christ, not the shadow (v. 17), and not disqualified (v. 18).

114. Col 1:22; 2:9, 11. In Colossians 2:11, Dunn, *Colossians*, 157–58 and O'Brien, *Colossians*, 116–17, argue for Christ's body here. Moo, *Colossians*, 198–200 and Sumney, *Colossians*, 137–38, take the alternative view, seeing here a reference to the destruction of the human fleshly nature by the circumcision of Christ. The resolution of this issue is not essential for this dissertation, as in either case it is not a metaphorical reference to the body of Christ.

115. Dunn, "Body of Christ," 148–53, notes the emphasis on one body, and on the "Christ-relatedness" of the theme.

116. Klingbeil, "Metaphors and Pragmatics," 273–93, develops a "metaphor map" of Ephesians, and argues that body is the main metaphor, occurring in 25.8% of verses.

Ἐκκλησία as Body

Three times in these letters, a direct link is made between the ἐκκλησία and the body, to indicate that the church is the body of Christ: in Colossians 1:28, Christ is the head of the body, τῆς ἐκκλησίας; in Colossians 1:24, Paul's sufferings are for the sake of Christ's body, ὅ ἐστιν ἡ ἐκκλησία; and in Ephesians 1:22-23, Christ is the head over all things for the church, which is his body. Twice in Ephesians 5,[117] in vv. 23 and 29, the link between the ἐκκλησία and the body of Christ can be seen, although the link is less explicit. Taken in conjunction with the uses of ἐκκλησία noted earlier, these references indicate that the body of Christ can be used in these two letters for the whole church, collectively for all believers,[118] and that these uses emphasize that the body is united with and belongs to Christ.

One Body

There is one place in Colossians where the image of the body of Christ is used to emphasize unit: Colossians 3:15. Some have taken this as a reference to the body of Christ as a whole,[119] while others take it to be a reference to the body of Christ in Colossae.[120] In the context of the exhortations in 3:12-17, an application of one body to intrachurch solidarity appears most likely here.[121]

There are two places in Ephesians where the image of the body of Christ is used to emphasize unity, with a focus on one body. In Ephesians 2:16, Jews and gentiles are both reconciled in one body.[122] This reconciliation

---

117. For a survey of Paul's creative use of body language here, see Marshall, "For the Husband," 165-77.

118. O'Brien, "Church," 108-10, argues that the references to the body in Colossians 1:18 and 1:24, and particularly Ephesians 1:22-23, point to a heavenly body in the heavenly realm with Christ. However, I have already rejected a heavenly sense to ἐκκλησία and temple, have argued that body can refer to the whole in 1 Corinthians, and have noted the flexibility of the imagery. I therefore see no need to posit a heavenly body here.

119. Lightfoot, *Colossians and Philemon*, 221.

120. O'Brien, *Colossians*, 205; Dunn, *Colossians*, 234-35. Sumney, *Colossians*, 221, argues that a universal or local reference is not the issue here, but rather the overcoming of differences due to social or ethnic status, the theme of 3:11.

121. Compare Moo, *Colossians*, 285.

122. I am taking this as a reference to the church, noting the significance of the adjective "one" here, with most commentators. See for example O'Brien, *Ephesians*, 201-2; Lincoln, *Ephesians*, 144-45; Hoehner, *Ephesians*, 382-83; Best, *Ephesians*, 255-56. Contra Barth, *Ephesians 1-3*, 298.

into one body is presented as an accomplished fact, for the whole body. In Ephesians 4:4, "one body" is one of seven "ones" mentioned in 4:4–6.[123] It is important to see these verses in the context of 4:1–3, where Paul exhorts the Ephesians to walk worthily (v. 1), before describing a set of behaviors which maintain unity (vv. 2–3), and which can be summarized as bearing with one another in love. The goal here is maintaining the unity of the Holy Spirit.[124] There is a unity which exists, but which also needs to be maintained, in the bond of peace.[125] Noticeably here the maintenance of unity takes place in the context of the local ἐκκλησία in Ephesus, as bearing with one another requires proximity to the other to have practical effect. At the same time, this local unity is related to the unity of the Spirit and the work of Christ, both of which transcend the local, whilst the activity of those in the local congregation has a wider effect, bringing glory to God throughout all generations (3:21). This exhortation to unity leads into a declaration in 4:4–6 of the reality of unity, which begins with the assertion that there is one body. "One body" is used in Ephesians 4:1–6 to emphasize the existing unity of the whole body; however, at the same time, that unity is to be maintained by activity taking place in the local ἐκκλησία.

"One body" language can be applied to activity in the local ἐκκλησία and to the whole ἐκκλησία, but can also be used to illuminate the relationship between the whole and the local, where the unity of the whole body is an encouragement to practice intrachurch solidarity.

Head and Body

In Colossians 1:18, Paul states that Christ is the head of the body.[126] I have already noted how headship language in Colossians and Ephesians occurs in contexts which imply Christ's rule, and how this passage would serve to reassure the Colossians as part of something translocal. Having made this

---

123. Some have sought to find a preexisting Christian hymn here; for example, Best, "Use of Credal," 65–66; Barth, *Ephesians 4–6*, 462–72. Whether this is a preexisting hymn or one that Paul wrote is not central to establishing the ecclesiology of Ephesians.

124. See Hoehner, *Ephesians*, 511–12, the Holy Spirit brings about the unity which exists.

125. Hoehner, *Ephesians*, 513, takes the genitive as epexegetical or appositional. See also Best, *Ephesians*, 365. The bond of peace is a reference back to 2:14–18, where Christ's work is described in terms of bringing peace between human beings and God and between human beings, specifically Jews and gentiles. Unity in the Spirit is then maintained both by the fact of Christ's death upon the cross, the peace which bonds, and by calling that fact to mind, as Paul does here.

126. See also Best, *One Body*, 126–28.

statement in Colossians 1:18, Paul applies the language of headship of the body in Colossians 2:19. Here there is a critique of those who are following the shadow of things to come, and who are puffed up (vv. 17–18), and are not holding to the head, who nourishes, knits together, and provides growth for the body (v. 19).[127] It is difficult to be certain about whether "body" here is primarily a reference to the local ἐκκλησία in Colossae, or to the whole ἐκκλησία, and the flexibility of body terminology would allow, and perhaps even encourage, a dual referent. However, the context of Colossians 1:18 and the use of "whole body" in v. 19 suggests that the translocal is in view here.[128] If that is the case, then here the translocal reality of the head and body is used to encourage the local body in Colossae to resist false teaching (vv. 20–22).

In Ephesians 4:15–16, the body is to grow into the head, into Christ. There are similarities here with Colossians 2:19, although in Ephesians 4:16 the activity of those in the body, as well as that of Christ the head, can be seen. The passage flows from the giving of gifted individuals (4:11) who are to equip the saints for ministry, whose ministry will build up the body of Christ (4:12). This equipping and ministry will continue until three parallel states are reached: unity of the faith and knowledge of the son of God, mature manhood, and fullness (4:13).[129] The equipping and ministry also have a purpose, so that the believers will not be vulnerable to human deceit, but instead will grow up into Christ (4:14–15). Ephesians 4:16 makes clear that as the body grows together, Christ is active in making the body grow.

Is the local ἐκκλησία or the whole body of Christ primarily in view here? In favor of taking the language to refer to the ἐκκλησία in Ephesus are the reference to speaking the truth in love in v. 15, which, taken with the exhortations to right conduct in the local congregation in 4:25–32, suggests a local reference, that the activity of speaking the truth leads to a local growing into Christ, and the reference to building up in love in v. 16, which has had a local focus elsewhere in Paul's letters, for example in 1 Corinthians 14. However, there are a number of reasons for seeing a reference to the whole body here. First, Christ's role as head of the body (or the ἐκκλησία) elsewhere in Ephesians is linked to the whole body. Second, the focus in Ephesians 4:7–10 is on Christ's gifts to all:[130] Christ who ascended to the heavens,

---

127. See O'Brien, *Colossians*, 147; Moo, *Colossians*, 231 for the Greek translations adopted here.

128. For a recognition of the dual reference here, but with a greater emphasis on the local, see Dunn, *Colossians*, 185–87; Sumney, *Colossians*, 157–59. O'Brien, *Colossians*, 147, takes "whole" to mean that no member is excluded.

129. See Hoehner, *Ephesians*, 551–59.

130. See Moritz, *Profound Mystery*, 63–76, for Paul's use of Psalm 68:18 here. Arnold,

who is above all things and will fill all things, and who descended to earth and died on the cross, gives gifts, as a result of taking the powers captive on the cross. Third, this translocal focus continues with the use of apostles (v. 11), saints (v. 12), and all (v. 13). Fourth, Paul uses "we" throughout this section. Fifth, in v. 16, Paul refers to the growth of all, or the whole body. This section is framed in language which begins with and presents a goal for the whole body, but the activity of speaking the truth in love and building up in love takes place locally. Rather than deciding between translocal and local here, I would argue that both are in view, that as the local ἐκκλησία works out the process of 4:11–16, they are building up the whole body, and by doing so they are participating in the making known and glorification of God described in 3:10 and 3:21, as they contribute to the unity and maturity of the body (4:13). Here we see that intrachurch solidarity expressed through loving relationships is both a response to the activity of Christ for the whole church in giving gifts, but also contributes to interchurch solidarity, as the whole body grows into Christ.

Conclusion

"The body of Christ" can be used in Colossians and Ephesians to refer to the whole church, and can be applied to activity in the local ἐκκλησία. It can also be used to illuminate the relationship between the whole and the local, where the unity of the whole body is an encouragement to practice intrachurch solidarity and where, in Ephesians, intrachurch solidarity contributes to interchurch solidarity, as the whole body grows into Christ. I have argued that this can be related to Paul's use of ἐκκλησία in Ephesians 3:10, where the church reveals God's plan both by its existence and activity. Here we see that, in Ephesians, behavior in the local ἐκκλησία is predicated on the existence, reality, and goal of the whole ἐκκλησία and body.

Imitation and Apostleship

Imitation

In chapters 3 to 5, I have argued that the language of imitation has been used to encourage intrachurch solidarity, through the use of Paul as an example who follows the example of Christ and makes other-regard central to his behavior, rather than self-interest. I have also noted a number of

---

Power and Magic, 51–59, notes how the captives referred to here are the powers, further reassurance in magic-dominated Ephesus of the universal authority of Christ.

occasions where interchurch solidarity has been encouraged through the use of the language of imitation: in 1 Thessalonians 1:6 and 2:14, where imitation operates from ἐκκλησία to ἐκκλησία; in 1 and 2 Corinthians, where the behavior of believers in other ἐκκλησίαι provides a model for the Corinthians, and where their behavior regarding the collection could set an example for others; and in Philippians 3:17-19, where Paul links imitation to heavenly citizenship. Imitation is to take place in reception of the gospel and in persevering through suffering, but also in imitating the behavior of others more generally.

In Colossians and Ephesians, the language of imitation is used in two ways. First, Paul uses the examples of God and Christ to encourage intrachurch solidarity. This can be seen most clearly and explicitly in Ephesians 5:1, where the Ephesians are urged to be imitators of God. This is the only place in Paul where imitation of God is urged,[131] although the imitation of God here is closely linked to the example of Christ in 5:2, and to the forgiveness received in Christ in 4:32.[132] The imitation is to be undertaken as beloved children, indicating that God is the example as a loving father.[133] The content of the imitation is love,[134] and the way in which this love is expressed can be seen in 4:17—5:6, for the imitation of God links with 4:24, and the new man being created after the likeness of God,[135] whilst the call to "walk in love" in 5:1 is one of five calls to walk in 4:17—6:9, and the content of this particular walking is spelled out in 5:1-6.[136] The focus of the exhortation in 4:17—5:6 is the local ἐκκλησία, and behavior which will strengthen intrachurch solidarity, through what is said and done.[137]

Second, Paul uses his own example to foster intrachurch solidarity. In Ephesians 4:1, Paul's imprisonment carries with it an implicit call to imitation: as one who has shown his love for others, even down to suffering imprisonment, he exhorts them to walk worthily and love one another

---

131. Clarke, "Imitators," 350-51.

132. Clarke, "Imitators," 351; de Boer, *Imitation*, 76-77, 80.

133. Copan, *Saint Paul*, 57; Clarke, "Imitators," 351; de Boer, *Imitation*, 78-79. Contra Michaelis, "μιμέοηαι," 671 who argues that "children" is used as a call to obedience.

134. de Boer, *Imitation*, 79.

135. de Boer, *Imitation*, 75.

136. See Hoehner, *Ephesians*, 643, on the structure of this passage.

137. Colossians 3:17 might also be noted here, although the imitation is much more implicit, in the name of Christ and giving thanks to the Father. Again, the focus in Colossians 3:12-17 is on activity within the local ἐκκλησία. de Boer, *Imitation*, 77, notes the parallel between Ephesians 4:32 and Col 3:13.

(4:1–2).¹³⁸ I have already noted how the exhortations in 4:1–6, although in the context of the whole church, are nevertheless directed to the local ἐκκλησία.¹³⁹

In Colossians 1:24—2:5, Paul reports on his ministry to the church and for the Colossians. In 1:24–29,¹⁴⁰ he writes of his suffering (v. 24) and toil (v. 29) for the sake of the gospel, and then in 2:1 he applies his behavior to the Colossians, the Laodiceans, and all who haven't seen his face in the flesh, a reference to all believers. All are to be encouraged by Paul's example to have their hearts knit together and to understand Christ. Whilst this may appear to be a case of interchurch solidarity, and aspects of the passage which tend in that direction have been noted here, the application of the example of Paul is that each group should be encouraged and knit together in intrachurch solidarity.

I have noted a number of passages and images in Colossians and Ephesians which indicate a concern for interchurch solidarity, and some of that language is found in the passages discussed in this section. However, the imitation motif is used with a primary focus on intrachurch solidarity.

Apostleship

I have argued that Paul's use of apostleship language implies an ongoing relationship with the churches he founded, and the sense of a wider grouping of churches. This wider grouping, whether founded by Paul or not, can speak through Paul to the local church with authority: there are different apostles, and yet all come with an apostolic message which is the gospel, the message of the cross. Paul's particular role to the gentiles has also been noted.

In Colossians 1:1, Paul writes as an apostle of Christ Jesus by the will of God. He distinguishes himself from his brother Timothy. His description of himself outlines both his authority as an apostle, writing to a church he did not found, and how he is under the authority of God, and one who is sent by Jesus.¹⁴¹ In Colossians 1:24–29, Paul outlines his behavior for the sake of the Colossians, and although he does not appeal to his apostolic role

---

138. Heil, *Ephesians*, 166.

139. If there is an implicit call to imitation in Paul's reiteration of the motif of chains in 6:19–20, it functions in a similar way: the Ephesians are called to share the gospel after the example of Paul. See also Colossians 4:18.

140. Copan, *Saint Paul*, 117n45, admonition is the act of a father in Colossians 1:28; 3:16.

141. Sumney, *Colossians*, 26.

here, his activity is consistent with what has been noted about his apostolic role elsewhere: sufferings for the sake of the church (v. 24); a particular role to bring good news to the gentiles (vv. 25-27);[142] a desire to teach all that they might reach maturity (v. 28);[143] and one who works through the power of Christ (v. 29).[144] Paul also writes as an apostle when he combats the false teaching in Colossae in 2:6-23.[145] Whilst Paul's use of the language of body (v. 24), ἐκκλησία (v. 24), saints (v. 26), and everyone (v. 28) in this passage are reminders of the wide scope of his apostleship, his application of it is primarily for the sake of the Colossians, seeking to knit them together in love, in intrachurch solidarity.

In Ephesians 1:1, Paul also writes as an apostle of Christ Jesus by the will of God. In addition, however, Paul makes a number of statements about the role of apostles in this letter.

Ephesians 2:20 states that the household of God is built upon the foundation of the apostles and prophets. I take apostles here to be a reference to the twelve mentioned in 1 Corinthians 15:5 and Paul,[146] although as the least of the apostles (1 Cor 15:9),[147] and the prophets are most likely NT prophets.[148] As I have already noted, saints and temple here are references to the whole, and there is an emphasis here on growth. The apostles here are the foundation for the household of God,[149] and that foundation is the message which has been revealed to the apostles and prophets (Eph 3:5), the mystery of Christ (3:4), the abolition of the dividing wall between Jew and gentile (2:14-15).[150] The apostles, then, in Ephesians 2:20 and 3:5, have a foundational role for the whole church; they preach a message which is the basis for interchurch solidarity.

In Ephesians 4:11, the apostles are listed as one of four or five[151] gifts given to the saints. As noted earlier, this section of the letter deals with the

---

142. Compare Gal 1:8; 2:1-10; Rom 1:5; 11:13.

143. Compare 1 Cor 9:2; 2 Cor 12:12.

144. Compare Gal 1:1. See also the list of functions noted in 3.3.2.1.

145. O'Brien, *Colossians*, 2.

146. McKelvey, *New Temple*, 113; Lincoln, *Ephesians*, 152.

147. Compare Ephesians 3:8, where the author refers to himself as "least of all the saints."

148. Lincoln, *Ephesians*, 153. McKelvey, *New Temple*, 113-14, allows the possibility of OT prophets here.

149. O'Brien, *Ephesians*, 213

150. O'Brien, *Ephesians*, 216; McKelvey, *New Temple*, 113.

151. For a recent survey of whether pastors/teachers should be considered separately or together see Hoehner, *Ephesians*, 543-45.

whole church, but with a focus on activity within the local ἐκκλησία.[152] Apostles are a gift to the whole church, as in Ephesians 2:20 and 3:5, but here that gift is applied for the benefit of the local ἐκκλησία which, in turn, contributes to unity for the whole.

In Colossians, Paul's apostolic role is seen primarily in the encouragement of intrachurch solidarity. In Ephesians 2:20, 3:5, and 4:11, the apostles, of whom Paul is one, foster interchurch solidarity by communicating to each local ἐκκλησία the mystery of Christ.

Conclusion

I have argued in this chapter that ἐκκλησία is used in Colossians for the domestic, local, and whole church. In Ephesians, the reality of the wider ἐκκλησία, and particularly the unity that wider reality expresses, is used to encourage unity and solidarity in the local ἐκκλησία, and behavior in the local ἐκκλησία is predicated on the existence, reality and goal of the whole ἐκκλησία.

In exploring Paul's use of imagery in these letters, I have noted the comparatively infrequent use of the language of brothers, but also a similarity with other letters in usage, and the comparative frequency of the use of "holy people," which I have argued is used to express interchurch solidarity, and may be being preferred in some contexts to ἐκκλησία or brothers.

I have also noted how some imagery is used in a similar way to the use of ἐκκλησία, particularly in Ephesians. In Ephesians 2:20, the translocal reality which is the temple has implications for the ἐκκλησία in Ephesus, as a spur to walk worthily. The body of Christ is the place where intrachurch solidarity contributes to interchurch solidarity, as the whole body grows into Christ: behavior in the local ἐκκλησία is predicated on the existence, reality and goal of the whole body.

I noted how imitation has a primarily intrachurch reference in these letters, and that Paul's apostolic role is seen in the encouragement of

---

152. Lincoln, *Ephesians*, 249–52, argues that the focus narrows to particular ministers from the ministries of Romans 12 and 1 Corinthians 12; that apostles and prophets have a past reference, as at Ephesians 2:10 and 3:5; and that evangelists perform the function of apostles in the post-apostolic period. He views evangelists, pastors, and teachers as a new triad of ministers to replace the ministries of 1 Corinthians 12:28. However, the context of this verse is significant. Ephesians 4:11 occurs in the context of Christ giving gifts to all. This verse then looks at five (or four if pastors and teachers are taken together) particular gifts, and shows how those gifts, despite their nature and diversity, serve to build unity. From the standpoint of the author of the letter, all four/five gifts have a present function in equipping the saints.

intrachurch solidarity and in the fostering of interchurch solidarity by communicating to each local ἐκκλησία the mystery of Christ.

I noted at the start of this chapter that these two letters are often considered to have a more developed ecclesiology than Paul's earlier letters, particularly in the idea of the "universal" church. I have argued that there is no uniform progression from the intrachurch to the interchurch in Colossians and Ephesians, and I have noted many similarities between the use of ἐκκλησία, imagery, and the language of imitation and apostleship here and in other letters. I have argued against the need for a "heavenly church concept" to understand ἐκκλησία here. However, in Ephesians, there is the development of a new argument: that behavior in the local ἐκκλησία is predicated on the existence, reality, and goal of the whole ἐκκλησία, body, and temple, and then also contributes to the goal of the whole ἐκκλησία, body, and temple. Interchurch solidarity is then the foundation and the result of intrachurch solidarity.[153]

---

153. Stenschke, "'Not the Only Pebble,'" 331–32, picks up on Thiselton, *First Epistle*, 74, who describes the Corinthians as not the only pebble on the beach, demonstrating how the Corinthians share in the privileges and responsibilities of the wider people of God. Here in Ephesians, the argument is not so much that "you are not the only pebble on the beach" as "see what the pebbles gathered together can create on the beach."

7. Conclusion

In chapter 1 of this book, I proposed an investigation of ecclesial solidarity in the nine letters in the Pauline corpus that were addressed to churches, exploring the beliefs and practices which Paul promoted to encourage solidarity. I argued that, although intrachurch solidarity has received considerable attention, interchurch solidarity has been neglected. I have addressed this neglect in a number of ways.

First, in chapter 1, I adopted an approach to examining the nine letter by splitting them into four groups arranged by approximate and relative chronological order. I have then explored these four groups in chapters 3 to 6. This has allowed an examination of these letters without a focus on authorship, or on a commonly adopted development scheme from "early" letters to Colossians and Ephesians to the pastoral letters, and therefore fostered a thorough examination of interchurch solidary from the earliest letters.

Second, building on the work of Horrell, Meeks, Trebilco, and others, I proposed an approach to terminology and imagery in chapter 1 and implemented it in chapters 3 to 6. This approach involved looking at the meaning of ἐκκλησία; the use of "brothers," holiness language (including temple imagery), and metaphorical use of the body of Christ; the use of the language of imitation; and Paul's understanding of apostleship. By examining a defined group of terms and images throughout the nine letters, I have been able to observe any differences or developments across the corpus.

Third, in chapter 2, I examined the use of ἐκκλησία in Greek literature and the Septuagint, arguing that, whilst the primary meaning of political assembly remains consistent through all the references I examined, nevertheless there is flexibility in usage. In chapter 3, I argued that Paul's earliest uses of ἐκκλησία were a departure from previous usage, that this flexibility needs to be recognized, and that Paul's terminology cannot be limited to an assembly as it is assembled. This has been further demonstrated in a large number of plural and singular translocal references to ἐκκλησία noted in chapters 4 to 6.

Fourth, in examining translocal usage of ἐκκλησία and other imagery in chapters 3 to 6, I have sought to avoid the terminology of "universal church," with its later connotations, and have explored both who Paul has in mind when he writes of "all the churches," or "the church (of God)." I have also noted regional usage, and the distinctions and overlap between domestic and local church in one city. This has revealed a more complex web of ecclesial solidarity than is often noted, and undermines a binary classification of the church as either local or universal. There are various links between churches, which can be described both as relationships between churches and as relationships within the church. Church can be used to describe that which is domestic, local, regional, multiregional, and also for the whole church, which can also be designated "all the churches."

Fifth, in chapters 3 to 6, I noted many examples of intrachurch solidarity, of how solidarity is encouraged within the local church. However, I also argued for a much greater appreciation of Paul's concern for interchurch solidarity, based his earliest letters.

In chapter 3, I argued that ἐκκλησία is used in both the singular and the plural with a translocal reference. This translocal reference can also be seen in the use of holiness language. In 1 Thessalonians 4:9–12, Paul commands the church in Thessalonica to live quietly and work hard for the sake of other churches, and uses imitation language to encourage a right response to the word of God and the behavior that entails (1 Thess 1:5, 2:14). I have argued, therefore, that in Paul's earliest letters, there is evidence of the promotion of a shared ethos across and between churches. Paul's earliest letters indicate a concern for interchurch solidarity shown through acting for the good of others, imitating others, and being a model for imitation.

In chapter 4, I argued that the Corinthian correspondence shows a highly developed regard for interchurch solidarity. This can be seen in the use of ἐκκλησία for the domestic, local, regional and whole church, and how the existence of the whole church and other churches is used to encourage the Corinthians to interchurch solidarity. There are indications of joint ventures between churches. It can also be seen in the use of the language of holiness, temple, brothers, and the body of Christ to remind the Corinthians that they are part of a wider grouping, imitation language which indicates that what happens elsewhere should influence them, and the language of apostleship, which indicates a group of apostles have wide authority over "the church," including Corinth. The focus on ecclesial solidarity in the Corinthian correspondence is on encouraging the Corinthians to believe and behave as those who are part of the whole church; that a shared ethos should exist between churches.

In chapter 5, I argued that Philippians and Romans break any apparent trajectory from the local to the "universal," because the general focus of both letters is on solidarity in the local church. This can be seen in the use of the language of brothers in both letters, of saints in Philippians and the body in Romans. There are indications of interchurch concerns in the language of heavenly commonwealth in Philippians and in Paul's role as apostle to the gentiles in Romans. However, the general focus on intrachurch solidarity should be noted.

In chapter 6, I addressed the question as to whether Paul writes of a heavenly church in Ephesians and Colossians, arguing instead for his use of whole church. I noted the translocal focus of the use of ἐκκλησία in these letters, which is mirrored in the use of body, saints, and temple. However, this translocal focus is not uniform, as the language of imitation and apostleship is used to foster intrachurch solidarity. Overall, I argued that, particularly in Ephesians, behavior in the local ἐκκλησία is predicated on the existence, reality, and goal of the whole ἐκκλησία, body, and temple and then also contributes to the goal of the whole ἐκκλησία, body, and temple. Interchurch solidarity is then the foundation for, and the result of intrachurch solidarity. Therefore, whilst the language of interchurch solidarity is just as prevalent in the Corinthian correspondence—if not more so—the focus is different: Paul seeks to show the Corinthians their responsibility to the whole, but encourages the Ephesians to see that interchurch solidarity establishes their identity in Christ, and is strengthened by intrachurch solidarity.

Across these six chapters, then, I have highlighted and addressed the neglect of interchurch solidarity, and argued that Paul promotes, in many and varied ways, an ethos across all the churches. I have noted how this is achieved through different language in different letters, and how there is not a uniform development in thought from the local to the universal. I have noted the flexible usage of ἐκκλησία and other imagery to address the particular needs of addressees. I wish now to highlight some of the implications of this study.

There are a number of implications for New Testament ecclesiology. First, by reexamining the use of ἐκκλησία in Greek and then tracing usage through nine letters in the traditional Pauline corpus, I have argued that there is no need to posit a heavenly church in any of these letters. Rather, ἐκκλησία can be used with confidence to refer to domestic, local, and translocal church. The argument that interchurch solidarity exists from beginning may also shed light on the use of ἐκκλησία in other New Testament books; for example, in Matthew 16:18.

Second, I argued that interchurch relationships are a neglected area, in part because of a desire to determine whether the local or universal church is prior. Instead, in the Pauline corpus, church is a local phenomenon with translocal implications; there are churches which can be considered together as church because of their interrelationships.

Third, I also noted how a concern with church structures has also caused neglect of translocal relationships. Church government has deliberately not been a focus of this thesis; however, the strong sense of interchurch solidarity evident from Paul's earliest letters means that any consideration of church leadership in the New Testament should consider how leadership structures would foster interchurch as well as intrachurch solidarity.

Fourth, I noted in chapter 6 a potential shift of language from "brothers" and ἐκκλησία to "saints." It has been beyond the scope of this study to analyze this further, and it remains a potentially interesting area for further investigation, in seeking to better understand Paul's ecclesiological terminology.

I would argue that there is an important implication for Pauline theology. I have sought in this study to engage with all nine of the Pauline letters to churches without too much focus on questions of authorship and development. However, given that ecclesiology is seen as one of the main areas where development happens in the Pauline corpus, there are potential implications for authorship and development in this thesis. I would argue that the different application of the same imagery in different letters, and the general flexibility with which terminology is used, would suggest that interchurch solidarity does not provide evidence which can be used to substantiate the case for different authorship; there is no uniform development from the local to the translocal application of terminology. Rather, the findings here are consistent with letters to different churches, addressing different issues, and spanning a significant time period, but deriving from the same principal author.

This may also have implications for wider New Testament study. Whilst the Pauline corpus offers a unique opportunity to explore the writings of one author spread over a number of years, and recognizing the distinct genres of letter and gospel, the issues raised here with regard to the thesis of ecclesiological development in the Pauline corpus may have wider implications in questioning whether differing emphases in different New Testament books are best seen as theological developments or particular applications of a more profoundly shared ethos than is sometimes suggested. The idea of a shared ethos may be worthy of further study, to examine whether other New Testament authors along with Paul worked with a wider conception of all the churches/the church of God, conscious of the needs of those outside their local community or communities.

In this study, I have sought to ground discussion of ecclesial solidarity in the settings of the various letters which Paul wrote, and the communities to which he wrote. As such, this study has a number of implications for understanding the history of earliest Christianity.

First, Horrell and Adams note that Baur's thesis on earliest Christianity has been extensively refuted;[1] nevertheless, the idea of division or distinction between Pauline Christianity and Jerusalem or other centers remains. Against this, I have argued that Paul's deep-rooted concern with interchurch solidarity extends beyond "his" churches, that he has a concern for all the churches, with the collection revealing a particular concern with Jerusalem. In addition, I have argued that Paul is concerned about interchurch solidarity from his earliest letters, which may indicate that this concern was a general feature of early Christianity. I would suggest, then, that the history of early Christianity should be one where continued efforts at interchurch solidarity are examined and appreciated.

Second, a very much related argument concerns the extent of communication which existed between churches in early Christianity. I have already noted how Thompson argues for extensive communicative links between early Christian centres.[2] This chapter forms part of a more general argument in the book that the gospels should be considered to be written for a more general audience, rather than for specific communities.[3] I would argue that the picture of earliest Christianity envisaged here is one which coheres with that which emerges from my examination of interchurch solidarity in the Pauline corpus, where the links rather than the distinctions between communities can be emphasized.

Third, I have already noted that I have not found evidence for significant development in ecclesiology within the Pauline corpus. As well as having implications for examining development within the New Testament, this may also have two implications for the idea of development within early Christianity:[4] first, to question how far different regions developed distinctly different theological identities given the identified links,[5] and second, to challenge assumptions about a move from the simple, local, and primitive to the complex, translocal, and developed.

Finally, this book may have a number of implications for understanding the church in the twenty-first century which may offer some directions for further study or reflection. Given the nature of this study, these implications can only be suggestive at best, but I offer them in a comparatively strong form to encourage that reflection (and no doubt disagreement).

---

1. Horrell and Adams, "Scholarly Quest," 13–16. See Baur, "Two Epistles to the Corinthians," 52–59.

2. Thompson, "The Holy Internet."

3. See for example, Klink, "The Gospel Community Debate," 60–85.

4. For a summary of various models of development within early Christianity, see Bingham, "Development and Diversity," 48–63.

5. Bingham, "Development and Diversity," 50–1.

First, I have frequently noted how intra- and interchurch solidarity in the Pauline corpus is unequivocally ethical, concerned both with right belief and right behavior, founded on a shared relationship in Christ. I would argue that any present-day discussions of church unity, whether that is considered locally, translocally, nationally, or internationally, need to take account of the strongly theological and ethical understanding of unity and solidarity in the Pauline corpus.

Second, the strong emphasis on interchurch solidarity which I have argued for in this thesis indicates that an exclusively congregational position on church polity, where emphasis falls solely on the needs and concerns of the local congregation, is at least discouraged by the Pauline corpus, if not prohibited; to adopt an exclusively congregational position on ecclesiology is not to rediscover the primitive church. More positively, churches which consider the ecclesiology of the New Testament to be worthy of emulation or regard need to take account of interchurch solidarity, and to ensure that whatever structures exist should foster interchurch cooperation. Furthermore, the Pauline pattern of the development and encouragement of links between local churches may challenge some institutional assumptions about how the "church universal" is to be realized.

Third, and finally, as noted in my introduction, "solidarity" has been used in this thesis due to its comparatively undeveloped meaning. This can be seen in the contemporary world, where the idea of showing solidarity is often referenced, with a variety of applications. This thesis presents a model of solidarity which may be worthy of further reflection: to examine and question how solidarity may look in the twenty-first century, both within and outside the church.

Bibliography

Aasgaard, Reidar. *My Beloved Brothers and Sisters! Christian Siblingship in Paul.* Journal for the Study of the New Testament Supplement Series 265: Early Christianity in Context. London: T. & T. Clark, 2004.

———. "'Role Ethics' in Paul: The Significance of the Sibling Role for Paul's Ethical Thinking." *New Testament Studies* 48.4 (2002) 513–30.

Adams, Edward. *Constructing the World: A Study in Paul's Cosmological Language.* Studies of the New Testament and Its World. Edinburgh: T. & T. Clark, 2000.

———. *The Earliest Christian Meeting Places: Almost Exclusively Houses?* The Library of New Testament Studies. London: Bloomsbury, 2013.

———. "First-century Models for Paul's Churches: Selected Scholarly Developments since Meeks." In *After the First Urban Christians: The Social-scientific Study of Pauline Christianity Twenty-five Years Later*, edited by Todd D. Still and David G. Horrell, 60–78. London: T. & T. Clark, 2009.

Aernie, Jeffrey W. *Is Paul Also Among the Prophets? An Examination of the Relationship between Paul and the Old Testament Prophetic Tradition in 2 Corinthians.* The Library of New Testament Studies. London: Bloomsbury, 2012.

Aeschines. *The Speeches of Aeschines.* Translated by Charles Darwin Adams. Loeb Classical Library. Cambridge: Harvard University Press, 1919.

Agnew, Francis H. "On the Origin of the Term *Apostolos*." *Catholic Biblical Quarterly* 38.1 (1976) 49–53.

———. "The Origin of the NT Apostle-Concept: A Review of Research." *Journal of Biblical Literature* 105.1 (1986) 75–96.

Aletti, Jean-Noel. "Le Status de l'Église dans les letters pauliniennes. Réflexions sur quelques paradoxes." *Biblica* 83.2 (2002) 153–74.

Alexander, Loveday. "Hellenistic Letter-Forms and the Structure of Philippians." In *The Pauline Writings: A Sheffield Reader*, edited by Stanley Porter and Craig Evans, 232–46. Biblical Seminar 34. Sheffield: Sheffield Academic, 1995.

Amador, J. D. H. "The Word Made Flesh: Epistemology, Ontology and Postmodern Rhetorics." In *The Rhetorical Analysis of Scripture: Essays from the 1995 London Conference*, edited by Stanley E. Porter and Thomas H. Olbricht, 53–65. Sheffield: Sheffield Academic, 1997.

Andocides. "Andocides." In *Minor Attic Orators, Volume I: Antiphon, Andocides*, translated by K. J. Maidment, 325–583. Loeb Classical Library. Cambridge: Harvard University Press, 1941.

Annas, Julia. "Plato." In *The Oxford Classical Dictionary*, edited by Simon Hornblower and Anthony Spawforth, 1190–91. 3rd ed. Oxford: Oxford University Press, 1996.

Aristophanes. *Aristophanes.* Translated by Jeffrey Henderson. 5 vols. Loeb Classical Library. Cambridge: Harvard University Press, 1998–2008.

Aristotle. *Aristotle*. Translated by H. Rackham et al. 23 vols. Loeb Classical Library. Cambridge: Harvard University Press, 1926–2011.

Arnold, Clinton E. *The Colossian Syncretism: The Interface between Christianity and Folk Belief at Colossae*. Grand Rapids: Baker, 1996.

———. *Ephesians Power and Magic: The Concept of Power in Ephesians in Light of Its Historical Setting*. Society for New Testament Studies Monograph Series 63. Cambridge: Cambridge University Press, 1989.

———. "Jesus Christ: 'Head' of the Church." In *Jesus of Nazareth Lord and Christ: Essays on the Historical Jesus and New Testament Christology*, edited by Joel B. Green and Max Turner, 346–66. Grand Rapids: Eerdmans, 1994.

Ascough, Richard S. "Translocal Relationships among Voluntary Associations and Early Christianity." *Journal of Early Christian Studies* 5 (1997) 223–41.

———. *What Are They Saying about the Formation of the Pauline Churches?* New York: Paulist, 1998.

Balch, David L. "Paul, Families, and Households." In *Paul in the Greco-Roman World: A Handbook*, edited by J. Paul Sampley, 258–92. Harrisburg: Trinity, 2003.

Banks, Robert J. *Paul's Idea of Community: The Early House Churches in Their Cultural Setting*. Rev. ed. Peabody: Hendrickson, 1994.

Barclay, John M. G. "Conflict in Thessalonica." *Catholic Biblical Quarterly* 55.3 (1993) 512–30.

Barnett, Paul W. *The Corinthian Question: Why did the Church Oppose Paul*. Nottingham: Apollos, 2011.

Barr, James. *The Semantics of Biblical Language*. Oxford: Oxford University Press, 1961.

Barth, Markus. *Ephesians 1–3*. Anchor Bible 34. New York: Doubleday, 1974.

———. *Ephesians 4–6*. Anchor Bible 34A. New York: Doubleday, 1974.

Barth, Markus, and Helmut Blanke. *Colossians: A New Translation with Introduction and Commentary*. Translated by Astrid B Beck. Anchor Bible 34B. New York: Doubleday, 1994.

Bartlett, John R. *1 Maccabees*. Guides to the Apocrypha and Pseudepigrapha. Sheffield: Sheffield Academic, 1998.

Baur, Ferdinand Christian. "The Two Epistles to the Corinthians." In *Christianity at Corinth: The Quest for the Pauline Church*, edited by Edward Adams and David G. Horrell, 51–59. Louisville: Westminster John Knox, 2004.

Beale, G. K. *The Temple and the Church's Mission: A Biblical Theology of the Dwelling Place of God*. New Studies in Biblical Theology 17. Leicester: Apollos, 2004.

Becker, Jürgen. *Paul, Apostle to the Gentiles*. Translated by O. C. Dean Jr. Louisville: Westminster John Knox, 1993.

Berkhof, Louis. *Systematic Theology*. Edinburgh: Banner of Truth, 1971.

Best, Ernest. *Ephesians*. International Critical Commentary. Edinburgh, T. & T. Clark, 1998.

———. *Essays on Ephesians*. Edinburgh: T. & T. Clark, 1997.

———. *One Body in Christ: A Study in the Relationship of the Church to Christ in the Epistles of the Apostle Paul*. London: SPCK, 1955.

———. *Paul and His Converts*. Edinburgh: T. & T. Clark, 1988.

———. "The Use of Credal and Liturgical Material in Ephesians." In *Worship, Theology and Ministry in the Early Church: Essays in Honour of Ralph P. Martin*, edited by Michael J. Wilkins and Terence Paige, 53–69. Journal for the Study of the New Testament Supplement Series 87. Sheffield: JSOT Press, 1992.

Bingham, D. Jeffrey. "Development and Diversity in Early Christianity." *Journal of the Evangelical Theological Society* 49.1 (2006) 45–66.
Bockmuehl, Markus. "1 Thessalonians 2:14–16 and the Church in Jerusalem." *Tyndale Bulletin* 52.1 (2001) 1–31.
Brookins, Timothy A. "The (In)frequency of the Name 'Erastus' in Antiquity: A Literary, Papyrological, and Epigraphical Catalog." *New Testament Studies* 59.4 (2013) 496–516.
Brower, Kent. *Living as God's Holy People: Holiness and Community in Paul*. The Didsbury Lectures. Milton Keynes: Paternoster, 2010.
Brown, Schuyler. "Apostleship in the New Testament as an Historical and Theological Problem." *New Testament Studies* 30.3 (1984) 474–80.
Bruce, F. F. *1 & 2 Thessalonians*. Word Biblical Commentary 41. Waco: Word, 1982.
———. *The Epistle to the Galatians*. The New International Greek Testament Commentary. Grand Rapids: Eerdmans, 1982.
———. *The Epistles to the Colossians, to Philemon, and to the Ephesians*. The New International Commentary on the New Testament. Grand Rapids: Eerdmans, 1984.
Bultmann, Rudolf. *Theology of the New Testament: Volume 1*. Translated by Kendrick Grobel. London: SCM, 1952.
Burke, Trevor J. *Adopted into God's Family: Exploring a Pauline Metaphor*. New Studies in Biblical Theology 22. Nottingham: Apollos, 2006.
———. *Family Matters: A Socio-Historical Study of Kinship Metaphors in 1 Thessalonians*. Journal for the Study of the New Testament Supplement Series 247. London: T. & T. Clark, 2003.
———. "Pauline Paternity in 1 Thessalonians." *Tyndale Bulletin* 51.1 (2000) 59–80.
———. "Paul's Role as 'Father' to his Corinthian 'Children' in Socio-Historical Context (1 Corinthians 4:14–21)." In *Paul and the Corinthians: A Study on A community in Conflict: Essays in Honour of Margaret Thrall*, edited by Trevor J. Burke and J. Keith Elliott, 95–113. Supplements to Novum Testamentum 109. Leiden: Brill, 2003.
Burton, Ernest DeWitt. *A Critical and Exegetical Commentary of the Epistle to the Galatians*. International Critical Commentary. Edinburgh: T. & T. Clark, 1921.
Calvin, John. *The Epistles of Paul the Apostle to the Romans and to the Thessalonians*. Calvin's New Testament Commentaries. Translated by Ross Mackenzie. Grand Rapids: Eerdmans, 1995.
———. *Galatians, Ephesians, Philippians and Colossians*. Calvin's New Testament Commentaries. Translated by Ross Mackenzie. Grand Rapids: Eerdmans, 1996.
———. *Institutes of the Christian Religion*. Edited by John T. McNeill. Translated by Ford Lewis Battles. Library of Christian Classics 20–21. 2 vols. Philadelphia: Westminster, 1960.
Campbell, J. Y. "The Origin and Meaning of the Christian Use of the Word ἐκκλησία." *Journal of Theological Studies* 49.195/196 (1948) 130–42.
Caragounis, Chrys C. *The Ephesian Mysterion: Meaning and Content*. Coniectania Biblica New Testament Series 8. Lund: Gleerup, 1977.
Carey, Christopher. "Attic Orators." In *The Oxford Classical Dictionary*, edited by Simon Hornblower and Anthony Spawforth, 212. 3rd ed. Oxford: Oxford University Press, 1996.
Castelli, Elizabeth A. *Imitating Paul: A Discourse of Power*. Louisville: Westminster John Knox, 1991.

Cerfaux, Lucien. *The Church in the Theology of St. Paul.* Translated by Geoffrey Webb and Adrian Walker. Edinburgh: Nelson, 1959.

Chester, Andrew. "The Pauline Communities." In *A Vision for the Church: Studies in Early Christian Ecclesiology in Honour of J. P. M. Sweet*, edited by Markus Bockmuehl and Michael B. Thompson, 105-20. Edinburgh: T. & T. Clark, 1997.

Chow, John K. *Patronage and Power: A Study of Social Networks in Corinth.* Journal for the Study of the New Testament Supplement Series 75. Sheffield: JSOT Press, 1992.

Chrysostom. *Homilies on the Epistles of St Paul the Apostle to the Galatians and Ephesians.* In *The Nicene and Post-Nicene Fathers: First Series*, edited by Alexander Roberts et al, 13:1-172. Reprint, Peabody: Hendrickson, 1996.

Clark, Andrew C. "Apostleship: Evidence from the New Testament and Early Christian Literature." *Vox Evangelica* 19 (1989) 49-82.

Clarke, Andrew D. "'Be Imitators of Me': Paul's Model of Leadership." *Tyndale Bulletin* 49.2 (1998) 329-60.

———. "Equality or Mutuality? Paul's Use of 'Brother' Language." In *The New Testament in Its First Century Setting*, edited by P. J. Williams et al., 151-64. Grand Rapids: Eerdmans, 2004.

———. *A Pauline Theology of Church Leadership.* Library of New Testament Studies. London: T. & T. Clark, 2008.

———. *Secular and Christian Leadership in Corinth: A Socio-Historical and Exegetical Study of 1 Corinthians 1-6.* Paternoster Biblical Monographs. Exeter: Paternoster, 2006.

———. *Serve the Community of the Church: Christians as Leaders and Ministers.* First-Century Christians in the Greco-Roman World. Grand Rapids: Eerdmans, 2000.

Coenen, L. "Church." In *The New International Dictionary of New Testament Theology*, edited by Colin Brown, 1:291-307. Grand Rapids: Zondervan, 1975-85.

Conzelmann, Hans. *1 Corinthians.* Hermeneia. Philadelphia: Fortress, 1975.

Copan, Victor A. *Saint Paul as Spiritual Director: An Analysis of the Concept of the Imitation of Paul with Implications and Applications to the Practice of Spiritual Direction.* Paternoster Biblical Monographs. Milton Keynes: Paternoster, 2007.

Cotterell, Peter, and Max Turner. *Linguistics and Biblical Interpretation.* London: SPCK, 1989.

Craigie, Peter C. *Psalms 1-50.* Word Biblical Commentary 19. Waco: Word, 1983.

Darko, Daniel K. *No Longer Living as the Gentiles: Differentiation and Shared Ethical Values in Ephesians 4:17—6:9.* Library of New Testament Studies. London: T. & T. Clark, 2008

Dawes, Gregor W. *The Body in Question: Metaphor and Meaning in the Interpretation of Ephesians 5:21-33.* Biblical Interpretation Series. Leiden: Brill, 1998.

Debanné, Marc J. *Enthymemes in the Letters of Paul.* Library of New Testament Studies. London: T. & T. Clark, 2006.

de Boer, Willis P. *The Imitation of Paul: An Exegetical Study.* Kampen: Kok, 1962.

Deming, Will. *Paul on Marriage and Celibacy: The Hellenistic Background of 1 Corinthians 7.* Society for New Testament Studies Monograph Series 83. Cambridge: Cambridge University Press, 1995

Demosthenes. *Demosthenes.* Translated by J. H. Vince et al. 7 vols. Loeb Classical Library. Cambridge: Harvard University Press, 1926-49.

Denniston, John Dewar. "Thucydides." In *The Oxford Classical Dictionary*, edited by Simon Hornblower and Anthony Spawforth, 1519. Oxford: Oxford University Press, 1996.
Derow, Peter Sidney. "Polybius." In *The Oxford Classical Dictionary*, edited by Simon Hornblower and Anthony Spawforth, 1209–11. 3rd ed. Oxford: Oxford University Press, 1996.
De Silva, David A. "Worthy of His Kingdom: Honor Discourse and Social Engineering in 1 Thessalonians." *Journal for the Study of the New Testament* 19.64 (1996) 49–79.
De Vos, Craig Steven. *Church and Community Conflicts: The Relationships of the Thessalonian, Corinthians, and Philippian Churches with Their Wider Civic Communities*. Society of Biblical Literature Dissertation Series 168. Atlanta: Scholars, 1999.
Dihle, Albrecht. *A History of Greek Literature: From Homer to the Hellenistic Period*. Translated by Clare Krojzl; London: Routledge, 1994.
Dinarchus. *Dinarchus*. In *Minor Attic Orators, Volume II: Lycurgus, Dinarchus, Demades, Hyperides*, translated by J. O. Burtt, 165–325. Loeb Classical Library. Cambridge: Harvard University Press, 1954.
Diodorus Siculus. *Diodorus Siculus*. Translated by C. H. Oldfather et al. Loeb Classical Library. 12 vols. Cambridge: Harvard University Press, 1933–67.
Dionysius of Halicarnassus. *Dionysius of Halicarnassus*. Translated by Ernest Carey and Stephen Usher. Loeb Classical Library. 9 vols. Cambridge: Harvard University Press, 1937–85.
Dodd, Brian. *Paul's Paradigmatic 'I': Personal Example as Literary Strategy*. Journal for the Study of the New Testament Supplement Series 177. Sheffield: Sheffield Academic, 1999.
Doran, Robert. "The First Book of Maccabees." In *The New Interpreter's Bible. Volume IV: The First Book of Maccabees, the Second Book of Maccabees, Introduction to Hebrew Poetry, the Book of Job, the Book of Psalms*, edited by Leander E. Keck et al., 1–178. Nashville: Abingdon, 1996.
Dover, Kenneth J. "Thucydides 'as History' and 'as Literature.'" In *Thucydides: Oxford Readings in Classical Studies*, edited by Jeffrey S. Rusten, 44–59. Oxford: Oxford University Press, 2009.
Downs, David J. *The Offering of the Gentiles: Paul's Collection for Jerusalem in Its Chronological, Cultural, and Cultic Contexts*. Wissenschaftliche Untersuchungen zum Neuen Testament 248. Tübingen: Mohr Siebeck, 2008.
Duggan, Michael W. *The Covenant Renewal in Ezra-Nehemiah (Neh. 7:72b—10:40): An Exegetical, Literary and Theological Study*. Society of Biblical Literature Dissertation Series 164. Atlanta: Society of Biblical Literature, 2001.
Dunn, James D. G. *Beginning from Jerusalem: Christianity in the Making Volume 2*. Grand Rapids: Eerdmans, 2009.
———. "'The Body of Christ' in Paul." In *Worship, Theology and Ministry in the Early Church: Essays in Honour of Ralph P. Martin*, edited by Michael J. Wilkins and Terence Paige, 146–62. Journal for the Study of the New Testament Supplement Series 87. Sheffield: JSOT Press, 1992.
———. *The Epistles to the Colossians and to Philemon*. The New International Greek Testament Commentary. Grand Rapids: Eerdmans, 1996.
———. *The Theology of Paul the Apostle*. Grand Rapids: Eerdmans, 1998.

Du Toit, Andrie. "*Paulus Oecumenicus*: Interculturality in the Shaping of Paul's Theology." *New Testament Studies* 55.2 (2009) 121–143.

Du Toit, Herman. "Contributions from Modern Linguistics to New Testament Exegesis." In *Focusing on the Message: New Testament Hermeneutics, Exegesis and Methods*, edited by Andrie du Toit, 267–304. Protea: Pretoria, 2009.

Ellicott, Charles J. *St Paul's Epistles to the Thessalonians.* 3rd edition. London: Longman, Green, Longman, Roberts & Green, 1866.

Fee, Gordon D. *The First Epistle to the Corinthians.* New International Commentary on the New Testament. Grand Rapids: Eerdmans, 1987.

———. *Paul's Letter to the Philippians.* New International Commentary on the New Testament. Grand Rapids: Eerdmans, 1995.

Finney, Mark. "Honour, Head-coverings and Headship: 1 Corinthians 11.2–16 in Its Social Context." *Journal for the Study of the New Testament* 33.1 (2010) 31–58.

Fitzgerald, John T. "Paul and Friendship." In *Paul in the Greco-Roman World: A Handbook*, edited by J. Paul Sampley, 319–43. Harrisburg: Trinity, 2003.

Fitzmyer, Joseph A. *First Corinthians.* Anchor Bible 32B. New Haven: Yale University Press, 2008.

Fowl, Stephen E. *Ephesians: A Commentary.* New Testament Library. Louisville: Westminster John Knox, 2012.

Friesen, Steven J. "Poverty in Pauline Studies: Beyond the So-called New Consensus." *Journal for the Study of the New Testament* 26.3 (2004) 323–61

Fulton, Karen E. "The Phenomenon of Co-Senders in Ancient Greek Letters and the Pauline Epistles." PhD diss., University of Aberdeen, 2011.

Furnish, Victor Paul. *2 Corinthians.* Anchor Bible 32A. New Haven: Yale University Press, 1984.

———. "Inside Looking Out: Some Pauline Views of the Unbelieving Public." In *Pauline Conversations in Context. Essays in Honour of Calvin J. Roetzel*, edited by J. C. Anderson et al., 104–24. Journal for the Study of the New Testament Supplement Series 221. London: Sheffield Academic, 2002.

Garland, David E. *1 Corinthians.* Baker Exegetical Commentary on the New Testament. Grand Rapids: Baker, 2003.

Gehring, Roger W. *House Church and Mission: The Importance of Household Structures in Early Christianity.* Peabody: Hendrickson, 2004.

Georgi, Dieter. *Remembering the Poor: The History of Paul's Collection for Jerusalem.* Nashville: Abingdon, 1992.

Giles, Kevin. "Apostles Before and After Paul." *Churchman* 99 (1985) 241–256.

———. *What on Earth Is the Church? An Exploration in New Testament Theology.* London: SPCK, 1995.

Gorman, Michael J. "'You Shall be Cruciform for I am Cruciform': Paul's Trinitarian Reconstruction of Holiness." In *Holiness and Ecclesiology in the New Testament*, edited by Kent E. Brower and Andy Johnson, 148–66. Grand Rapids: Eerdmans, 2007.

Gray, John. *I & II Kings: A Commentary.* Old Testament Library. 2nd ed. London: SCM, 1970.

Green, Gene L. *The Letters to the Thessalonians.* Pillar New Testament Commentary. Grand Rapids: Eerdmans, 2002.

———. "Lexical Pragmatics and Biblical Interpretation." *Journal of the Evangelical Theological Society* 50.4 (2007) 799–812.

Gupta, Nijay K. "Towards a Set of Principles for Identifying and Interpreting Metaphors in Paul: Romans 5:2 (Προσαγωγή) as a Test Case." *Restoration Quarterly* 51 (2009) 169–81.
Guthrie, Donald. *New Testament Theology*. Leicester: InterVarsity, 1981.
Hall, David R. *The Unity of the Corinthian Correspondence*. The Library of New Testament Studies. London: T. & T. Clark, 2003.
Hanks, Patrick. "Do Word Meanings Exist?" In *Practical Lexicography: A Reader*, edited by Thierry Fontelle, 125–34. Oxford: Oxford University Press, 2009.
Harrington, Daniel J. *God's People in Christ: New Testament Perspectives on the Church and Judaism*. Overtures to Biblical Theology. Philadelphia: Fortress, 1980.
Harris, Murray J. *The Second Epistle to the Corinthians*. The New International Greek Testament Commentary. Milton Keynes: Paternoster, 2005.
Harsh, Philip Whaley. *A Handbook of Classical Drama*. Stanford: Stanford University Press, 1944.
Hawthorne, Gerald F. "The Imitation of Christ: Discipleship in Philippians." In *Patterns of Discipleship in the New Testament*, edited by Richard N. Longenecker, 163–79. McMaster New Testament Studies. Grand Rapids: Eerdmans, 1996.
Heil, John Paul. *Ephesians: Empowerment to Walk in Love for the Unity of All in Christ*. Studies in Biblical Literature. Atlanta: Society of Biblical Literature, 2007.
Hellerman, Joseph H. *When the Church was a Family: Recapturing Jesus' Vision for Authentic Community*. Nashville: B&H Academic, 2009.
Hoehner, Harold W. *Ephesians: An Exegetical Commentary*. Grand Rapids: Baker, 2002.
Holland, Tom. *Contours of Pauline Theology: A Radical Survey of the Influence of Paul's Biblical Writings*. Fearn: Mentor, 2004.
Horrell, David G. "Domestic Space and Christian Meetings at Corinth: Imagining New Contexts and the Buildings East of the Theatre." *New Testament Studies* 50.1 (2004) 349–69.
———. "From ἀδελφοί to οἶκος θεοῦ: Social Transformation in Pauline Christianity." *Journal of Biblical Literature* 120.2 (2001) 293–311.
———. *The Social Ethos of the Corinthian Correspondence: Interests and Ideology from 1 Corinthians to 1 Clement*. Studies of the New Testament and Its World. Edinburgh: T. & T. Clark, 1996.
———. *Solidarity and Difference: A Contemporary Reading of Paul's Ethics*. London: T. & T. Clark, 2005.
Horrell, David G., and Edward Adams. "The Scholarly Quest for Paul's Church at Corinth: A Critical Survey." In *Christianity at Corinth: The Quest for the Pauline Church*, edited by Edward Adams and David G. Horrell, 1–43. Louisville: Westminster John Knox, 2004.
Hossfeld, Frank Lothar, and Erich Zenger. *Psalms 3: A Commentary on Psalms 101–150*. Hermeneia. Translated by Linda M. Maloney. Minneapolis: Fortress, 2011.
Hughes, Frank Witt. *Early Christian Rhetoric and 2 Thessalonians*. Journal for the Study of the New Testament Supplement Series 30. Sheffield: Sheffield Academic, 1993.
Isocrates. *Isocrates*. Translated by George Norlin and La Rue Van Hook. 3 vols. Loeb Classical Library. Cambridge: Harvard University Press, 1928–45.
———. *Isocrates II*. Translated by Terry L. Papillon. The Oratory of Classical Greece. Austin: University of Texas Press, 2004.
Japhet, Sara. *1 and 2 Chronicles*. Old Testament Library. London: SCM, 1993.

Jervis, L. Ann. "Becoming like God through Christ: Discipleship in Romans." In *Patterns of Discipleship in the New Testament*, edited by Richard N. Longenecker, 143–62. McMaster New Testament Studies. Grand Rapids: Eerdmans, 1996.

Jewett, Robert. "Ecumenical Theology for the Sake of Mission: Romans 1:1–17 and 15:14—16:24." In *Pauline Theology, Volume III: Romans*, edited by David M. Hay and E. Elizabeth Johnson, 89–108. Atlanta: Society of Biblical Literature, 2002.

———. *Romans*. Hermeneia. Minneapolis: Fortress, 2007.

———. *The Thessalonian Correspondence: Pauline Rhetoric and Millenarian Piety*. Foundations and Facets. Philadelphia: Fortress, 1986.

Johnson, Andy. "The Sanctification of the Imagination in 1 Thessalonians." In *Holiness and Ecclesiology in the New Testament*, edited by Kent E. Brower and Andy Johnson, 275–92. Grand Rapids: Eerdmans, 2007.

Johnston, George. *The Doctrine of the Church in the New Testament*. Cambridge: Cambridge University Press, 1943.

Käsemann, Ernst. "Ephesians and Acts." In *Studies in Luke-Acts: Essays Presented in Honour of Paul Schubert*, edited by Leander E. Keck and J. Louis Martyn, 288–97. London: SPCK, 1968.

King, Justin D. "Paul, Zechariah, and the Identity of the 'Holy Ones' in 1 Thessalonians 3:13: Correcting an Un'fee'sible Approach", *Perspectives in Religious Studies* 39.1 (2012) 25–38.

Kirk, J. Andrew. "Apostleship since Rengstorf: Towards a Synthesis." *New Testament Studies* 21.2 (1974–75) 249–64.

Klein, Gunter. "Paul's Purpose in Writing the Epistle to the Romans." In *The Romans Debate*, edited by Karl P. Donfried, 29–43. Rev. and exp. ed. Peabody: Hendrickson, 1991.

Klingbeil, Gerald A. "Metaphors and Pragmatics: An Introduction to the Hermeneutics of Metaphors in the Epistle to the Ephesians." *Bulletin for Biblical Research* 16.2 (2006) 273–93.

Klink, Edward W., III. "The Gospel Community Debate: State of the Question." *Currents in Biblical Research* 3.1 (2004) 60–85.

Kloha, Jeffrey. "The Trans-Congregational Church in the New Testament." *Concordia Journal* 34.3 (2008) 172–90.

Knowles, Michael P. "'Christ in You, the Hope of Glory': Discipleship in Colossians." In *Patterns of Discipleship in the New Testament*, edited by Richard N. Longenecker, 180–201. McMaster New Testament Studies. Grand Rapids: Eerdmans, 1996.

Knox, D. Broughton. *Selected Works Volume II: Church and Ministry*. Edited by Kirsten Birkett; Kingsford: Matthias Media, 2003.

———. *Sent by Jesus: Some Aspects of Christian Ministry Today*. Edinburgh: Banner of Truth, 1992.

Kruse, Colin G. *New Testament Foundations for Ministry*. Marshalls Theological Library. Basingstoke: Marshall, Morgan & Scott, 1983.

———. *Paul's Letter to the Romans*. Pillar New Testament Commentary. Nottingham: Apollos, 2012.

Lampe, Peter. "Rhetorical Analysis of Pauline Texts – Quo Vadit? Methodological Reflections." In *Paul and Rhetoric*, edited by J. Paul Sampley and Peter Lampe, 3–21. London: T. & T. Clark, 2010.

———. "The Roman Christians of Romans 16." In *The Romans Debate*, edited by Karl P. Donfried, 216–30. Rev. and exp. ed. Peabody: Hendrickson, 1991.

Lategan, Bernard. "New Testament Hermeneutics (Part II): Mapping the Hermeneutical Process." In *Focusing on the Message: New Testament Hermeneutics, Exegesis and Methods*, edited by Andrie du Toit, 65–109. Protea: Pretoria, 2009.

Lee, Michelle V. *Paul, the Stoics, and the Body of Christ*. Society for New Testament Studies Monograph Series 137. Cambridge: Cambridge University Press, 2006.

Levering, Matthew. *Ezra and Nehemiah*. SCM Theological Commentary on the Bible. London: SCM, 2008.

Liddell, Henry George, et al. *A Greek-English Lexicon*. 9th ed. Oxford: Clarendon, 1940.

Lightfoot, J. B. *Saint Paul's Epistle to the Galatians*. London: Macmillan, 1900.

———. *Saint Paul's Epistles to the Colossians and to Philemon*. London, Macmillan, 1897.

Lincoln, Andrew T. *Ephesians*. Word Biblical Commentary 42. Dallas: Word, 1990.

———. *Paradise Now and Not Yet: Studies in the Role of the Heavenly Dimension in Paul's Thought with Special Reference to His Eschatology*. Society for New Testament Studies Monograph Series 43. Cambridge: Cambridge University Press, 1981.

Linton, Gregory. "House Church Meetings in the New Testament Era." *Stone-Campbell Journal* 8 (2005) 229–44

Longenecker, Bruce W. *Remember the Poor: Paul, Poverty, and the Greco-Roman World*. Grand Rapids: Eerdmans, 2010.

Longenecker, Richard N. *Galatians*. Word Biblical Commentary 41. Dallas: Word, 1990.

———. *Introducing Romans: Critical Issues in Paul's Most Famous Letter*. Grand Rapids: Eerdmans, 2011.

———. "The Metaphor of Adoption in Paul's Letters." *The Covenant Quarterly* 72.3–4 (2014) 71–78.

Luther, Martin. *Commentary on the Epistle to the Galatians*. London: Clarke, 1953.

Lyons, George. "Church and Holiness in Ephesians." In *Holiness and Ecclesiology in the New Testament*, edited by Kent E. Brower and Andy Johnson, 238–56. Grand Rapids: Eerdmans, 2007.

Lysias. *Lysias*. Translated by W. R. M. Lamb. Loeb Classical Library. Cambridge: Harvard University Press, 1930.

MacDonald, Margaret Y. *The Pauline Churches: A Socio-historical Study of Institutionalization in the Pauline and Deutero-Pauline Writings*. Society for New Testament Studies Monograph Series 60. Cambridge: Cambridge University Press, 1988.

Magda, Ksenija. *Paul's Territoriality and Mission Strategy: Searching for the Geographical Awareness Paradigm Behind Romans*. Wissenschaftliche Untersuchungen zum Neuen Testament 266. Tubingen: Mohr Siebeck, 2009.

Malherbe, Abraham J. "Exhortation in 1 Thessalonians." *Novum Testamentum* 25 (1983) 238–56.

———. *The Letters to the Thessalonians*. Anchor Bible 32B. New Haven: Doubleday, 2000.

———. *Paul and the Thessalonians: The Philosophic Tradition of Pastoral Care*. Philadelphia: Fortress, 1987.

Malina, Bruce J. "Collectivism in Mediterranean Culture." In *Understanding the Social World of the New Testament*, edited by Dietmar Neufeld and Richard E. DeMaris, 17–28. London: Routledge, 2010.

Marcos, Natalio Fernandez. *The Septuagint in Context: Introduction to the Greek Version of the Bible*. Translated by Wilfred G. E. Watson. Leiden: Brill, 2000.

Marshall, I. Howard. "'For the Husband Is Head of the Wife': Paul's Use of Head and Body Language." In *The New Testament in Its First Century Setting: Essays on Context and Background in Honour of B.W. Winter on His 65th Birthday*, edited by P. J. Williams et al., 165-77. Grand Rapids: Eerdmans, 2004.

Martin, Dale B. *The Corinthian Body*. New Haven: Yale University Press, 1995.

Martin, Troy. "Circumcision in Galatia and the Holiness of God's Ecclesia." In *Holiness and Ecclesiology in the New Testament*, edited by Kent E. Brower and Andy Johnson, 219-37. Grand Rapids: Eerdmans, 2007.

Martyn, J. Louis. *Galatians*. Anchor Bible 33B. New York: Doubleday, 1997.

McConville, J. G. *Deuteronomy*. Apollos Old Testament Commentary. Leicester: Apollos, 2002.

McKelvey, R. J. *The New Temple: The Church in the New Testament*. Oxford Theological Monographs. Oxford: Oxford University Press, 1969.

Meeks, Wayne A. "The Circle of Reference in Pauline Morality." In *Greeks, Romans, and Christians: Essays in Honour of Abraham J. Malherbe*, edited by David L. Balch et al., 305-17. Philadelphia: Fortress, 1990.

———. *The First Urban Christians: The Social World of the Apostle Paul*. 2nd ed. Haven: Yale University Press, 2003.

Meggitt, Justin J. "The Social Status of Erastus (Rom. 16:23)." In *Christianity at Corinth: The Quest for the Pauline Church*, edited by Edward Adams and David G. Horrell, 219-25. Louisville: Westminster John Knox, 2004.

———. *Paul, Poverty and Survival*. Studies of the New Testament and Its World. Edinburgh: T. & T. Clark, 1998.

Michaelis, W. "μιμέοηαι μιμητής σθμμιμητής." In *Theological Dictionary of the New Testament*, edited by Gerhard Kittel and Gerhard Friedrich and translated by Geoffrey W. Bromiley, 4:659-74. Grand Rapids: Eerdmans, 1964-76.

Minear, Paul S. *Images of the Church in the New Testament*. London: Lutterworth, 1961.

Mitchell, Margaret M. *Paul, the Corinthians and the Birth of Christian Hermeneutics*. Cambridge: Cambridge University Press, 2010.

Moo, Douglas J. *The Epistle to the Romans*. New International Commentary on the New Testament. Grand Rapids: Eerdmans, 1996.

———. *The Letters to the Colossians and to Philemon*. Pillar New Testament Commentary. Nottingham: Apollos, 2008.

Morgado, Joe. "Paul in Jerusalem: A Comparison of His Visits in Acts and Galatians." *Journal of the Evangelical Theological Society* 37.1 (1994) 55-68.

Moritz, Thorsten. *A Profound Mystery: The Use of the Old Testament in Ephesians*. Novum Testamentum Supplement 85. Leiden: Brill, 1996.

Mouton, Elna. *Reading a New Testament Document Ethically*. Academia Biblica. Atlanta: Society of Biblical Literature, 2002.

Muddiman, John. *The Epistle to the Ephesians*. Black's New Testament Commentaries. London: Continuum, 2001.

Munck, Johannes. "The Church Without Factions: Studies in 1 Corinthians 1-4." In *Christianity at Corinth: The Quest for the Pauline Church*, edited by Edward Adams and David G. Horrell, 61-70. Louisville: Westminster John Knox, 2004.

Murphy-O'Connor, Jerome. "House-Churches and the Eucharist." In *Christianity at Corinth: The Quest for the Pauline Church*, edited by Edward Adams and David G. Horrell, 129-38. Louisville: Westminster John Knox, 2004.

Nicholl, Colin R. *From Hope to Despair in Thessalonica*. Society for New Testament Studies Monograph Series 126. Cambridge: Cambridge University Press, 2004.

Nussbaum, Martha C. "Aristotle." In *The Oxford Classical Dictionary*, edited by Simon Hornblower and Anthony Spawforth, 165–69. 3rd ed. Oxford: Oxford University Press, 1996.

Oakes, Peter. "Contours of the Urban Environment." In *After the First Urban Christians: The Social-scientific Study of Pauline Christianity Twenty-five Years Later*, edited by Todd D. Still and David G. Horrell, 21–35. London: T. & T. Clark, 2009.

―――. *Philippians: From People to Letter*. Society for New Testament Studies Monograph Series 110. Cambridge: Cambridge University Press, 2001.

―――. *Reading Romans in Pompeii: Paul's Letter at Ground Level*. London: SPCK, 2009.

O'Brien, Peter T. "The Church as a Heavenly and Eschatological Entity." In *The Church in the Bible and the World*, edited by D. A. Carson, 87–119. Grand Rapids: Baker, 1987.

―――. *Colossians, Philemon*. Word Biblical Commentary 44. Waco: Word, 1982.

―――. *The Epistle to the Philippians*. New International Greek Testament Commentary. Grand Rapids: Eerdmans, 1991.

―――. *Introductory Thanksgivings in the Letters of Paul*. Novum Testamentum Supplement 49. Leiden: Brill, 1977.

―――. *The Letter to the Ephesians*. Pillar New Testament Commentaries. Grand Rapids: Eerdmans, 1999.

Ogereau, Julien M. "The Jerusalem Collection as Κοινωνία: Paul's Global Politics of Socio-Economic Equality and Solidarity." *New Testament Studies* 58.3 (2012) 360–78.

Oropeza, B. J. "Running in Vain, but Not as an Athlete (Galatians 2:2): The Impact of Habakkuk 2:2–4 on Paul's Apostolic Commission." In *Jesus and Paul: Global Perspectives in Honor of James D. G. Dunn: A Festschrift for his 70th Birthday*, edited by B. J. Oropeza et al., 139–50. London: T. & T. Clark, 2009.

Osiek, Carolyn, and David L. Balch. *Families in the New Testament World: Households and House Churches*. The Family, Religion and Culture. Louisville: Westminster John Knox, 1997.

Perry, Greg. "Phoebe of Cenchreae and 'Women' of Ephesus: 'Deacons' in the Earliest Churches." *Presbyterion* 36.1 (2010) 9–36.

Peterson, David. "The 'Locus' of the Church—Heaven or Earth?" *Churchman* 112.3 (1998) 199–213.

―――. *Possessed by God: A New Testament Theology of Sanctification and Holiness*. New Studies in Biblical Theology 1. Leicester: Apollos, 1995.

Phillips, Thomas E. *Paul, His Letters, and Acts*. Library of Pauline Studies. Peabody: Hendrickson, 2010.

Philo. *Philo*. Translated by F. H. Colson et al. 12 vols. Loeb Classical Library. Cambridge: Harvard University Press, 1929–1962.

Pickett, Raymond. *The Cross in Corinth: The Social Significance of the Death of Jesus*. Journal for the Study of the New Testament Supplement Series 143. Sheffield: Sheffield Academic, 1997.

Piñero, Antonio, and Jesús Peláez. *The Study of the New Testament: A Comprehensive Introduction*. Translated by David E. Orton and Paul Ellingworth. Tools for Biblical Study 3. Leiderdorp: Deo, 2003.

Plato. *Plato*. Translated by Harold North Fowler et al. 12 vols. Loeb Classical Library. Cambridge: Harvard University Press, 1914–2013.

Plutarch. *Plutarch*. Translated by Bernadotte Perrin et al. 28 vols. Loeb Classical Library. Cambridge: Harvard University Press, 1914–2004.

Polybius. *Polybius*. Translated by W. R. Paton and S. Douglas Olson. 6 vols. Loeb Classical Library. Cambridge: Harvard University Press, 2010–12.

Porter, Stanley E., and Bryan R. Dyer. "Oral Texts? A Reassessment of the Oral and Rhetorical Nature of Paul's Letters in Light of Recent Studies." *Journal of the Evangelical Theological Society* 55.2 (2012) 323–41.

Rebenich, Stefan. "Historical Prose." In *Handbook of Classical Rhetoric in the Hellenistic Period: 330 B.C—A.D. 400*, edited by Stanley E. Porter, 265–337. Leiden: Brill, 1997.

Rengstorf, Karl Heinrich. "ἀπόστολος, ἀποστολή." In *Theological Dictionary of the New Testament*, edited by Gerhard Kittel and Gerhard Friedrich and translated by Geoffrey W. Bromiley, 1:407–47. Grand Rapids: Eerdmans, 1964–76.

Reumann, John. *Philippians*. Anchor Bible 33. New Haven: Yale University Press, 2008.

Richards, E. Randolph. *Paul and First-century Letter Writing: Secretaries, Composition and Collection*. Downers Grove: InterVarsity, 2004.

Robinson, Donald. *Selected Works Volume 1: Assembling God's People*. Edited by Peter G. Bolt and Mark D. Thompson. Camperdown: Australian Church Record, 2008.

Roetzel, Calvin J. *Judgement in the Community: A Study of the Relationship between Eschatology and Ecclesiology in Paul*. Leiden: Brill, 1972.

Roloff, Jürgen. "ἐκκλησία." In *Exegetical Dictionary of the New Testament*, edited by Horst Balz and Gerhard Schneider, 1:410–15. Grand Rapids: Eerdmans, 1993.

Rusten, Jeffrey S. "Thucydides and His Readers." In *Thucydides: Oxford Readings in Classical Studies*, edited by Jeffrey S. Rusten, 1–28. Oxford: Oxford University Press, 2009.

Sacks, Kenneth S. "Diodorus Siculus." In *The Oxford Classical Dictionary*, edited by Simon Hornblower and Anthony Spawforth, 472–73. 3rd ed. Oxford: Oxford University Press, 1996.

Sampley, J. Paul. *'And the Two Shall Become One Flesh': A Study of Traditions in Ephesians 5:21–33*. Society for New Testament Studies Monograph Series 16. Cambridge: Cambridge University Press, 1971.

———. *Pauline Partnership in Christ: Christian Community and Commitment in Light of Roman Law*. Philadelphia: Fortress, 1980.

Samra, James George. *Being Conformed to Christ in Community: A Study of Maturity, Maturation and the Local Church in the Undisputed Pauline Epistles*. Library of New Testament Studies. Edinburgh: T. & T. Clark, 2006.

Sanday, William, and Arthur C. Headlam. *Romans*. International Critical Commentary. 5th ed. Edinburgh: T. & T. Clark, 1902.

Schmidt, Karl Ludwig. "ἐκκλησία." In *Theological Dictionary of the New Testament*, edited by Gerhard Kittel and Gerhard Friedrich and translated by Geoffrey W. Bromiley, 3:501–36. Grand Rapids: Eerdmans, 1964–76.

Schmithals, Walter. *The Office of Apostle in the Early Church*. Translated by John E. Steely. London: SPCK, 1971.

Schnackenburg, Rudolf. *The Church in the New Testament*. London: Burns & Oates, 1974.

Schnelle, Udo. *Apostle Paul: His Life and Theology.* Translated by M. Eugene Boring. Grand Rapids: Baker, 2005.

Schütz, John Howard. *Paul and the Anatomy of Apostolic Authority.* Society for New Testament Studies Monograph Series 26. Cambridge: Cambridge University Press, 1975.

Sharples, Robert William. "Theophrastus." In *The Oxford Classical Dictionary*, edited by Simon Hornblower and Anthony Spawforth, 1504–5. 3rd ed. Oxford: Oxford University Press, 1996.

Silva, Moises. *Interpreting Galatians: Explorations in Exegetical Method.* 2nd ed. Baker: Grand Rapids, 2001.

Skehan, Patrick W., and Alexander A. Di Lella. *The Wisdom of Ben Sira.* Anchor Bible 39. New York: Doubleday, 1987.

Spivey, Steven W. "Colossians 1:24 and the Suffering Church." *Journal of Spiritual Formation & Soul Care* 4.1 (2011) 43–62.

Stenschke, Christoph W. "'Not the Only Pebble on the Beach': The Significance and Function of Paul's References to Christians Other Than the Addressees in 1 and 2 Corinthians." *Neotestimenica* 45.2 (2011) 331–57.

———. "The Significance and Function of References to Christians in the Pauline Literature." In *Paul and His Social Relations*, edited by Stanley E. Porter and Christopher D. Land, 185–228. Pauline Studies 7. Leiden: Brill, 2013.

Summers, Charlie. "Nehemiah 5:1–13." *Interpretation* 65.2 (2011) 184–85.

Sumney, Jerry L. *Colossians: A Commentary.* New Testament Library. Louisville: Westminster John Knox, 2008.

———. "'I Fill Up What is Lacking in the Afflictions of Christ': Paul's Vicarious Suffering in Colossians." *Catholic Biblical Quarterly* 68.4 (2006) 664–80.

———. *'Servants of Satan', 'False Brothers' and Other Opponents of Paul.* Journal for the Study of the New Testament Supplement Series 188. Sheffield: Sheffield Academic, 1999.

Tate, Marvin E. *Psalms 51–100.* Word Biblical Commentary 20. Dallas: Word, 1990.

Theissen, Gerd. "Social Conflicts in the Corinthian Community: Further Remarks on J. J. Meggitt, Paul, Poverty and Survival." *Journal for the Study of the New Testament* 25.3 (2003) 371–91.

———. *The Social Setting of Pauline Christianity: Essays on Corinth.* Edited and translated with an introduction by John H. Schultz. Edinburgh: T. & T. Clark, 1982.

Theophrastus. *Theophrastus.* Translated by Arthur F. Hort et al. 6 vols. Loeb Classical Library. Cambridge: Harvard University Press, 1916–2003.

Thiselton, Anthony C. *The First Epistle to the Corinthians.* New International Greek Testament Commentary. Grand Rapids: Eerdmans, 2000.

———. "Semantics and New Testament Interpretation." In *New Testament Interpretation*, edited by Howard Marshall, 75–104. Carlisle: Paternoster, 1977.

Thompson, James W. "Paul, Plutarch and the Ethic of the Family." *Restoration Quarterly* 52 (2010) 223–26.

Thompson, Michael B. "The Holy Internet: Communication between Churches in the First Christian Generation." In *The Gospel for all Christians: Rethinking the Gospel Audiences*, edited by Richard Bauckham, 49–70. Edinburgh: T. & T. Clark, 1998.

Thucydides. *Thucydides.* Translated by C. F. Smith. 4 vols. Loeb Classical Library. Cambridge: Harvard University Press, 1919–23.

Trebilco, Paul. "Creativity at the Boundary: Features of the Linguistic and Conceptual Construction of Outsiders in the Pauline Corpus." *New Testament Studies* 60.2 (2014) 185–201.

———. *Self-designations and Group Identity in the New Testament*. Cambridge: Cambridge University Press, 2012.

Tuplin, Christopher J. "Xenophon." In *The Oxford Classical Dictionary*, edited by Simon Hornblower and Anthony Spawforth, 1628–29. 3rd ed. Oxford: Oxford University Press, 1996.

Turretin, Francis. *Institutes of Elenctic Theology*. Edited by James T. Dennison. Translated by George Musgrave Giger. 3 vols. Phillipsburg: P. & R., 1997.

Van Kooten, George H. "Ἐκκλησία τοῦ θεοῦ: the 'Church of God' and the Civic Assemblies (ἐκκλησία) of the Greek Cities in the Roman Empire: A Response to Paul Trebilco and Richard A. Horsley." *New Testament Studies* 58.4 (2012) 522–48.

Verhey, Allen. "Able to Instruct One Another: The Church as a Community of Moral Discourse." In *The Community of the Word: Toward an Evangelical Ecclesiology*, edited by Mark Husbands and David Treier, 146–70. Leicester: Apollos, 2005.

Wanamaker, Charles A. *The Epistles to the Thessalonians*. New International Greek Testament Commentary. Grand Rapids: Eerdmans, 1990.

Ward, Roy Bowen. "Ekklesia: A Word Study." *Restoration Quarterly* 2.4 (1958) 164–79.

Watson, Francis. "The Two Roman Congregations: Romans 14:1—15:13." In *The Romans Debate*, edited by Karl P. Donfried, 203–15. Rev. and exp. ed. Peabody: Hendrickson, 1991.

Weima, Jeffrey A. D. "'How You Must Walk to Please God': Holiness and Discipleship in 1 Thessalonians." In *Patterns of Discipleship in the New Testament*, edited by Richard N. Longenecker, 98–119. McMaster New Testament Studies. Grand Rapids: Eerdmans, 1996.

———. *Neglected Endings: The Significance of the Pauline Letter Closings*. Journal for the Study of the New Testament Supplement Series 101. Sheffield: JSOT Press, 1994.

———. "What Does Aristotle Have to Do with Paul? An Evaluation of Rhetorical Criticism." *Calvin Theological Journal* 32.2 (1997) 458–68.

White, L. Michael. "Paul and Pater Familias." In *Paul in the Greco-Roman World: A Handbook*, edited by J. Paul Sampley, 457–87. Harrisburg: Trinity, 2003.

Wiarda, Timothy. "Plot and Character in Galatians 1–2." *Tyndale Bulletin* 55.2 (2004) 231–52.

Wills, Lawrence M. "The Book of Judith." In *The New Interpreter's Bible Volume III: 1 & 2 Kings, 1 & 2 Chronicles, Ezra, Nehemiah, Esther, Tobit, Judith*, edited by Leander E. Keck et al., 1073–183. Nashville: Abingdon, 1999.

Wilson, Deirdre. "Relevance and Lexical Pragmatics." *UCL Working Papers in Linguistics* 16 (2004) 343–60.

———. "Relevance Theory." *UCL Working Papers in Linguistics* 26 (2014) 129–48.

Winter, Bruce. *After Paul Left Corinth: The Influence of Secular Ethics and Social Change*. Grand Rapids: Eerdmans, 2001.

———. "The Problem with 'Church' for the Early Church." In *In The Fullness of Time: Biblical Studies in Honour of Archbishop Donald Robinson*, edited by David Peterson and John Pryor, 203–17. Homebush: Lancer, 1992.

Witherington, Ben, III. *1 and 2 Thessalonians: A Socio-Rhetorical Commentary*. Grand Rapids: Eerdmans, 2006.

———. *Conflict & Community in Corinth: A Socio-Rhetorical Commentary on 1 and 2 Corinthians*. Grand Rapids: Eerdmans, 1995.

———. *Paul's Letter to the Philippians: A Socio-Rhetorical Commentary*. Grand Rapids: Eerdmans, 2011.

Xenophon. *Xenophon*. Translated by Walter Miller et al. 7 vols. Loeb Classical Library. Cambridge: Harvard University Press, 1914–2013.

www.ingramcontent.com/pod-product-compliance
Lightning Source LLC
Chambersburg PA
CBHW070255230426
43664CB00014B/2543